Mass Communication and Everyday Life

A Perspective on Theory and Effects

Dennis K. Davis
Cleveland State University
Stanley J. Baran
University of Texas at Austin

Wadsworth Publishing Company
Belmont, California
A Division of Wadsworth, Inc.

Senior Editor: Becky Hayden
Production Editor: Helen Sweetland
Designer: Joe de Chiarro
Copy Editor: John Eastman
Cover Design: Patricia Girvin Dunbar

Printed in the United States of America

1 2 3 4 5 6 7 8 9 10—85 84 83 82 81

Library of Congress Cataloging in Publication Data

Davis, Dennis K
Mass communication and everyday life.

Bibliography: p.
Includes index.
1. Mass media—Social aspects—United States.
2. Mass media—United States—Psychological aspects.
3. Mass media—Political aspects—United States.
I. Baran, Stanley J., joint author. II. Title.
HN90.M3D36   302.2'3   80-20050
ISBN 0-534-00883-6

You people and 62 million other Americans are listening to me right now. Because less than three percent of you read books. Because less than 15 percent of you read newspapers. Because the only truth you know is what you get over this tube.

Right now there is a whole, an entire generation that never knew anything that didn't come out of this tube. This tube is the Gospel. The Ultimate Revelation. This tube can make or break presidents, popes, prime ministers. This tube is the most awesome, Goddamned force in the whole Godless world. And woe is us if it ever falls into the hands of the wrong people. . . .

So you listen to me. Listen to me! Television is not the truth. Television is a Goddamned amusement park. Television is a circus. A carnival. A travelling troupe of acrobats, story-tellers, dancers, singers, jugglers, side-show freaks, lion tamers and football players. We're in the boredom killing business.

So if you want the truth, go to God. Go to your gurus. Go to yourselves. But man, you're never going to get any truth from us. We'll tell you anything you want to hear; we lie like hell. We'll tell you that Kojak always gets the killer. That nobody ever gets cancer at Archie Bunker's house. And no matter how much trouble the hero is in, don't worry. Just look at your watch. At the end of the hour he's going to win. . . .

We deal in illusions, man. None of it is true. But you people sit there day after day. Night after night. All ages, colors, creeds. We're all you know. You're beginning to believe the illusions we're spinning here. You're beginning to think that the tube is reality and that your own lives are unreal. You do whatever the tube tells you. You dress like the tube. You eat like the tube. You raise your children like the tube. You even think like the tube. This is mass madness! You maniacs!

In God's name, you people are the real thing. We are the illusion. So turn off your television sets. Turn them off right now. Turn them off and leave them off. Turn them off in the middle of the sentence I'm speaking to you now. Turn them off!

Howard Beale, The Mad Prophet of the Airwaves, reporting on "The Network News Hour" of the fictional UBS Television Network in the MGM movie Network. *Printed by permission of Simcha Productions, Inc. © Simcha Productions, Inc., 1976.*

Preface

This is an innovative book about mass communication and its role in American society. It focuses on how mass communication contributes to and intrudes upon everyday life. Unlike many past textbook efforts at understanding mass communication theory and effects, this book offers few statistics and no tables of scientific data. Yet we are engaging in and reporting legitimate social science research. We believe that there are good reasons for this approach.

Much contemporary mass communication research consists of short reports that offer and interpret statistical analyses of data collected from relatively small, geographically isolated groups of individuals. Eventually someone attempts to make sense of these discrete studies by synthesizing their results and drawing conclusions from that synthesis. The end product is a text that lists findings and generalizes from them.

This book is different. We will summarize, evaluate, and elaborate the most useful efforts made toward understanding, not studies but how our personal and societal definitions of media content arise in everyday life. We will examine the consequences of applying these definitions to ourselves and others. Our goal is to create a synthesis of the best work that has been done, a synthesis that will provide a useful introduction to mass communication theory and effects for students. We hope too that it will serve as a source of research questions for communication scholars. Above all, we want to stimulate creative and critical thought about the role of mass communication in everyday life.

Why does so much existing social science research appear of so little practical use to intelligent, interested students? Why are most research findings so fragmentary and contradictory? Is a broad, unified, coherent approach to understanding mass communication possible? These are questions that we will try to answer. We do not expect our answers to be accepted without evaluation, but we hope they will initiate debate and discussion. We offer no final proof of our perspective; but if it is taken seriously, we believe that it can provide useful insights into how individuals use mass media and the role played by the media in our society.

An important objective is to initiate and structure classroom discourse that will benefit all participants. Each of us has grown up in qualitatively different media environments, so we can learn from one another. There are no experts in the understanding of the ways in which mass communication intrudes upon our personal lives. No theory can accurately predict what we will do when we turn on the television or enter a movie theater. No theory can accurately predict our behavior once we leave those situations. And yet our experience of and reaction to mass communication is usually not unique. We share likes and dislikes with millions of other people; we respond to media messages in ways that are very similar to the responses of others in the audience. Why? How is our experience related to theirs? We need to talk with each other about what we are doing when we respond. We need to share experiences and what understanding of mass communication we have managed to acquire. If this book can help us communicate about mass communication, we will have achieved our most important objective.

The book is divided, roughly, into three parts. In the first section, we contrast our approach with the more traditional approaches to understanding mass communication, outlining the strengths and weaknesses of the differing approaches. We want to stress that we do not view our approach as antithetical to other approaches. In fact, we believe that most existing approaches to understanding media effects and theory can complement rather than compete with one another. In the second section, beginning with chapter 3 and ending with chapter 8, we detail our own approach centering on frame analysis. Each chapter presents highlights and discusses sets of concepts that can be used to understand mass communication. In the last section (chapter 9) we consider how our approach can be used to develop a social science study of mass communication.

Some readers might label our approach "humanistic" because it draws on scholarly methods and concepts that are more common in the humanities than in the social sciences. But we also cite and rely upon findings and theories developed by empirical social science researchers; and we use the social theories developed by symbolic interactionists and phenomenologists to guide our own theory building efforts. We argue that such an integrated approach to the understanding of mass communication could overcome existing shortcomings in isolated approaches and could revitalize the study of mass communication.

To aid readers in understanding the various approaches—ours and others, we raise fundamental questions in chapters 1 and 3 and consider possible answers; in an effort to clarify and supplement the main text, we provide key definitions and explanations of theories and concepts in boxed inserts throughout the book; and, at the end of the table of contents, we have added a handy reference guide to the mass communication theories discussed in the text.

We are grateful for the assistance of others in completing this project. We have benefited from the advice of colleagues at both Cleveland State University and the University of Texas at Austin. These institutions have provided us with the resources that helped to make this book possible. Perhaps the most important resource that we have consumed has been our own time. To be able to work for extended periods of time on a personally significant project has been a fulfilling and rewarding experience. This would not have been possible without the implicit and explicit support of our respective chairpersons, Sidney Kraus and Robert Davis.

Manuscript reviewers are often a necessary curse inflicted upon authors, but in our case the curse has proved to be a blessing. Our reviewers have been very understanding, even as they identified and criticized major flaws in our early manuscripts. We have generally followed and benefited from their advice, but of course they bear no responsibility for advice rejected or for any remaining errors in the approach we have developed. We wish to acknowledge the criticism and advice of these professors: Jennings Bryant, University of Massachusetts; Steven H. Chaffee, University of Wisconsin, Madison; T.R. Donohue, University of Hartford; David Eshelman, Central Missouri State University; Dan Nimmo, University of Tennessee; Gregory P. Stone, University of Minnesota; Gaye Tuchman, Graduate Center, City University of New York; and Ellen Wartella, University of Illinois, Urbana-Champaign. The comments of Bryant, Stone, and Nimmo were especially useful to us in the final stages of this book's revision. We have been encouraged to find such people willing to give generously of their time and knowledge to help us produce a more useful book. We hope that the product justifies their concerns and contributions.

D. K. D. and S. J. B.

Contents

Reference Guide to
Mass Communication Theories

To our parents:
Melville and Lydia Davis
Stanley and Margaret Baran

Chapter 1

Toward a Critical Understanding of Mass Communication

TV VIOLENCE HELD UNHARMFUL TO YOUTH. The Office of the United States Surgeon General has found that violence in television programming does not have an adverse effect on the majority of the nation's youth. . . .

> From a *New York Times* story on the *Surgeon General's Report on Television and Social Behavior,* 11 January 1972

For we now know there is a causal relation between televised violence and antisocial behavior which is sufficient to warrant immediate remedial action. . . .

> Senator John Pastore, Chairman of the Senate Subcommittee on Communications, commenting on the *Surgeon General's Report on Television and Social Behavior,* 1972

1.1 Introduction

We live in an era of lightning social change. The changes happen mostly without our consent and seemingly even without our understanding. But unless we understand these changes, we are powerless to control or even influence them.

The mass media—radio, television, film, newspapers, and magazines—with their capacity for instant dissemination of information are symbolic of this mercurial era. They also represent a change that we

1

do not really understand. They are magical in their power to transform our experiences. But that magic has become so commonplace that we forget the awe that we (or our parents or grandparents) felt upon first hearing recorded music, watching moving pictures, or gazing at tiny images on a television screen. The ubiquitous mass media intrude so routinely into our lives that we tend to take them for granted and ignore the industries that structure their content and control their development. We forget they are magic.

Understanding the role of mass media in modern society is much more complicated than many of us assume. When we turn to media professionals for explanations, we find that they have only a limited capacity to explain what they are doing. They say that they are only seeking to make a profit. The advertisers who subsidize the production and distribution of most media content maintain that they only want to ensure efficient mass distribution of their products. Audiences are generally satisfied with media content and enjoy simply being entertained by media. Social scientists have tended to dismiss the mass media as mere conveyor belts for information and entertainment content.

Does all this mean that we can safely ignore the magic of the media? Can we trust business and scientific leaders to provide us with all we need to know about mass communication, the process by which we receive and interpret mass media messages? Does magic cease to be powerful when it becomes commonplace?

The two excerpts that open this chapter should make clear that these questions have no easy answers, that fact is sometimes hard to separate from fiction. Yet they should also make clear that understanding how the mass media may affect us is important to our everyday functioning and to our quality of life. If we are being influenced, we ought to know how. If we must all consume mass media messages, can we become more efficient consumers, making a virtue of necessity? The mass media are an integral part of our lives. If we do not understand them and their impact, our lives are that much poorer.

People have at least tried to understand the mass media for a very long time. The influence of mass communication upon everyday life has been debated for more than a century. Predictably, the most intense discussions about effects have broken out immediately after new media were introduced. The appearance of each new medium—newspapers, movies, comic books, radio, and television—generated widespread argument about its purpose and consequences. Equally predictably, concern about effects tended to decline as each medium was made more effective in communicating to larger audiences and as its usage became more commonplace and socially accepted. It is important, then, to remind ourselves of the arguments that proponents, critics, and students of the mass media have advanced. A critical examination of these arguments can provide a starting point for developing our understanding of mass communication theory and effects.

1.2   The Debate Over Media Effects

Almost twenty years ago, Bernard Berelson wrote an intriguing discussion of mass media effects titled "The Great Debate on Cultural Democracy" (Berelson 1961). He summarized three major viewpoints on the effects of mass media on audiences, and he labeled them *Practicus* (mass media representatives and researchers), *Academicus* (elite critics of media content, especially those in universities), and *Empiricus* (empirical social science researchers). In Berelson's view of the debate, Practicus people sought to justify their efforts to satisfy the desire of mass audiences for popular culture. Academicus was cynical about the actions of Practicus and pessimistic about the long-term effects on values of widespread exposure to popular culture. Empiricus took a moderate position in the debate; scientific evidence supported the view that mass audiences wanted popular culture and also supported some of the less extreme views of the elite critics.

Berelson's "Great Debate" has persisted. Indeed, it has intensified in recent years with the development of special and public interest groups like Action for Children's Television and Morality in Media. Drawing on the elite critics' arguments, such groups have renewed the strength of these critics. At the same time, tremendous growth of the media industries has increased the Practicus power to use popular culture for self-serving ends despite growing criticism. Empirical researchers find themselves caught between ever more powerful antagonists. Their moderate position is under attack. Elite critics charge that Empiricus has sold out to the media industries, while industry leaders fear that some researchers are asking the wrong research questions and using unscientific methods to substantiate irresponsible criticisms of their actions.

The rest of this chapter summarizes the most important arguments advanced by the different sides in the effects debate. Some of the arguments are quite old, predating Berelson's summary, while others are more recent. We have structured our presentation of the three effects perspectives by constructing hypothetical answers to seven often-asked questions about effects. These answers are based upon arguments found in the sources cited at the end of each answer section. After presenting the answers, we will offer our own answers to the questions.

1.3 Seven Questions and Three Different Answers

The many concerns that people voice about mass media effects and the issues that Practicus, Academicus, and Empiricus have so hotly debated can be combined into seven basic questions:

1. Does mass communication have any effects?

2. How does mass communication affect us?

3. What are its most important and significant effects?

4. Which mass communication effects are positive—beneficial to us as individuals and to our society?

5. Which mass communication effects are negative—harmful to us as individuals and to our society?

6. How can positive effects of mass communication be increased and negative effects limited for us as individuals? How can we as individuals use mass communication more effectively?

7. How can positive effects of mass communication be increased and negative effects reduced for our society? How can our society use mass communication more effectively?

Answers to Question One: Does mass communication have any effects?

Practicus: Mass communication has few if any major political and social effects. The mass media simply provide services that are more or less useful to individuals. If we examine attitudes toward the media and their services, we find that the large majority of people are satisfied with what the media do for them. They enjoy the entertainment that the media provide and place a good deal of trust in the news and information made available. People even find most advertising useful in making purchase decisions. Beyond providing such useful and important services, the media have minimal impact on society.

The primary reason for this lack of effect is that the media are not a powerful means of transmitting messages. Face-to-face conversations are a much more effective means of persuading people to change their thoughts and actions. But because the media are the bearers of bad news, because they reflect those social changes that are occurring, the mass media are blamed for effects and for social changes over which they have no control (Klapper 1960). Much of the violence that was directed at media news people during civil rights and anti-Vietnam war protests is a good example of this misdirected blame-the-media thinking.

4

Academicus: Yes, the media have direct and powerful effects that influence the lives of everyone. Average people trust and depend upon the mass media far too heavily. They readily accept media reports of events as true. They waste much of their time being entertained by trivial, quite meaningless mass media content. These media effects touch the lives of all of us and make our society a worse place in which to live (Glynn 1956). Laverne and Shirley have replaced Romeo and Juliet as primary cultural characters.

Empiricus: Mass media have some effects on some types of people under some conditions. Society and individuals themselves create the conditions that increase the likelihood of media effects. Thus the media alone are not the cause of effects (Schramm, Lyle, and Parker 1961). A commercial might be able to influence your purchase of a new toothpaste by reminding you of your lack of sex appeal, but it is you who have that need. The ad would fail without it.

Our Perspective: All the forms of communication that touch us are likely to influence the way we view ourselves, plan our actions, and conduct our everyday lives. Some of this influence is positive whereas some is negative; some is subject to our control and some is beyond our control. We need a perspective on effects that can help us understand and control how we use mass media.

Mass communication has become one of the most potent forms of communication in our society. The way we use the mass media has probably transformed our other uses of communication; and as we transform our means of communicating, we transform ourselves in very real and important ways.

The invention, diffusion, and acceptance of new mass media technologies and the potential for restructuring the media industries that may soon exist make possible many new ways for us to understand ourselves and our world. Existing perspectives on effects fail to take new possibilities into account.

Answers to Question Two: How does mass communication affect us?

Practicus: Most of the significant media effects are the result of personal choices. These effects are initiated by media users themselves and should not be blamed on the media. The public chooses to allow the media to perform certain services—primarily news gathering and entertainment. These services are so important that if the media did not exist, people would develop and turn to other sources for them (Lazarsfeld and Stanton 1941). Television has simply replaced the minstrel, the traveling vaudeville show, and the neighborhood gossip, doing their jobs more efficiently and effectively. Any effects of these services occur only when media users seek such effects. People may change their style of dress, for example, because they looked to advertising to inform them of new fashions.

Academicus: Mass media produce effects by their immense power to attract and hold the attention of millions of people. People see the mass media as mystical, virtually omnipotent sources of compelling messages. They look to the media for messages that can transform their drab and humdrum personal lives. Average people have no ability or motivation to critically evaluate what they get from the mass media. They simply accept whatever they are offered and are grateful. They consume enormous quantities of media messages that fill their thoughts with trivial, meaningless content. They trust whatever they read in media news reports, which provide their bases for understanding themselves and their world. They look to the mass media for intellectual and emotional fulfillment; as such, the media affect their lives (Adorno 1954).

Empiricus: Mass media produce effects by *reinforcing* or supporting the status quo or already existing social trends. The majority of media messages simply describe things as they are; the mass media serve as a *mirror of society*. When dramatic social changes are initiated by social groups or organizations, mass media messages reflect these changes for the public and, in doing so, make these changes likelier to become widespread. In these cases, social groups or organizations must work to make their publics receptive to media influence. They must alert their people to the desirability of change so that they will look to the mass media for useful information about how the changes are best made. In other words, social groups or organizations must establish the conditions that allow the media to reinforce changes. The cancer society, heart fund, and other health organizations attempt to do this with their televised announcements about various health hazards such as smoking and high blood pressure.

The mass media have power only to reinforce, because people are generally *selective* in their use of the media. They expose themselves only to types of content that they see as consistent with what they already believe. The audiences for John Wayne's movie *The Green Berets* was markedly different from those that viewed *The Deer Hunter* and *Apocalypse Now*. This is called *selective exposure*. People systematically interpret messages to make those messages consistent with what they already believe. Some viewers see Archie Bunker as a bigot, some as a hero. This is called *selective perception*. Finally, people quickly forget content that is inconsistent with their beliefs. This phenomenon is called *selective retention*. Only the interpersonal communication that is possible in groups or organizations can overcome the barriers created by audience selectivity. For this reason, mass media alone can do little or nothing to alter beliefs and actions. The media can simply reinforce what people already believe and do (Klapper 1960).

Our Perspective: Mass communication probably affects our lives and our society because it has become so much a part of our everyday communication. This intrusion is usually very subtle. For children born in the 1950s or later, television becomes a routine means of engaging in communication as they mature. Many of us would feel uncomfortable about starting a day without at least reading the newspaper front page or the sports pages. Others would miss seeing "The Today Show," and children might miss viewing "Captain Kangaroo." Few parents can resist the break from child care provided by letting their children watch "Sesame Street" or the afternoon cartoon programs.

In some homes, Walter Cronkite's news stories replaced family dinnertime conversation—knowing the latest in Washington happenings is as important as knowing what happened to the other family members today. Walter was part of our lives, and some of us depended upon his reassurance that a cruel and crazy outside world would not invade our private corner of reality. When these intrusions become imminent—when crime, inflation, oil shortages, nuclear meltdowns, or tax increases threaten—the media show us solutions to the problems or show us how other people are coping. We turn to mass media messages when we want our emotions soothed or stimulated in certain ways. We can rely on certain television programs to make us feel good about other people. We can dispel sadness by playing a favorite record or turning on our favorite radio station. Socially acceptable stories and images of sex and violence are readily available to stimulate our imaginations or divert our attention from troublesome everyday problems. A comprehensive perspective on effects should explain how mass communication has transformed everyday communication.

Answers to Question Three: What are the most important and significant effects that mass communication might have?

Practicus: Media inform people and develop public understanding of events, especially the importance of these events for people's own lives. The media alert the public to potential problems so that people can act to prevent them from arising. Advertising gives consumers information that can save them money and help them make better buying decisions. Entertainment content provides an easily accessible, low-cost, yet very satisfying form of recreation (Lazarsfeld and Stanton 1941).

Academicus: The most important media effects result from the power of the media to corrupt culture. Media make the least useful, most meaningless, and trivial elements of a culture attractive, dramatic, and interesting. The media create a debased and amoral popular culture in which things are valued for the sensations they create, the emotions they arouse. Sex in films, for example, is often used for its sensational value, not to tell the viewer anything about the characters or their motives. This popular culture is attractive to the public because it asks nothing of them. It is simple to understand. It does not require that they think or critically interpret what they read, see, or hear. After prolonged exposure to popular culture, people lose whatever capacity they once had to understand and appreciate more complex and worthwhile forms of content. Content that provokes thought or requires careful intellectual or aesthetic interpretation is misunderstood or ignored. Instead, people come to demand content that gives them simple, easy, and quick solutions to life's problems. The simplest and most commonly offered of these solutions is escape into attractive, dramatic, but meaningless fantasies.

Social institutions that are responsible for transmitting useful forms of culture—entities such as religious, political, and educational institutions—find that people are less and less willing to understand or even pay attention to the complex messages that they try to communicate. We are in danger of becoming a nation of children mesmerized by hucksters who fill our heads with pretty stories (Porter 1977).

Empiricus: The media have little or no independent ability to produce direct effects. In the strictest sense, then, media have no significant or important effects. It is the action of groups or organizations that determines whether media will encourage significant social changes or simply help preserve the status quo. The media are not inherently disruptive to the social order. If anything, the mass media tend to have a conservative influence on society because social groups or organizations rarely try or are able to use media to produce changes.

The most consistent source of media effects is the ability of media to enhance the power of social groups and organizations. Groups and organizations can use the media to achieve a wide variety of effects— to get people to vote, to stop smoking, to contribute money, and so on. These effects, however, are the responsibility of the groups or organizations that initiate them, not of the media, which simply serve to enhance them.

The mass media, however, occasionally do have important effects upon certain types of people. For example, children predisposed to aggression may choose to watch more violence on television, and they may be likely to imitate it or be stimulated by it. Similarly, socially isolated adults may become dependent on the mass media for information about life and other people. Ordinarily, though, the average adult is not influenced (Himmelweit, Oppenheim, and Vince 1958).

Our Perspective: A comprehensive perspective on effects should discuss the power of mass communication to transform how we experience ourselves, other people, and the social environment. All of us live in a world where others use mass communication even if we ourselves do not. To what extent do we use mass communication as a means of controlling ourselves, as a means of maintaining everyday routines, and as a means of coping with problems and planning our futures? Do we use the media to manipulate ourselves, to prop ourselves up when we feel down, to divert our attention from our anxieties, to help us solve immediate, practical problems? As long as we use the media in only these ways, they will seem to have no observable influence on our lives.

Equally important, none of the existing effects perspectives discuss how we use mass communication to help us avoid doing certain things. But mass communication can help us avoid reflecting upon ourselves, other people, or our social environment. We can easily avoid conversations with other people or even conversations with ourselves by turning on the television set or by picking up a newspaper. Mass communication is usually quite pleasurable, while interpersonal communication or introspection is often troublesome. Mass communication helps us believe that we live in an unchangeable, objective real world and that we must adjust ourselves to it. This world makes many demands on us and creates problems for us that we must cope with as well as we know how. We will get through life with the fewest problems if we can just determine how to cope effectively, and we learn to cope by devising many short-term solutions. The media often tell us to buy products, take vacations, use more media, join clubs, or take up a hobby. The media's most significant effects, then, are not necessarily the most observable or dramatic. They may be those that alter our lives in subtle but meaningful ways.

Answers to Question Four: Which mass communication effects are positive—beneficial to us as individuals and to our society?

Practicus: (The news, information, and entertainment services that mass media provide have many positive effects on individuals and society. If people use the media properly for news and information, they can get a very useful understanding of what is going on in the world around them.) Unfortunately, not all people take advantage of these services. Much news content goes unused. But this is not the fault of the news media industries. People who use mass media wisely can make better decisions in their everyday lives. Remember, however, that the media do not directly influence these decisions. People decide what they do with the help of the mass media, not because of the mass media.

Entertainment content, on the other hand, gives individuals a chance to divert their attention temporarily from the anxieties and problems of everyday life and recreate themselves by listening to, reading, or watching pleasant and interesting stories. They can then return to their everyday activities with renewed strength and enthusiasm.

By providing entertainment, mass media help society function more smoothly. Potential social problems caused by unsatisfied or frustrated individuals are attenuated or avoided entirely. People complain less and cooperate more when they have easy access to entertainment. Similarly, news and information content serve important social purposes. News and information help people make decisions about who to vote for in elections and what types of organized social action to support. By helping people in their voting decisions, the media help them act more responsibly and make better choices. Ultimately, better public officials are elected and the social order is better administered. If poor choices are made, the mass media can publicize them and thus increase the likelihood of good choices next time (Stephenson 1967).

Academicus: The mass media have few if any positive effects. Any positive effects that do exist are far outweighed by negative ones. Media could transmit important educational, religious, or political messages, but good content is usually rendered useless by the presence of bad content. If the public is allowed to choose between popular culture messages and complex but enlightening messages, it will almost always choose the simple, easy-to-understand, easy-to-enjoy content. An occasional outstanding program has positive effects, but such programs are rare and must struggle against immense odds to succeed. Television documentaries are a good example of meaningful content that is ignored. By contrast, the media transmit a continuing flood of trivial, useless content that has overwhelmingly negative effects (Van den Haag 1957).

Empiricus: Groups and organizations have many positive effects on our lives that the mass media enhance. The most basic of these groups in our society is the nuclear family. The powerful tool of media can aid parents in socializing their children, helping them grow up in the world. Parents initially explain to children how they should act. When children use the media, they see that what their parents told them is correct. Right actions are rewarded and wrong behavior is punished.

This observation reinforces the parents' explanations. The socialization efforts of religious and educational organizations are often similarly enhanced by the mass media (Schramm, Lyle, and Parker 1961).

Our Perspective: A comprehensive perspective on effects should recognize that the mass media are neither inherently good nor bad. They can be used by individuals to transform their experience of everyday life or they can be used to cope with a very narrowly defined existence. Mass communication makes available messages that can be used to stimulate and develop human capacities for feeling, imagination, and conceptualization. Through the enlargement of these capacities, we can develop as moral, reasoning beings capable of planning our lives in personally meaningful ways and of developing futures that benefit ourselves and those around us. In short, mass communication holds the promise of helping us become more fully human. That promise may be lost, however, in poor content and a lack of media consumer understanding.

Such a comprehensive perspective on mass communication should recognize that the development of better, more just, and more humane social orders depends on developing each individual's capacities to be more fully human. Social orders depend on the capacity of their members to engage in rational communication and, through this discourse, on their capacity to determine moral actions for themselves and for others. A smoothly functioning social order should be based on a moral consensus derived from free, public, rational communication.

Although we can build essentially static social orders that will survive by means of constrained social action made possible by controlled communication, these social orders would not be humane ones. A useful understanding of mass communication theory and effects should help us apply that communication to build dynamic, democratic social orders in which public communication can provide an effective means of creating individual and social good.

Answers to Question Five: Which mass communication effects are negative—harmful to us as individuals and to our society?

Practicus: Mass media content is occasionally misused or abused. But this is also true of many vital services provided elsewhere in our society. People abuse medical care by consuming large quantities of unnecessary drugs. Should we therefore ban the sale of all drugs? Americans tend to eat too much. Should we restrict the sale of food?

There are two common misuses of media content. Some individuals may depend too much on the information they receive from one media source. They fail to evaluate the information properly and to compare it with news from other sources. As a result, they are sometimes misled by irresponsible sources and consequently make bad plans and decisions. The second misuse is that some people seek out too much entertainment content and spend too much time consuming it. They constantly seek to avoid involvement in the real world. As a result, such people occasionally fail to meet their responsibilities to others. These abuses, however, can easily be corrected if individuals take the time and trouble to educate themselves to a better use of the media. Only the individual can be blamed for failing to evaluate media messages adequately. The mass media should not be blamed because some people use bad judgment (Rosten 1962).

Academicus: Most effects of the mass media are negative. Heavy media consumers risk ruining their lives. They are never likely to develop into responsible, thoughtful, creative adults. Instead they will tend to remain egocentric, irresponsible, thoughtless children who follow the simple advice offered by the mass media and who seek only to be constantly entertained by its generally pleasant stories. Media users are likely to develop as unreflective hedonists, ready to obey the demands of any demagogue who gains control of the mass media. They are concerned only about where their next entertaining message is coming from and will avoid participation in groups or organizations that might serve to stabilize their thoughts and actions. Any society that contains large numbers of these people is inherently unstable. Whenever a demagogue can seize control of the mass media, he or she can command the instant loyalty and respect of media addicts (Ortega y Gasset 1932).

Empiricus: Groups do not always use the media wisely. Some parents, for example, let children watch television with little or no guidance. As a result, children become confused about what they see. They may develop idiosyncratic and antisocial behavior. They may imitate aggressive behavior because parents failed to prepare them adequately for the violent actions they see on television. When schools fail to instruct students about the value of democracy or the free enterprise system, adolescents may seek out bad content or misinterpret content that accurately portrays these things. Thus whenever groups fail to prepare their members for media use, effects may result that are harmful to individuals, to groups, and to the society as a whole (Bogart 1956).

Our Perspective: The existing perspectives on effects fail to note that most negative effects occur when we believe what we see in the media windows, when we uncritically accept what is represented in the media as reality. Unquestioningly accepting a reporter's evaluation of a news event is one example. The consequences of this uncritical acceptance are harmful to us and to our society.

Media representations of reality are a form of controlled truth. Most representations are not deliberate lies but show only a part of what could have been shown. They are necessarily selective, and the media professionals who produce them have become expert at developing representations that show us only certain things about ourselves, other people, and the social environment. We need an understanding of mass communication that sensitizes us to the selectivity of media representations and enables us to be critical of them.

Answers to Question Six: How can positive effects of mass communication be increased and negative effects limited for us as individuals? How can we as individuals use mass communication more effectively?

Practicus: We can increase the positive and decrease the negative effects of mass media by learning how to become discriminating users of the media. We can learn to seek out high-quality, trustworthy sources of information and entertainment. We can learn how to avoid low-quality, sensational, or biased media messages. If individuals become discriminating media users, they will put bad media sources out of business. Advertisers will not buy ads in media that audiences do not use. Without advertising revenue, these media will go out of business. Television programs with consistently low ratings, for example, will be taken off the air and replaced with other programs. Our individual media choices can shape media content as surely as our individual votes are critical to our democratic political system (Bauer 1964).

Academicus: The only way that we can increase the positive effects of mass communication for ourselves is simply to ignore most media content. We must search very carefully for the few books, magazines, or television programs that contain high-quality, personally useful content. This content, however, is so rare in the mass media that, as a general rule, people are safest if they ignore the mass media entirely and concentrate on specialized media, such as narrow-interest magazines and some of public television, that serve small, select audiences (Adorno 1954).

Empiricus: We can help increase the positive effects of mass communication most efficiently by educating groups in the use of media to serve their purposes. If parents, teachers, ministers, politicians, and business people were trained to use media more effectively, most negative effects would be avoided. If groups fulfilled their responsibilities in preparing their members for media use, the positive effects of mass communication for those individuals would be greatly increased (Donohue, Meyer, and Henke 1979).

Our Perspective: Existing perspectives provide little help in developing our skills as communicators. A useful understanding should allow us to educate ourselves to the role of communication in our lives. Although we cannot avoid being influenced by communication from the media, we can choose the role that it will play in our lives. We may be able to use the media to develop our capacities to feel, to imagine, and to conceptualize. As we develop these capacities, we should be better able to assume control over our personal lives, to reflect on and understand ourselves, to develop personally meaningful solutions to everyday problems, to detect significant problems that we would otherwise have ignored, and to plan our future. We live in almost constant communication with our environment and the things in it. That communication defines us and how we live. Understanding it will help us understand ourselves; because mass communication is a large portion of our daily communication, it demands such reflection and understanding.

Answers to Question Seven: How can positive effects of mass communication be increased and negative effects reduced for our society? How can our society use mass communication more effectively?

Practicus: The existing commercial mass media industries are self-regulating and self-correcting. Media governed by a free market system usually transmit those forms of content that the greatest number of people find useful. When new media entrepreneurs come along with a more useful product, a large audience tends to develop for their product, and their less resourceful competitors fail. Ultimately individuals make the choices that determine the structure of media industries and their bureaucracies. A bureaucratic structure that was not responsive to the needs and desires of most individuals, and thus to the needs and desires of society as a whole, could not survive.

Our media industries are among the most responsive and flexible bureaucracies in our society. There is no need for regulatory actions that would only impair their ability to provide services that the public expects. The high levels of public satisfaction with media service and performance are sufficient evidence that the mass media industries are operating in a manner that best serves the interests of society. Any operational changes resulting from government or other outside regulation would do more harm than good. Governments are notoriously bad decision makers in the area of media content. Our present system is doing its job and will continue to develop and improve as time goes on (Helffrich 1970).

Academicus: Control of the mass media should be given to those social institutions that will use them to transmit useful, high-quality content. Universities or public corporations made up of leaders drawn from many social organizations might be suitable. In any case, the profit motive must be removed, as in the case of public television. The quest for profits results in the worst forms of popular culture content. Direct public financing of content production is necessary to eliminate the unwholesome influence of advertisers by removing all advertising content from the mass media. Advertising content is among the most corrupting and useless of all mass media content (Lee 1969).

Empiricus: We can help increase the positive effects and curtail the negative effects of mass communication for our society in the same way as for individuals. We must educate groups to use media more effectively in meeting their own needs. If groups can socialize their members to good, effective media use, all levels of society will function better and the social system as a whole will operate at peak efficiency. Responsible group leaders can effectively use the media to maintain the status quo when appropriate or to encourage changes when these are deemed useful (Donohue, Meyer, and Henke 1979).

Our Perspective: The Practicus, Academicus, and Empiricus perspectives do not provide a useful basis for determining how mass communication should be controlled and used to benefit society. An alternative approach should describe how we can initiate and structure a broad, rational public debate on the nature of the media industries and their content. This discourse could provide a means of reaching a moral consensus concerning the role of mass communication in society. The current debate over effects is unlikely to produce this consensus. Instead it is likely to produce, as it has for decades, continued bickering over specific effects, while important broader influences continue to be ignored.

1.4 Conclusion

We have tried to revitalize the debate over media effects by summarizing its most prevalent arguments and offering our criticisms of them. These criticisms are not directed at specific antagonists or their views. Rather, we have faulted all sides for failing to develop a sufficiently broad, insightful perspective on media effects. Industry spokespersons answer all criticisms with the same defense: They are performing a public service by giving the people what they want. Elite critics cling to obsolete notions about culture; they see most media content as popular culture and popular culture as the debased product of an amoral industry. Empirical researchers have confined their studies to concepts that can be easily observed and measured. In doing this, they ignore broader issues of morality and important human values. Moreover, their work is often interpreted by the other antagonists to support their own views.

What these three perspectives on effects most obviously miss—and what we hope to provide—is a basis for helping each of us determine for ourselves whether and when we are influenced and if that influence is good or bad, alterable or not.

We examined the effects debate in terms of seven often-asked questions:

1. Does mass communication have any effects?

2. How does mass communication affect us?

3. What are its most important and significant effects?

4. Which mass communication effects are positive—beneficial to us as individuals and to our society?

5. Which mass communication effects are negative—harmful to us as individuals and to our society?

6. How can positive effects of mass communication be increased and negative effects limited for us as individuals? How can we as individuals use mass communication more effectively?

7. How can positive effects of mass communication be increased and negative effects reduced for our society? How can our society use mass communication more effectively?

We should begin to question and criticize the bases on which the existing effects perspectives rely for their answers to these important questions. Through this critical appraisal, we should be able to develop an understanding that avoids the assumptions and biases implicit in the existing perspectives.

In the following chapter, we offer such a critical appraisal. We will trace the historical development of the three different perspectives, focusing on the factors that narrowed each approach and made it less useful in helping us to understand mass communication theory and effects.

References

Adorno, T. W. 1954. How to look at television. *Q. Film, Radio, and Television* 8: 213–35.

Bauer, R. A. 1964. The obstinate audience. *Am. Psychol.* 19: 319–28.

Berelson, B. 1961. The great debate on cultural democracy. In *Values in America*, ed. D. N. Barrett, pp. 147–68. Notre Dame, Ind.: Univ. of Notre Dame Press.

Bogart, L. 1956. *The age of television*. New York: Ungar.

Donohue, T. R.; Meyer, T. P.; and Henke, L. L. 1979. Learning about TV commercials: the impact of instructional units on children's perceptions of motive and intent. Paper presented to Annual Convention of International Communication Association, May 1979, at Philadelphia, Pennsylvania.

Glynn, E. D. 1956. Television and the American character: a psychiatrist looks at television. In *Television's impact on American culture*, ed. W. Y. Elliott, pp. 175–82. Lansing: Michigan State Univ. Press.

Helffrich, S. 1970. The radio and television codes and the public interest. *J. Broadcasting* 4: 267–74.

Himmelweit, P. F.; Oppenheim, A. N.; and Vince, P. 1958. *Television and the child: an empirical study of the effects of television on the young*. London: Oxford Univ. Press.

Klapper, J. T. 1960. *The effects of mass communication*. New York: Free Press.

Lazarsfeld, P. F., and Stanton, F. N. 1941. *Radio research, 1941*. New York: Duell, Sloan & Pearce.

Lee, R. E. 1969. Self-regulation or censorship. *Educ. Broadcasting Rev.* 3: 17–20.

Ortega y Gasset, J. 1932. *The revolt of the masses*. New York: Norton.

Porter, D. 1977. Soap time: thoughts on a commodity art form. *Coll. English* 38: 782–88.

Rosten, L. 1962. A disenchanted look at the audience. In *The eighth art*, ed. R. L. Shayon, pp. 31–38. New York: Holt, Rinehart & Winston.

Schramm, W.; Lyle, J.; and Parker, E. 1961. *Television in the lives of our children*. Stanford, Calif.: Stanford Univ. Press.

Stephenson, W. 1967. *The play theory of mass communication*. Chicago: Univ. of Chicago Press.

Van den Haag, E. 1957. Popular culture. In *The fabric of society*, ed. E. Van den Haag and R. Ross, pp. 167–91. New York: Harcourt, Brace.

Additional Readings on the Effects Debate

Davis, R. E. 1976. *Response to innovation: a study of popular argument about new mass media.* New York: Arno.

Haselden, K. 1968. *Morality and the mass media.* Nashville, Tenn.: Broadman.

Head, S. W. 1976. *Broadcasting in America.* Boston: Houghton Mifflin.

Hertzler, J. O. 1961. *American social institutions.* Boston: Allyn & Bacon.

Rivers, W. L., and Schramm, W. 1969. *Responsibility in mass communication.* New York: Harper & Row.

U.S. Surgeon General's Scientific Advisory Committee on Television and Social Behavior. 1972. *Television and growing up: the impact of televised violence.* Washington, D.C.: U.S. Government Printing Office.

Wright, C. 1959. *Mass communication: a sociological perspective.* New York: Random House.

Chapter 2

A History of Our Understanding of Mass Communication

We're a success, and there's nothing wrong with that. So we're not going to be embarrassed by it, or ashamed of it, either. And we're certainly not going to apologize for what we're presenting to the American public.

Fred Silverman, President of NBC

The networks have determined that children control the TV set and the rest of the family simply watches what the kids choose. So they turn their programs into pap, in order to appeal to these youngsters.

Tony Randall, former television actor. Both quotations from Gary Deeb's "The Man Who Destroyed Television," *Playboy,* October 1979

2.1 Introduction

In this chapter we will begin our search for an understanding of mass media theory and effects by reviewing the mass communication research of the past half century. This is a difficult task not only because those years have seen changes in theory construction and research performance, but because even greater changes have taken place in the society that this theory and research were trying to explain.

Even the basic motivation for doing research and developing theories has changed. Many of the men and women who studied mass communication in the 1920s and 1930s were trying to understand something that they believed could profoundly change human society. In some cases, this motivation bordered on a fear that media-induced changes might bring an end to civilized society.

Most of us are no longer so afraid of mass communication. Recent media research has been reassuring, leading us to conclude that mass media ordinarily do not threaten society. It tells us that mass media typically support and preserve the existing social order. This has been an immensely important and useful perspective, but it is no longer completely adequate. It is not enough to know that the media will not destroy society as we know it; we want to know whether media have any positive effects. We want to know whether the mass media can help us discover and develop new human potentials. Our generation is asking new questions about mass communication, but we should not forget the past in our haste to explore the future. We can learn a great deal from considering how the past two generations of mass communication theorists and researchers worked to understand mass media. They have left us a useful legacy of mass communication theories and research tools, and we should understand this legacy if we hope to use it wisely.

2.2 From Libertarianism to Mass Society Theory

When our nation was founded, some of the most rational and enlightened men of their generation wrote a constitution outlining a system of government consistent with their view of human beings and their capacities. This document stood the test of time well, partly because its framers did not try to establish a static government that would simply administrate an unchanging social order. As visionaries, they sought to create a system of government that would accommodate social change. But they differed greatly in their visions of the eventual American social order. In spite of these differences, however, they agreed that the new system of government should make possible the development of a variety of social orders.

One essential safeguard of this freedom and flexibility was the First Amendment to the Constitution, guaranteeing freedom of speech, press, religion, peaceful assembly, and petition. The founders had learned the value of these freedoms during their struggle for national independence. They had learned that these freedoms could not be taken for granted, that they were essential if governments were to be peacefully reformed. They resented British colonial rule partly because they believed that it imposed a social order upon them over which they had no control. One of their revolutionary slogans was "no taxation without representation." In other words, people should not be required to support a form of government in which they had no participation.

The philosophy of the founders has come to be called *libertarianism*. This seventeenth-century philosophy and its relationship to the press was articulated by John Milton in *Areopagitica* (see Rivers, Peterson, and Jensen 1971 for an extended discussion of how libertarian thought developed). Milton argued that if freedom of speech and the press were permitted, a marketplace of ideas would develop. People would be free to discuss, proclaim, print, and distribute a wide variety of ideas. Milton was not a total idealist. He knew that if complete freedom were permitted, some people would intentionally or unintentionally tell lies. Without censorship, which Milton rejected, how was such falsehood to be dealt with? Milton argued that innate human reason provided a basis for discerning truth from falsehood. If people were educated to use their capacity for reason, they would be able to enter the marketplace of ideas, engage in rational discussion and debate, and then make correct moral decisions about their actions. Education was fundamental to libertarianism. Milton believed that people were by nature rational, but to use their rational powers wisely they must be educated to develop and exercise reason.

The founders were pragmatic idealists. They realized that most people living in the thirteen colonies were uneducated and thus unlikely to act wisely. Their system of government, then, did not provide for equal participation by all people in politics or the marketplace of ideas. In post-revolutionary America, property and education were closely related. It was practical to limit the voting right to males with property because only they could be assumed to have enough education to engage in the rational public debate essential for responsible participation in politics. The founders saw this as a practical starting point for developing a new social order.

Although the founders could not foresee the dramatic social change that the next two centuries would bring, the Constitution they had written proved adaptable enough to the demands for participation by unpropertied males, women, and racial minorities. The marketplace of ideas and politics was gradually opened to broader participation.

For more than a century, libertarianism persisted with few important vocal dissenters, and the freedom to engage in rational public discussion and debate was taken for granted. This does not mean that troublesome problems did not arise. Many varieties of libertarian thought existed, some in fact that were more libertarian than others—the Civil War proved that. Individuals sometimes altered their own understanding of the concept based on events of the day and their own experiences. Despite the abuses that created many political problems, few people who were engaged in politics doubted that rational

Libertarianism

Libertarianism is a theory of public communication that makes certain important assumptions about human capacities for communication and how society should be structured to develop and serve these capacities. Milton described what he called a "self-righting process" of public communication, in which people endowed with reason would have easy access to competing ideas so that they could engage in a personally meaningful search for truth. This conception of public communication contrasted sharply with the authoritarian theories and practices of his era. Governments placed little trust in the capacity of individuals to seek truth, and censorship was considered a necessary means for protecting the state from the irresponsible expression of subversive ideas. Milton argued that such censorship might unduly interfere with an individual's relationship with God by preventing him from coming to a knowledge of truth. It was more important, he thought, for individuals to know truth than for specific governments to survive.

Libertarian ideas had been discussed for more than a century when they were seized upon and developed by American revolutionaries seeking to overthrow British colonial rule. These ideas provided a justification for revolution by asserting the primacy of individual rights over the rights of government. In libertarian thinking, governments exist to serve individuals and to provide them with the resources that enable them to develop their innate capacities. When governments are unjust and threaten individual rights, people may justifiably revolt and institute better forms of government.

Libertarian theory was especially important to the development of mass communication in the United States. From the beginning, newspapers were considered essential to the success of a libertarian social order. Jefferson noted that the press was "the best instrument for enlightening the mind of man, and improving him as a rational, moral, and social being." But libertarian theory did not explain how the press should develop so that it could best serve as a marketplace of ideas. In the early nineteenth century, libertarianism was wedded to the economic theories of Adam Smith to create a theory of media development. This theory argued that mass media would develop best if individual publishers were forced to earn profits by selling content in a free and open marketplace; the public would then seek out the best content, and the publishers of this content would earn the largest profits, while publishers of less useful content would fail. Competition between publishers would assure that someone would publish the truth to serve their own self-interest as well as the public good. This argument has persisted until today and is now used to justify the television ratings as a means of determining what should be broadcast. Profits are equated with public service.

public discussion and debate were essential to the American system of government.

Why did libertarianism work reasonably well for almost a century? There are many possible explanations. First, only a small, elite segment of the total population could participate in politics. Then, as more segments of the population were educated and given the vote, these people tended to vote as their political leaders urged them to vote. Control of politics was limited to those people who knew how to engage in rational public discussion and debate, to leaders who knew the rules of this game. Temporary crises occurred whenever new leaders emerged who were not participants in the existing public communication. For example, the rise of Andrew Jackson aroused concern among eastern and southern politicians who had not communicated much with Jackson or the men around him.

A second reason why libertarianism worked was that the national system of government in eighteenth- and nineteenth-century America touched the everyday lives of most people so little. To Westerners, for example, policies set in Washington, D.C., seemed far from their lives. There were much more important things for them to be concerned about—life itself was constantly threatened. At best, the federal government could provide little protection from the weather and insects. Similarly, urban workers did not expect government to legislate better working conditions for them. Most workers were simply resigned to conditions that we now consider quite inhumane.

A final reason why libertarianism worked was the absence of mass media as we now know them. The only mass media operating throughout most of the nineteenth century were the urban daily newspapers, and their control was very decentralized. Many separately owned newspapers were published in most cities. These newspapers reflected many different political viewpoints or tended not to emphasize politics at all. They dealt with current events and sensationalized human interest stories. They were more often sought out for their entertainment value than for their politics. Also, in order to use a newspaper, one had to be literate or know someone who was literate. This requirement tended to limit newspaper access to literate people who valued the concept of rational debate and discussion, even if they did not fully understand it.

As the twentieth century began, however, there were growing signs that libertarian philosophy might prove unworkable. Politicians began to complain about the growing power of urban press lords like Pulitzer and Hearst. Some claimed that these editors had pushed Congress into declaring an unnecessary and costly war with Spain in 1898. Less than two decades later, World War I further undermined trust in libertarianism. It was the first mass war in which Americans became involved, and for the first time Americans were exposed to war-inspired propaganda. Social and political leaders began to grow concerned over the apparent power of this propaganda to mobilize immense armies and to maintain their morale for long periods of time. Social philosophers had argued through much of the nineteenth century that the industrial revolution was creating a mass society that would behave differently than previous social orders. World War I provided evidence that this speculation might be true. Efforts were begun to explain what was happening to society.

The Legacy of Libertarianism

There are many inconsistencies in the libertarians' arguments. History has proven many of their notions—such as limiting political participation to landed gentry—to be naive and impractical. But it is important to understand the very useful insights into public communication found in libertarianism while rejecting its less useful notions. The libertarians struggled with questions about how public communication should be structured for societies in which traditional elites (royalty, clergy, military) were no longer capable of exercising absolute control over human action. They sought to establish the rules that could be used to decide (a) who is able to communicate, (b) what should be communicated, (c) by which communication media, and (d) to whom.

The libertarians favored rules that placed minimal restrictions on the freedom of individuals to search for and communicate content that they believed to be true. They based their arguments for liberal rules on a belief in natural laws assuring that individuals would communicate responsibly and that ideal mass media systems would develop. Today little basis exists for believing that such natural laws operate. Free access to a wide variety of media content does not assure that wise choices will be made, nor does open competition between media entrepreneurs assure that only those who produce the best content will earn profits.

In its worst forms, traditional libertarianism (not to be mistaken with the philosophy of the contemporary Libertarian political party) is used to justify the mass media status quo—a status quo that is assumed to result from a natural process. But this libertarianism can also be used to justify many changes that can remove barriers to communication, that encourage individuals to develop their capacities to understand themselves and their society so that the quality of their lives is improved. Libertarianism can be viewed as either a conservative philosophy or a radical faith. It can be used to justify television ratings or to justify demands that mass media be reformed.

In later chapters we will develop a theory of public communication that we believe shares several basic assumptions with libertarian theory. We will argue that individuals can develop communication skills that enable them to become responsible users of public communication; and that mass media can be restructured to help individuals use communication skills to achieve personally meaningful objectives and to make responsible contributions to society.

Harold Lasswell: A Theory of Propaganda— The Hypodermic-Needle Model

Harold Lasswell developed an innovative conceptualization of the impact of mass communication during World War I. He is, for several reasons, regarded as the first modern mass communication theorist and researcher. Lasswell drew on Freudian theory to explain how World War I propaganda came to be created, why it was so effective, and how it could be counteracted. Perhaps the most significant feature of Lasswell's theory was the extent to which it contradicted libertarian philosophy. To fully understand this theory, we must understand something about Freudian theory and the way in which Lasswell interpreted Freud. Freud had argued that humans are motivated not by reason but by primitive, unconscious, irrational forces that are only partly controlled by the conscious mind. Consequently human behavior is nonrational. The conscious mind itself is fragmented into an ego and a superego that vie for control over these irrational forces. Only when the superego is able to maintain full control will somewhat rational action take place.

From Freudian theory Lasswell developed a theory labeled the *hypodermic-needle model* of mass communication because it assumed that media messages have direct effect, just as hypodermic needles inject their serum directly into the individual. Lasswell believed that nonrational people would be easy targets for political propaganda and that innate urges might be aroused by powerful propaganda symbols. When this happened, people would fall in love with the symbol just as nonrationally as they fall in love with a member of the opposite sex (Lasswell 1935, pp. 29–35). He argued that certain "dominating personalities" would be motivated by their nonrational urges to express powerful symbols that would radiate throughout a society. These symbols would be received by those people with "unconscious receptivities," and would arouse, in turn, nonrational urges in them. In Lasswell's time, the dominating political personalities were men like Adolf Hitler, Franklin D. Roosevelt, Joseph Stalin, and Benito Mussolini. It was these men's voices that radiated throughout entire nations through the power of radio.

Lasswell's theory signaled an important change in how public communication was perceived in America. Libertarian philosophy had assumed that people were innately rational and would develop rational capacities if they were not inhibited by censorship. Lasswell suggested that rationality was not to be taken for granted. Even the leaders of large social movements or entire nations could act nonrationally. They could also be expected to communicate symbols that might cause many other people to adopt their personal form of nonrationality. Thus entire nations might become paranoid or obsessed by primitive desires. In those nations, rational public communication would be impossible.

Since democracy was thought to depend upon rational discussion and debate, it must somehow be protected from abuse. But how? Lasswell suggested analyzing the potential of propaganda messages for causing widespread public nonrationality. If an objective means could be found for determining that potential, messages could be censored or their propagators prosecuted.

Lasswell's theory and the research based upon it deserve attention because they illustrate an important but often overlooked point about mass communication theory and research: It was based upon a negative assessment of the average person's capacity to reason. It argued that mass media had the power to transform the social order by radiating the symbols of nonrational leaders. This theory encouraged the development of research methods that could be used to validate it and make it applicable in a variety of settings. Methods were thus developed to detect the existence of nonrational symbols in propaganda and to provide an objective basis for censoring them.

Mass communication research has tended to be an "applied" social science in the sense that theories were developed in response to practical problems. In the case of Lasswell's work, the social disruptions apparently linked to mass-communicated propaganda messages were the problem that necessitated a solution. Later mass communication researchers have similarly limited their theories and research methods to somewhat narrow, albeit important research problems. Mistakes have sometimes been made when theories that were developed and applied toward specific research problems were used to explain problems in quite different contexts. In particular, mistakes were made when these theories were used to "prove" that human nature was limited in specific ways, or that mass communication must be structured in certain ways to assure that a desired social order would be developed or maintained.

In the years since Lasswell, we have developed many ingenious notions about mass communication and have created many complex research methods to aid our understanding; but it would be a mistake to say that we have found definitive answers to the broad questions concerning the role of mass communication in the lives of individuals or the social order in which we live. Such an understanding remains to be developed, and the long-term promise of mass communication research remains to be fulfilled, though many important steps have already been taken in this exploration. Our ability to answer the broader questions in useful ways depends upon the vision and work of the people considered in the following pages of this chapter.

Paul Lazarsfeld: Founder of Mass Communication Research

If one person deserves the title of founder of the field of mass communication research, that person is Paul Lazarsfeld. No one has done more to determine the way in which theory and research methods would be developed to aid our understanding of mass communication. His ideas have influenced such diverse areas as audience research, consumer research, opinion leadership and diffusion research, and studies of the uses and gratifications of mass media.

Lazarsfeld's main legacy rests in an area he labeled *administrative research* (Lazarsfeld 1941). This research deals with how mass media industries should be structured and operated in order to serve the sometimes conflicting interests of investors, media professionals, and the public. Lazarsfeld believed that effective research would allow the interests of all to be well served. For example, he surveyed radio audiences to discover their program preferences, believing that larger numbers of listeners (benefiting broadcasters and investors) would be drawn by the improved programming (benefiting listeners) that resulted from his analysis. The commercial nature of mass media, he reasoned, need not preclude serving the significant needs and concerns of the public.

The full significance of Lazarsfeld's work cannot yet be evaluated. In some ways, he probably succeeded beyond his own expectations. His work now provides the basis for multimillion-dollar research industries the world over. But he would likely have been disappointed that most of the research activity he inspired has been administrative in nature, because he considered another type equally important— *critical research* (Lazarsfeld 1941). Critical research means evaluating the role of mass media in society and in the lives of individuals. It is research that seeks answers to the larger, broader questions involving human existence and the role of mass media in it. Critical research has no apparent immediate economic value for media industries.

Lazarsfeld thought that critical research would be an essential complement to administrative research. Administrative research sought to make the existing social order function more effectively to serve the needs of all parties in the mass communication situation, while critical research sought to lay a basis for necessary and useful change. If administrative research was successful, it would generate the resources to implement the changes suggested by critical research. Administrative research was concerned with the present, while critical research analyzed both past and present as a means of planning the future. While the theories and research methods used in both types of research may have had similarities, there were important differences in their respective goals.

Lazarsfeld's radio research (Lazarsfeld and Stanton 1941) is a good example of the sharing of common methods. Random sampling, sophisticated interview and survey techniques, detailed statistical analyses, and a perspective on effects that saw radio's influence as dependent on audience wants and needs were employed—both in those portions of his work that he saw as having long-term value for the medium and its listeners, and in those portions he saw as immediately benefiting his associates at the CBS Radio Network. He felt that the same tools could be used to produce different but related products.

Much of our current confusion about mass communication theory and effects, however, stems from a failure to differentiate between administrative and critical research. Administrative research has become so dominant that it is often assumed to be the only legitimate form of research possible. The balance between critical research and administrative research should be restored. This is a balance that Lazarsfeld would have wanted maintained (though he might have disagreed with this book's proposals for restoring that balance).

One of Lazarsfeld's earliest administrative research endeavors was in the area of marketing and advertising research. This type of inquiry highlights the strength (its ability to provide information that results in more profitable media service) and the limitation (its inability to search beyond that information for a broader understanding of the media and their audience) of administrative research. Marketing and advertising research was directed toward the solution of a very practical business problem: how to motivate consumers to purchase specific products. The solution to this problem would serve the interests of businesspeople directly—their profits would increase if they could more efficiently match their production and distribution of products to public consumption. At the same time, administrative researchers felt that the public would have its interest served. Effective marketing techniques would alert people to the existence of products they might want; and, by increasing the efficiency of marketing, these techniques could actually lower the cost of consumer goods. Through marketing research, business people might discover public needs that were not being met, then develop products to meet them. Of course, marketing research could easily be abused. Unethical business people could use this research to market useless or even dangerous products. Market research was only a practical administrative tool; how businesses used it was up to them. Researchers like Lazarsfeld had little control over how such tools were applied.

Lazarsfeld also pioneered in audience analysis. In 1937 he established the Office of Radio Research at Princeton University with a grant from the Rockefeller Foundation. By 1940 he moved this research unit to Columbia University in New York City. There Lazarsfeld developed a working relationship with Frank Stanton, a young radio audience researcher at the Columbia Broadcasting System. Stanton had recently completed a doctoral thesis at Ohio State University titled "A Critique of Present Methods and a New Plan for Studying Radio Listening Behavior." His ideas earned him a job with the CBS Radio Network and the opportunity to collaborate with Lazarsfeld in a variety of research projects that examined the audiences of radio programs.

The 1930s and early 1940s were radio's golden age. Radio was the nation's premiere entertainment medium, enjoyed nightly by gigantic audiences that listened to network programming from coast to coast. Industry leaders were very interested in any research tools that might enable them to reach and serve ever larger audiences and in research data that might encourage advertisers to increase their sponsorship of radio programming. The relationship between Lazarsfeld and Stanton was of great mutual advantage. Stanton was able to secure cooperation from CBS for research designed by Lazarsfeld, and Lazarsfeld helped Stanton develop new concepts and research methods for studying audiences (Metz 1975, pp. 61–62).

Administrative research for the radio industry filled many of the same practical functions that marketing research filled for consumer product manufacturers. The radio industry was also producing a "product," but the selling price of this product was determined by the number of people who would listen to it. Advertisers would pay more to sponsor programs that reached larger audiences. As in the marketing of consumer products, those programs that best served important audience needs were expected to attract the most listeners. In the 1930s, the networks thought the predominant need was for entertainment programming, and this was supplied in large quantities.

Lazarsfeld, however, realized that audiences needed more than just entertainment, that entertainment programming itself served other needs that were often not realized or understood either by audience members or the professionals who created the programming. One of his hopes was to conduct research that would encourage the radio networks to develop new forms of programming that would serve the unmet needs of the public, or that would alter existing programming to better serve needs that were already partially served. These research concerns were the goals of critical research. They sought to make a medium—radio—of new and greater value to people.

As time passed, however, Lazarsfeld was to complain of the unwillingness of industry leaders to adopt suggestions for program improvements that were derived from his critical as well as administrative research. His relationship with Stanton, while important and useful, ultimately proved to have its limitations. Stanton was a businessman as well as a researcher. Victor Ratner, one of Stanton's first bosses at CBS, described Stanton's gradual transformation from researcher to businessman: "In time an interesting thing happened to Frank psychologically. He began looking for data that could be used by salesmen. It was quite a different thing from looking for data showing the facts as they really were. Frank said a year or two later that he could never go back to honest research again. He had been corrupted like us. He had been an academic, he said, and we turned him into a salesman" (Metz 1975, p. 59).

The Voter Studies: Administrative Research
Applied to Critical Questions

One of Lazarsfeld's most important accomplishments during the 1940s was the design and execution of three large-scale surveys that made all previous social research efforts look unsophisticated and meager. In 1940 in Erie County, Ohio; in 1945 in Decatur, Illinois; and in 1948 in Elmira County, New York, Lazarsfeld's people interviewed hundreds of respondents.

The goal of all three research projects was to assess the role of mass communication in society, particularly people's media message consumption and the power of mass media to influence important decisions about politics. Partly as a result of the Lasswell work, mass communication was generally considered very powerful. Lazarsfeld expected that he could fully document this power. He was surprised, however, when his research data indicated that the media had relatively little influence. In the presidential elections of 1940 and 1948, for example, the power of the mass media to persuade the public to vote in certain ways was found to be very limited. Most voters made up their minds before election campaigns began, and they voted along strict party lines. If mass communication influenced voting at all, it was not through the direct influence that Lasswell had suggested. At best, mass media messages might have had indirect influence through people who talked a lot to others who, in turn, influenced others through personal conversations. The influential people or opinion leaders were shown to be above average in their consumption of mass media messages, so it was argued that they tended to be influenced by media messages and in turn influenced others. This notion of indirect media influence was formalized in the *two-step flow* theory. According to this theory, *opinion leaders* mediate mass media influence by passing along information and ideas from mass media messages to *opinion followers* (Lazarsfeld, Berelson, and Gaudet 1944).

For example, a person in a church organization might have particular access to mass media information about a certain matter. That person would gather as much information on that issue as he or she wanted, and others in the organization, knowing of that person's access, would seek him or her out. The media messages, therefore, have no direct effect; they flow from step one (the opinion leader) to step two (the opinion follower).

The two-step flow theory was tested in an elaborate study in Decatur, Illinois. There, in 1945, more than 1,400 housewives were questioned about their opinion leadership and followership. First, 800 women were questioned; then those women who claimed to be leaders were further investigated by questioning 634 other women whom the leaders had designated as their followers. The most important conclusion derived from the Decatur study was that opinion leadership was found at all levels of society (Katz and Lazarsfeld 1955). This proved important because it demonstrated that any relatively heavy media consumer, not only those who occupied socially elevated positions in the community, could be an opinion leader. Media professionals, then, discovered that they need not aim their persuasive and informational messages at only the elite.

Lazarsfeld's theoretical and research efforts served to illustrate several additional characteristics of much of the research conducted on mass communication. He designed his research projects not only to yield data that would be of immediate interest to the companies or foundations that financed these projects, but also to test theory, advance knowledge, and give rise to new theory. This new theory, however, was often constructed only long after the data were collected. In the case of the Decatur study, almost ten years passed before Lazarsfeld and Elihu Katz collaborated in developing a theory that explained the 1945 data.

The question that must be asked about Lazarsfeld's research approach is how often he was forced to study narrow research problems directed by the interests of sponsors. This is a question Lazarsfeld himself discussed when he wrote:

> Consider the advertiser, or the radio executive, or the propagandist or the educator. The sponsors of research are interested, simply, in the effect of their message on the public. . . . Moreover, if we reflect on these patrons of research and their motivations for a moment longer, we can sharpen this notion of effect. We have been talking as if effect were a simple concept when, in fact, there are a variety of possible effects that the mass media may have upon society, and several different dimensions along which effects may be classified. . . . The sponsors of research . . . have selected, by and large, just one kind of effect for exclusive attention. (Katz and Lazarsfeld 1955, pp. 18–19)

There is an important insight in this statement. Katz and Lazars-feld noted the narrow research interests of research sponsors. These sponsors were interested in the *short-term* persuasion effects of specific types of mass media messages. To secure and satisfy sponsors, these effects needed to be studied. But there were other effects—for example, long-range effects of the media upon society—that were not usually studied. Katz and Lazarsfeld speculated that these effects might be significant and that the media might be very potent in creating them. This speculation now takes on historic significance because the Decatur study was interpreted by many subsequent researchers as definitively establishing the *impotence* or weakness of mass media. The Decatur study, it was said, firmly established that personal influence by opinion leaders is ordinarily more important than influence by mass media. But Lazarsfeld himself had reservations about drawing such conclusions.

The research traditions that were spawned by Lazarsfeld's work have produced many apparently inconsistent findings that continue to trouble the field of mass communication research. Why does research on information campaigns produce findings that suggest that the mass media are weak, while marketing research suggests that advertising messages are powerful? How can mass media messages be powerless to produce certain short-term effects but still be capable of producing important long-term effects? The answers to these questions appear to rest in the different kinds of research questions asked, the different theories used to design research projects, the different methods used to collect data, and the different statistical and mathematical models used to draw conclusions from this data. Marketing research is concerned with prediction and control, not with explanation. For the marketer, it is enough to find that, as exposure to advertising messages increases, sales increase. The marketer does not need a complex theory to provide an elaborate explanation of the intervening mechanisms that transform media exposure into desired consumption.

Information campaign researchers have had similarly limited objectives. If their messages failed to produce immediate conversions among audience members, they were willing to conclude that media were impotent. Long-term effects had no immediate payoff or benefit and thus held no interest for them. Here again the dichotomy between administrative and critical research is apparent. Administrative research is interested in short-term effects because knowledge of these effects aids in making immediate decisions about effectively organizing actions under existing social conditions. Critical research speculates about long-term effects. It is concerned with the fate of people, not in terms of weeks or months, but of decades. It is interested, not in today's consumption habits, but in long-term development of basic human capacities.

As we might expect, these distinct research orientations produce inconsistent findings and generate very different sorts of theory. But the theories and findings of each approach are not wrong, nor is one too practical while the other is too idealistic. If a misconception arose from the work of Lazarsfeld, it was that researchers came to expect that the data from administrative research could be used to build theories for developing critical perspectives. Perhaps this was possible to some extent, but the severe limitations imposed by administrative research prevented it from being very useful to the critical researcher.

It is very costly to gather accurate information to predict and control existing human behavior. It is also not yet clear how it is possible to explain the past and project the future. This does not mean that administrative research should cease because it costs too much and requires too much work; nor should critical research be abandoned because we have not yet established firm rules for its conduct. Both efforts are necessary and useful. Neither needs to establish superiority over the other. The approach chosen should depend upon the personal values and career objectives of researchers, not the fear that one approach is too limited and uncreative while the other is too undefined or innovative. In the box on pages 33 and 34, we have contrasted administrative and critical research, pointing out the strengths and limitations of each.

Comparison of Administrative and Critical Approaches to Research

	Administrative	*Critical*
Primary objective	To improve status quo by increasing the efficiency of existing ways of doing things.	To guide useful change by evaluating existing ways of doing things and developing alternative actions.
Assumptions about Status Quo	Status quo is fundamentally adequate and can be gradually improved by making minor changes which minimize the worst problems.	Status quo is fundamentally inadequate and must be radically changed if human potentials are to be realized.
Assumptions about the Future	If present developments continue, the future will be an improvement over the present.	If present developments continue, the future is likely to be worse than the present.
Assumptions about the Mass Media	Media are simply conduits for messages. New technologies simply inrease the efficiency of the message transmission, making possible better service at lower cost.	Media create a communication environment. New technologies fundamentally alter this environment.

Primary Objective of Mass Media Research	To evaluate specific media uses and short-term effects so that existing needs can be better served and the most harmful effects can be minimized.	To evaluate the role of mass media in the lives of the individuals and in society so that fundamental changes in mass media that will benefit individuals and society can be made.
Purpose of Mass Media Theory	To detail and precisely describe the status quo, including empirical generalizations useful in increasing profits and improving services.	To create awareness of and provide insight into everyday use of mass media so that these uses can be critically evaluated and alternate uses considered.
Research on Media Effects	Studies short-term, easily observed, easily controlled effects and uses this knowledge to plan minor changes that serve administrative purposes.	Studies long-term, unobservable, hard-to-control effects and uses this knowledge to plan social changes that benefit individuals throughout a social order.
Purpose of Policy	Policy should seek to preserve the status quo during a period of rapid technological change. An open and competitive marketplace must be maintained so that the present responsive and efficient provision of media content continues.	Policy should aim to reform how mass media are structured and used. Development of new technologies increases the necessity for basic reforms that can usefully transform the role of mass communication in our society.

The World War II Years: Administrative Research Comes of Age

Throughout the 1930s, the rise of Hitler in Nazi Germany puzzled outside observers. Lasswell explained it by Freudian theory: Hitler was a psychologically unstable individual who had succeeded in using mass media to spread his madness to the entire German nation. Hitler himself had a somewhat different explanation for his success, and many American observers took this explanation seriously. He claimed to be waging psychological warfare, warfare not with bombs and guns, but with words and ideas. Joseph Barnes (1943, p. 34), a deputy director of the U.S. Office of War Information, described psychological warfare as "A war of words in which men's loyalties and convictions are manipulated on a mass scale, and with controls which make falsehoods as effective as truths in influencing people."

Because psychological warfare made falsehoods as effective as truths in influencing people, it directly challenged libertarian notions. Controlled falsehoods appeared to create a social order that operated more effectively than social orders based on uncontrolled truth. How then was this psychological warfare to be combated?

Here was a problem for administrative researchers that had enormous significance. In a time when the existing social order was under severe external threat, any means of making it more effective in resisting this threat was of supreme importance. The question that faced administrative researchers during the war years was not whether controls on the marketplace of ideas were necessary, but what types of controls would facilitate winning the war. According to Barnes, debates over the controls to be placed on truth and even over the possibility of disseminating falsehood raged for more than a year within the Office of War Information, the U.S. propaganda agency in World War II.

A useful description of how this debate was resolved was provided by Carl J. Friedrich (1943), a professor of government at Harvard, consultant to the Office of War Information, and director of Harvard's Radio Broadcasting Research Project. He outlined a strategy that had two objectives: the detection of psychological barriers to persuasion, and the assessment of how effectively a particular set of informative messages could overcome those barriers. This "informational strategy" approach, as he called it, provided a means of scientifically imposing useful controls on truth with the goal of making truth more effective.

It is important to recognize that the notion of an informational strategy was developed in an attempt to find a compromise between Hitler's immoral use of controlled falsehood and the libertarian ideals of a completely uncontrolled marketplace of ideas. America chose to oppose controlled falsehood with controlled truth because, as Friedrich explained, "A call for action will not be heeded, no matter how well supported by moral principles, unless the knowledge of men makes them consider such actions feasible and practical in the end" (Friedrich 1943, p. 89).

Thus World War II provided the incentive to develop new forms of administrative research. This research would enable us to defend ourselves effectively against what was seen as immoral external subversion. While the Office of War Information itself was the foremost practitioner, administrative research was also conducted by many different wartime bureaucracies. Smaller efforts were undertaken by the War Department, War Production Board, Office of Civilian Requirements of the War Production Board, and research units within various branches of the military. Some of the most intelligent, ambitious young social scientists in the nation were recruited to serve in these agencies, names that included Bernard Berelson, Carl Hovland, Samuel Stouffer, Arthur Lumsdaine, Fred Sheffield, Irving Janis, Nathan Maccoby, and M. Brewster Smith. Consultants to various wartime agencies included Paul Lazarsfeld, Robert Merton, John Dollard, and Quinn McNemar. Many of these people emerged from their wartime experience with a new vision of the role of administrative research in modern society.

Carl Hovland: A Vision of Effective Communication in a Peacetime Democracy

During World War II, Carl Hovland worked for the Research Branch of the army's Information and Education Division. He was noted for his research on a series of American war propaganda films, produced by Frank Capra, titled *Why We Fight*. In 1949, Hovland and his army co-workers published a report of their wartime work; their *Experiments in Mass Communication* (Hovland, Lumsdaine, and Sheffield 1949) detailed the development of a theory and set of research methods that Hovland used in most of his later research work in the Communication and Attitude Change Program that he established at Yale University after the war. Hovland was concerned with how and why individuals responded to persuasive messages. He gradually developed theories about what went on inside people's heads when they were exposed to such messages, and he developed a set of research tools to enable him to validate these theories. One of Hovland's earliest ideas was that some people are more easily persuaded than others. Therefore, he reasoned, their minds must be structured differently and work differently than those of people who resist persuasion. He gradually sought to identify and understand these differences in persuasibility.

Hovland began with some traditional notions about differences. In his war research, he studied whether individual characteristics, education and self-esteem, for example, made a difference in a person's persuasibility—how easily he or she is persuaded. DeFleur (1970, pp. 119–22) labeled this theory and research approach the *individual differences perspective*. Where Lasswell had assumed that powerful propagandists using mass media could effectively persuade anyone, no matter how seemingly rational, Hovland's understanding of the media partially contradicted this. Various personality and social factors could serve as barriers to persuasion, although it was possible to develop strategies for overcoming these barriers. Choosing credible communicators or designing two-sided messages, for example, were two such strategies. This implied that people were not defenseless against manipulative media messages. Their ability to judge and reason influenced possible media effects.

But Hovland's study of media, like Lasswell's, was accepted for its administrative rather than critical research value. It was concerned with making communication more effective for immediate, short-term persuasion. These persuasion effects were likely to be of most interest and usefulness to administrators. Hovland, Janis, and Kelley (1953, p. 1) argued that administrative applications were not only possible but were of societal importance. They pointed out that "executives in many organizations feel the need to improve their communication systems in order to achieve widespread acceptance of the standards and values necessary to the success of their enterprises. In the sphere of international relations, numerous communication problems are posed by the 'cold war,' particularly for government policy makers who wish to increase our 'influence' on the people of foreign countries and to counteract potentially disruptive foreign propaganda."

But Hovland and his colleagues also hoped that their research would be useful in answering more basic and critical research questions. They wrote: "Study of the way in which opinions and beliefs are affected by communication symbols provides an excellent means for examining the role of higher mental processes in assimilating the numerous and often contradictory influences impinging upon the individual in everyday life" (Hovland, Janis, and Kelley 1953, pp. 1–2).

Thus, like Lazarsfeld, they sought to find some accommodation between administrative and critical research. They wanted to answer two different sorts of research questions with the same theories and research tools.

Postwar Marketing, Advertising, and Public Relations Research: Administrative Research Reaches Maturity

Postwar America offered many challenges and rewards to business. An entire production and distribution system built to serve wartime needs had to be quickly restructured to serve the needs of peacetime consumers. How could such an enormous administrative task be accomplished efficiently and effectively? One answer was the use of surveys. Many companies that had been making wartime goods returned to the production of consumer goods. They had to decide what products to make, how they should be priced, whether and where they could be sold, and how they could best be sold.

Just as administrative research had been vitally important during the war, it could now be applied to the practical problems facing American business after the war. But how was this research tool to be used? Many business people feared that this research might make administrative decision making obsolete. The research tool might become the master rather than the servant if it dictated how marketing decisions were made. Market researchers were careful to calm these fears and argue that science would always be subservient to decision makers. One postwar market researcher argued that such research was "a subservient science," and that "while market research can help management, it should not attempt to usurp the functions or responsibilities of management" (Lockley 1946, p. 11).

What did this subservience entail? For one thing, researchers were rarely able to control their research objectives. Management decided what they would study and how. Sometimes these decisions were controlled directly; at other times they were controlled simply by limiting research funding. Market researchers were often forced to conduct "quick and dirty" research of limited validity to answer the practical research questions of specific clients. Moreover, business executives tended to utilize this research in very idiosyncratic ways. Some of them based important decisions on it, while others conducted research only to ignore the findings when they contradicted their commonsense understanding.

In postwar America, administrative research was also used in the field of public relations. Public relations sought to solve another set of practical problems that plagued business people. Steinberg (1975, pp. 13–18) provided a cogent description of these problems and the mission of public relations when he wrote that public relations "has to do with the way institutions communicate with their publics, both internal and external. . . . The prime function of public relations in practice is to create understanding and good will among these publics, to take necessary steps for the successful engineering of consent."

The engineering of consent described by Steinberg was to be accomplished through the use of scientific research methods. These research methods effected the techniques described by Friedrich in his discussion of informational strategies that controlled truth. The public's existing attitudes were measured and its resistance to persuasion was assessed. Then a set of persuasive messages was carefully developed, and their effectiveness was studied before and after transmission via the mass media. Efforts were then made to improve the effectiveness of those messages. Public relations people, like their counterparts in marketing research, were ultimately subservient to business executives who established the operating policies of their companies, and the researchers trusted the decisions of their employers.

Public relations people relied on administrative research to guide their efforts. They sought out those areas of social action that were likely to produce the greatest public relations benefits, not those of ultimate usefulness to society. They were concerned with improving the effectiveness of their persuasive messages by creating a receptive audience for them. Sometimes this would lead them to encourage the company to act in ways beneficial to all concerned, but sometimes such actions were designed primarily to benefit the company. The public relations people were seeking answers to administrative, not critical, questions. They were, however, advising companies to take actions of potential effect on the future of society and its members.

Motivation Research in Advertising: A New Style of Administrative Research

Perhaps no type of message is more characteristic of modern mass communication in America than the ubiquitous advertisement. While advertising existed prior to World War II, the advertising industry reached maturity only during the 1950s and 1960s. This rise to prominence was partially fueled by the efficient exploitation of a new mass medium, television. One of the primary research tools for this exploitation was an approach known as *motivation research*, the use of psychological research to investigate the causes, either conscious, unconscious, or both, of consumer behavior and the motives that elicited that behavior.

For advertisers to utilize television effectively, they needed to devise messages that would use not only words but pictures. Most previous administrative research had been devoted to using the written or spoken word more effectively. Television required insight into visual images and nonverbal cues, and this was provided by motivational research. Pierre Martineau's book *Motivation in Advertising: Motives That Make People Buy* (1957) established the precepts of motivational research.

Martineau, director of research and marketing for the *Chicago Tribune,* was disdainful of the reliance that advertisers had placed on verbal messages. They might inform but, according to Martineau (1957, p. 4), they did not motivate. He wrote: "The visual symbols communicate much faster, much more directly than any long involved argument in words. There is no work called for, no mental effort."

This was an advertising philosophy for the age of television. Martineau argued that words alone were becoming ineffective in persuading the average person because words were part of the traditional educational process that modern people resented. He stated that an individual did not "really like copy and words because he's been punished all his school life for not being skilled in things stated in words. . . . But nobody was ever punished for not understanding pictures" (Martineau 1957, p. 6).

There were some striking resemblances between Martineau's arguments and those of Lasswell a generation earlier. Like Lasswell's hypodermic-needle model, motivational research was grounded in

Freudian theory and assumed the primacy of nonrational motivational forces. The research question that faced the motivational researcher was how to use visual images and nonverbal cues to motivate people to consume specific products. This was clearly a question with important administrative implications. If consumers could be motivated to buy more of certain products, the companies that manufactured and distributed those products would find it easier to make large profits.

The debate over motivational research has at times been intense. Some critics, like Vance Packard (1957), have argued that this work motivates people to buy too much of things they do not really need. It convinces them of the need for material goods that do not really prove useful in satisfying important needs. From the point of view of administrative research, however, motivational research was useful because it worked. Advertising campaigns guided by motivational research proved enormously successful to the companies that sponsored them.

How does motivational advertising work? What makes it effective? These have been questions of limited interest, in fact, to motivational researchers. As with most applied administrative research, motivational research was not concerned with explaining human action, only with predicting and controlling it. Martineau himself, however, speculated a great deal on why motivational advertising worked. He believed that its power lay in imagery:

> Imagery plays a highly significant part in motivating our daily behavior. It is far more vivid and compelling than abstract ideas; it generates many emotional accompaniments which become translated into strong drives. . . . The semblance of truth is more important in advertising than truth itself. We believe what we want to believe. Actually, this is true about most things. . . . A woman luxuriating in her first mink is certain that she has been completely transformed. The product that has no other meaning except its functional uses is dull and uninteresting. . . . I don't wear dark glasses just to keep the sun out of my eyes. I'm much more interested in the overtones: being, for the moment, a racer, a movie star, a mountain climber, a skiing champion, an airline pilot. These are by far the most impelling product benefits to me, not some dull mumbo-jumbo about what the glasses are made of. (Martineau 1957, p. 50)

It is clear what motivational advertising attempted to do. It sought to create an association between fantasies that people had and specific products. These associations would motivate product purchases. Truth was irrelevant to these associations; people believed whatever associations they wanted to believe. The motivational researcher's task was to discover the fantasies that people wanted to believe, identify the people who wanted these fantasies, and then convince them to associate specific products with those fantasies. And one way of finding people who wanted to believe fantasies was to identify people who experienced everyday life as restrictive or meaningless. The motivational researcher used research tools to identify these people. Messages were then designed that conveyed those fantasies as well as information about a specific product.

Vance Packard (1957) offered this fine example. A maker of home bakery products developed a totally instant cake mix; all the preparer had to do was add water. The manufacturer wanted to use this fact as a major selling point in its commercials—no muss, no fuss. Motivational researchers discovered, however, that many women still clung to the fantasy of the "hardworking, protective homemaker." While a totally instant cake mix would seem to be thrifty and time-saving, it denied these women full participation in their fantasy—it was simply too easy. The manufacturer, heeding the researchers' advice, made the mix *almost* instant. As the new commercial campaign revealed, the preparer now had to add an egg as well as water. The cake mix was a success.

Motivational research gave rise to the same problems as had other forms of administrative research. In its concern for effective administration of an existing mass media industry, it tended to perpetuate the status quo. Motivational researchers were not concerned with changing the situation of the suburban housewife, for example, or in helping her develop her human potential. They wanted to sell her a cake mix that needed eggs as well as water. They were concerned with giving her fantasies that served to alleviate her frustrations and make her more content with her existing situation. Motivational researchers asked a very narrow research question and received quite narrow answers. These answers might have been useful in selling products, but they were not useful in dealing with larger questions about human existence.

2.3 The Mass Society and Mass Culture Critics: Traditional Elites Strike Back

Administrative researchers laid the basis for change that served the particular interests of their employers, and they believed that their work also served the public. This belief, however, was challenged by the elite critics, who argued that the changes being produced in the interest of business were perversions of traditional culture and would eventually result in the creation of an unstable, amoral social order. These elite critics were usually members of social groups or institutions that sought to preserve traditional culture. Religious leaders, school-teachers, university professors, even some small-town midwestern politicians and small-businesspeople were drawn into a very loosely structured alliance that opposed the changes being introduced. They based their opposition on their conviction that *they* understood what form of culture was best for society. Generally they favored older forms of culture including specific religious beliefs, certain forms of music and literature, certain ways of doing business and politics. They found new forms of culture offensive and judged them as potentially dangerous. They feared that their traditional culture was being "sold out" by Eastern establishment businesspeople and the mass media professionals they controlled. These businesspeople were said to be amoral, concerned only with profits, and not sufficiently concerned with the long-term consequences of what they were doing.

An editorial from the *Christian Century* (1930, p. 1271) offers an example of the form taken by that criticism when first advanced: "The cesspools of Hollywood are being piped unchecked to the minds of children everywhere. Their poison consists not in the bathing beauties, who are comparatively harmless, because so dumb, but in the movies' sentimentality, their false views of life, their glorification of the acquisitive instincts, their financial rewards for virtue, their never ending portrayal of stupid and mean people doing stupid and mean things to one another."

Three related criticisms of mass media were developed during the 1930s. Variations have been repeated many times during the past half-century.

The first criticism was that the media corrupted public taste and promoted popular culture and low taste content. Proponents of this particular criticism were usually creators and users of what they themselves called high culture content—"good books," "fine music," "good literature." They saw the mass media as threatening to reduce the market for their preferred content. Control of content would allow them to ensure the presence of high culture media material, and they maintained that this content control would serve the best interest of the whole or mass audience because it would educate people to the values presented in this superior material (see Davis 1976 for a thorough review of this and the following criticism).

The second indictment was that mass media content served to undermine the efforts of educational institutions by fostering values antithetical to education, such as anti-intellectualism, hedonism, and lack of discipline. Witness the Marx Brothers' humorous (and pointedly titled) attack on the pomposity of higher education and its misplaced value, the film *Horse Feathers*. The media, it was argued, also served to divert attention from academic study. These critics were traditional academics, concerned about the apparent threat to their institution.

The third charge was that the mass media created juvenile delinquents by fostering antisocial values that conflicted with norms and precepts advocated by the family, school, and religious leaders. The 1930s were golden years for movie and radio gangsters, and they were seen as disrupting the normal socialization process of young people and leading them astray. These critics were typically leaders of religious or educational organizations. The most valuable research stemming from this criticism were the Payne Fund studies of the movies (see Blumer and Hauser 1933) that claimed to demonstrate a direct relationship between movies and juvenile delinquency.

These elite critics proved powerless to stop the development of new forms of mass communication and the new social order based on these media—the mass society. The social organizations that they led had once wielded great influence and exercised much control over the everyday lives of individuals. Gradually, as schoolchildren and religious believers alike were transformed into radio and movie fans, into media message consumers, this power was eroded. Teachers complained that children were spending more time with the media and less with school. Clergy complained that parishioners had become more concerned with the next car they would buy than with their salvation. The operators of small local factories found that people did not want their products but preferred the brand-name items they heard about on radio or saw in newspapers or magazines. Politicians found the people's attention diverted away from local political party activities to state and national political leaders. The mass media had created, in the eyes of the elite critics, a base and amoral mass society.

The power of the elite critics was greatly impaired because they were unified only by their agreement of what was bad in American society. Each set of critics offered its own traditional culture as the alternative, but no strong coalition of critics formed to argue for a comprehensive and practical alternative. Yet, while no acceptable alternative to mass society was ever formulated and promoted, the criticisms of mass society became increasingly sophisticated. In time, these criticisms ceased to be miscellaneous comments inspired by current events and became a coherent critical theory of mass society and mass culture. The people who were most responsible for the development of this theory were humanistic scholars and thinkers. Before considering their theory, however, it is important to note how it differed from the critical research approach discussed earlier.

Mass society theory was developed primarily to answer the question, "What is wrong with the *current* changes in society and the culture that is experiencing those changes?" What the mass society critics failed to ask, however, was "What is wrong with *traditional* culture and *traditional* forms of society?" They assumed that what they saw as traditional culture and society brought about the best possible development of human potential. If they had any doubts about traditional forms of social order and traditional culture, they were certain that minor reforms could remedy any problems. The mass society critics were not searching for an answer to the question of how to best develop human capacities to act humanely and morally; they believed they already knew the answer. They were concerned instead with demonstrating the depravity of society and the popular culture that undermined their power and threatened their work.

Mass society critics gradually evolved several arguments, which appeared in most of their important statements. First, society was being "massified" by businesspeople and mass media professionals who had no respect for the traditional values and morality that had given human beings dignity and high purpose for centuries; instead, they permitted these values to be forgotten, and they presented morality as naive and silly. Second, businesspeople and media professionals were creating a new form of culture to replace traditional culture, and this popular culture was nothing more than a debased parody of traditional culture; nevertheless, it had wide appeal for the masses once they were deprived of their traditional culture. Finally, people who bought and used mass culture products were gradually transformed into these "mass people."

One of the most cogent and articulate statements of mass society and mass culture theory was written by Dwight Macdonald (1953, p. 2): "Mass Culture is imposed from above. It is fabricated by technicians hired by businessmen; its audiences are passive consumers, their participation limited to the choice between buying and not buying. The Lords of *kitsch*, in short, exploit the cultural needs of the masses in order to make a profit and/or to maintain their class rule."

He also criticized the administrative researchers whom he held partially responsible for the success of mass culture. These people, he believed, were helping create an amoral social order in which humans were being reduced to the statistics with which administrative researchers were so entranced. He wrote, "This collective monstrosity, 'the masses,' 'the public,' is taken as a human norm by the scientific and artistic technicians of our Mass Culture. They at once degraded the public by treating it as an object, to be handled with the lack of ceremony and the objectivity of medical students dissecting a corpse" (Macdonald 1953, p. 14).

Macdonald's statements offer evidence of a deep rift between humanistic scholars and social science researchers, a rift that was to continue growing throughout the 1950s and 1960s. The social changes of those years were viewed with deep concern by scholars in the humanities who had a limited capacity to interpret and no capacity to control them. At the same time, they saw social scientists who had those capacities as being unconcerned with social change. It appeared to the humanists that the social scientists had betrayed the traditional culture upon which their science was based. To the social scientists, the humanists were too biased by their commitments to tradition to assess objectively what was going on in the real world or its culture.

Edward Shils (1959, pp. 505–28), for example, argued that whatever problems that did exist could not be attributed to the mass media. Rather, he wrote, there was something "wrong with our intellectuals and their institutions and with some of our cultural traditions, which have little to do with the culture created for and presented by the mass media." He called on intellectuals "to look after intellectual things," to concentrate their powers on high culture; in doing that, they would have nothing to fear from the mass society's new culture.

The debate between elite critics and media defenders has persisted for decades with both sides seeming to move further apart with each new attack and counterattack. The two sides are both right and wrong. But as they struggle, the social changes that they debate continue to occur. Today the social scientists appear to be winning because the social order they defended is now well established. Yet the elite critics are in a position to counterattack because the problems and flaws of this social order grow ever more evident. The two sides no longer debate whether a new social order should be established; the focus of the debate has changed. They now debate whether the existing social order requires fundamental changes. As time has passed, increasing numbers of social scientists have joined the elite critics in suggesting the necessity for changes that can reform this social order, but they have yet to rediscover and revive the critical research tradition that could serve to guide those reforms.

2.4 The Rise of Functional, Middle-Range Theory: The Creation of a Dominant Paradigm

Throughout the 1950s, research on mass communication generated many discrete findings. Much of this research, as already noted, was sponsored by companies or agencies that had little interest in developing theory but a good deal of interest in specific findings that could guide administrative decision making. By 1960, concern was voiced by people who wanted to understand the media for other reasons. They expressed the need to integrate and interpret the findings derived from the many scattered research projects. Joseph Klapper (1960, p. 2) wrote about the inadequate answers given to questions raised by the public: "To these questions we have not only failed to provide definitive answers, but we have done something worse: we have provided evidence in partial support of every hue of every view. . . . It is surely no wonder that a bewildered public should regard with cynicism a research tradition which supplies, instead of definitive answers, a plethora of relevant but inconclusive and at times seemingly contradictory findings."

How could these discrete findings generated by different projects that were guided by divergent theoretical notions somehow be gathered in a form which made sense? A social theorist named Robert K. Merton, a colleague of Paul Lazarsfeld at Columbia University, answered this question. He argued that it was possible to integrate the many findings of scientific research into what he called *middle-range theories* (Merton 1967, pp. 39–40). He described these middle-range theories as follows:

> Middle-range theory is principally used in sociology to guide empirical inquiry. It is intermediate to general theories of social systems which are too remote from particular classes of social behavior, organization and change to account for what is observed and to those detailed orderly descriptions of particulars that are not generalized at all. Middle-range theory involves abstractions, of course, but they are close enough to observed data to be incorporated in propositions that permit empirical testing. Middle-range theories deal with delimited aspects of social phenomena, as is indicated by their labels. One speaks of a theory of reference groups, of social mobility, of role-conflict and of the formation of social norms just as one speaks of a theory of prices, a germ theory of disease, or a kinetic theory of gases.

In other words, middle-range theories offer explanations of phenomena that are very difficult to observe, measure, and classify into a precise theory. These middle-range theories take an assortment of disparate attempts at understanding the phenomena and, combining them, come to some reasonable conclusions that are somewhat less definite than hard-and-fast theories.

One of the best examples of middle-range theory developed by communication researchers was provided by Joseph Klapper. Klapper labored for many years to create a somewhat broader theoretical framework from discrete research findings. The result was the development of his *phenomenistic* or *reinforcement theory*, which argued that the media are usually agents of social reinforcement, not social change. This theory proved important during the 1960s and early 1970s in influencing researchers' conceptions about theory construction and the goals of social research. Klapper was quite modest about his efforts. Though he had reviewed hundreds of research articles and labored to make sense of them, he was careful to present his theory as a tentative effort that might have serious shortcomings. He was careful to note that his theories might overlook phenomena that needed to be accounted for. Klapper warned that, although his middle-range theory argued that mass communication usually seems to be a *contributory* cause of effects, it could often be a major or necessary cause—and in some instances even a sufficient cause of effects. But Klapper also believed that a practical need existed for his ideas, that the theory could serve important useful purposes.

The essence of Klapper's theory can be briefly stated. He argued that mass communication ordinarily does not affect people directly, nor does it initiate new audience effects. Instead, mass communication has indirect influence and tends to reinforce the effects of other, more powerful factors. Klapper (1960, p. 8) summarized his theory in the form of five generalizations drawn from the research that he reviewed:

1. Mass communication *ordinarily* does not serve as a necessary and sufficient cause of audience effects, but rather functions among and through a nexus of mediating factors and influences.

2. These mediating factors are such that they typically render mass communication as a contributory agent, but not the sole cause, in the process of reinforcing existing conditions. . . .

3. On such occasions as mass communication does function in the service of change, one of two conditions is likely to exist. Either:
   a. the mediating factors will be found to be inoperative and the effect of the media will be found to be direct; or
   b. the mediating factors, which normally favor reinforcement, will be found to be themselves impelling toward change.

4. There are certain residual situations in which mass communication seems to produce direct effects, or directly and of itself to serve certain psychophysical functions.

5. The efficacy of mass communication, either as a contributory agent or as an agent of direct effect, is affected by various aspects of the media and communications themselves or of the communication situation.

What conclusions can be drawn about middle-range theories such as this? Middle-range theories have proven difficult to interpret. On the one hand, they are based upon and summarize empirical findings; on the other, they provide rather narrow, restricted explanations of phenomena. Proponents of middle-range theory point out its virtues: It is based on empirical findings; it is logically structured; it can be evaluated by using scientific research methods; it can be used to guide research efforts or even to develop solutions to practical problems.

Critics of middle-range theory point out that it suffers from the same limitations of the research findings that it integrates. It is concerned with short-term, immediate, often trivial effects of communication, while ignoring long-term, significant, delayed consequences of communication. Middle-range theories lend themselves to administrative applications but fail to provide critical insight. Critics of middle-range theory do not usually dispute its usefulness because this usefulness is easily established and is one of its great virtues. Their concern centers around the argument of some social scientists that this is the only way in which legitimate social theory can be constructed.

The middle-range approach represents one way of constructing and using theory. Other approaches to theory construction and use may not have the same virtues as middle-range theory, but they also may not have the same flaws. It is possible to conceive of theory construction efforts that will complement middle-range theory rather than refute or reject it. In the following chapters of this book, we will present such a theory construction effort. We hope that it can provide us with sufficient guidance in answering critical research questions like the seven effects questions raised in Chapter 1.

2.5 Conclusion: An Alternate Way to Understand Mass Communication

In the remaining chapters of this book, we will develop and explain an alternate approach to the study of mass communication that could serve to guide critical rather than administrative research. The two previous chapters have illustrated the necessity for this approach. Existing research is typically administrative in intent or unduly restricted by the theories, research methods, and research standards developed for administrative research. This research has tended to produce inconsistent, frequently contradictory findings.

In Chapter 1, we described the three different perspectives on mass media effects that have persisted for more than two decades. Advocates of these perspectives are easily able to locate research findings that support their views. Because of this, no definitive conclusions about mass communication effects have been reached, nor do any appear to be very likely.

The critical research tradition discussed by Lazarsfeld offers an alternate approach that may overcome the limitations inherent in most of the work of Practicus, Empiricus, and Academicus. This tradition suggests that we turn at least a part of our attention away from specific, short-term media effects and direct it toward the long-term role of mass communication in society. But in order to do this, we cannot rely only upon middle-range theories that codify empirical generalizations. Instead we must construct a different form of theory that can provide insight into mass communication and serve as a guide for innovative use of the media.

We live in a society in which powerful institutions have conducted and continue to conduct administrative research seeking to perpetuate a social order useful to themselves. Our federal and state governments, too, rely increasingly upon administrative research to formulate policy for dealing with social problems. Some of us, however, should begin to ask questions that seek more than perpetuation of the existing social order or its simple reform. This does not mean that we are proposing anything revolutionary or proposing the destruction of this social order. We are proposing to generate forms of knowledge about mass communication that have no immediate application for societal bureaucracies concerned with administering the social order.

That such a proposal should be seen as bold or innovative is simply a sign of our times and the present state of our understanding of mass communication. The physical sciences have well-established traditions of pure, unapplied research, and it is assumed that this research will eventually yield findings that can be applied. Critical research offers the same advantage. It explores potential uses of mass communication that serve a wide range of human needs and purposes. Many of these needs and purposes are currently viewed as impractical or idealistic. Without further serious consideration of these needs and purposes and how they might be served by mass communication, they *will* remain utopian. Our argument throughout this book is that people create their own future, either as a simple linear extension of the present social order or through qualitative revisions of the existing social order. These qualitative revisions are made possible in large part by reforming the way in which communication is conducted.

This is perhaps our most controversial view. Communication is more than a simple nervous system or conveyor belt for society. If it is kept constrained within certain narrow limits, communication will simply serve the social order. But if new constraints are implemented, it can be used to transform our social order. Communication is always constrained—it is never free. To a large extent, though, people are free to choose the constraints they will impose on communication. It might be wise, then, to re-explore some of the old libertarian notions in our search for knowledge about how to constrain communication. The concept of rational public discussion and debate is as useful and rich today as it was three centuries ago.

Public communication in an era of mass communication, however, is difficult to understand because it takes so many forms. We can visualize (and we already have the technology for) national voting for political representatives via cable television or even direct voting for the creation of laws. New forms of communication technology offer people the possibility of overcoming many established communication constraints. These possibilities, however, bring with them the problems of deciding what new constraints to impose.

Will we become in the next few decades a nation of shoppers mesmerized by a marvelous electronic marketplace that we can visit at the touch of a button? Or will we become a nation of people dedicated to enriching our lives and the lives of others through the exploration of our potential to be rational, to make wise choices concerning ideas, stories, images, and actions? Will we remain comfortably settled between these two poles? What is the lesson to be learned from the past? Must we conclude that the bold libertarian experiment in rational public communication was naive and misguided? Must we conclude, as did Martineau and Lasswell, that people are inherently unstable, the victims of unconscious forces that cannot be controlled? Must we control the truth that is communicated to us so that we can protect ourselves from ourselves? Or must these controls be imposed, as Friedrich and Barnes suggested, so that we can resist some powerful external enemy who uses controlled falsehood as well as controlled truth? These are questions that a truly useful mass communication theory should help us answer. We risk answering these questions by default if we do not explicitly raise them and search for their alternative answers. This is the challenge that motivates us, the questions for which we seek answers and an understanding.

References

Barnes, J. 1943. Fighting with information: OWI overseas. *Pub. Opinion Q.* 7: 34–45.

Blumer, H., and Hauser, P. M. 1933. *Movies, delinquency, and crime.* New York: Macmillan.

Christian Century. 1930. 23 October, p. 1271.

Davis, R. E. 1976. *Response to innovation: a study of popular argument about new mass media.* New York: Arno.

DeFleur, M. L. 1970. *Theories of mass communication.* New York: David McKay.

Friedrich, C. J. 1943. Principles of informational strategy. *Pub. Opinion Q.* 7: 77–89.

Hovland, C. I.; Janis, I. L.; and Kelley, H. H. 1953. *Communication and persuasion.* New Haven: Yale Univ. Press.

Hovland, C. I.; Lumsdaine, A. A.; and Sheffield, F. D. 1949. *Experiments in mass communication.* New York: Wiley.

Katz, E., and Lazarsfeld, P. F. 1955. *Personal influence.* New York: Free Press.

Klapper, J. T. 1960. *The effects of mass communication.* New York: Free Press. Quotations used by permission.

Lasswell, H. D. 1935. *World politics and personal insecurity: a contribution to political psychiatry.* New York: McGraw-Hill.

Lazarsfeld, P. F. 1941. Remarks on administrative and critical communications research. *Studies Philos. Soc. Sci.* 9: 2–16.

Lazarsfeld, P. F.; Berelson, B.; and Gaudet, H. H. 1944. *The people's choice.* New York: Duell, Sloan & Pearce.

Lazarsfeld, P. F., and Stanton, F. N. 1941. *Radio research, 1941.* New York: Duell, Sloan & Pearce.

Lockley, L. C. 1946. Market description—quantitative and qualitative. In *How to conduct consumer and opinion research,* ed. A. B. Blankenship, pp. 11–28. New York: Harper.

Macdonald, D. 1953. A theory of mass culture. *Diogenes* 3: 1–17.

Martineau, P. 1957. *Motivation in advertising: motives that make people buy.* New York: McGraw-Hill. Quotations used by permission.

Merton, R. K. 1967. *On theoretical sociology.* New York: Free Press.

Metz, R. 1975. *CBS: reflections in a bloodshot eye.* New York: New American Library.

Milton, J. 1644. *Areopagitica.* Hammersmith, England: Doves Press, 1907.

Packard, V. 1957. *The hidden persuaders.* New York: David McKay.

Rivers, W. L.; Peterson, T.; and Jensen, J. W. 1971. *The mass media and modern society.* New York: Holt, Rinehart & Winston.

Shils, E. 1959. Mass society and its culture. In *Reader in public opinion and communication,* ed. B. Berelson and M. Janowitz, pp. 505–28. New York: Free Press.

Steinberg, C. S. 1975. *The creation of consent: public relations in practice.* New York: Hastings House.

Additional Readings

Libertarianism and the First Amendment

Emerson, T. I. 1970. *The system of freedom of expression.* New York: Random House.

Schmidt, B. C. 1976. *Freedom of the press vs. public access.* New York: Praeger.

Siebert, F.; Peterson, T.; and Schramm, W. 1963. *Four theories of the press.* Urbana: Univ. of Illinois Press.

Administrative and Critical Research

Adorno, T. W. 1945. A social critique of radio music. *Kenyon Rev.* 7: 208–17.

Blumler, J. G. 1978. Purposes of mass communication research: a transatlantic perspective. *Journalism Q.* 55: 219–30.

Dawe, A. 1970. The two sociologies. *British J. Sociol.* 21: 207–18.

Gerbner, G. 1958. On content analysis and critical research in mass communication. *Audiovis. Comm. Rev.* 16: 85–108.

McQuail, D. 1969. *Toward a sociology of mass communication.* London: Collier.

Mass Society and Mass Culture

Bauer, R. A., and Bauer, A. H. 1960. American "mass society" and mass media. *J. Soc. Issues* 16: 3–56.

Jacobs, N. 1959. *Culture for the millions?* Princeton, N.J.: Van Nostrand.

Kornhauser, W. 1959. *The politics of mass society.* New York: Free Press.

Wilensky, H. L. 1964. Mass society and mass culture. *Am. Sociol. Rev.* 29: 173–97.

Chapter 3

A Frame Analysis Theory of Mass Communication

Our mental diets consist very largely of cultural junk food. We eat it up regularly, because we are under the misapprehension that it is actually health food. The harm it does is hidden from us for years, like that of environmental carcinogens. We do not connect the workings of these intellectual pollutants with those strange buzzings in our brains—that erratically sounding, endlessly distracting static that prevents contemporary men and women from hearing one another's voices clearly, and therefore from making the connections they desperately need.

Film critic Richard Schickel's interpretation of the Woody Allen movie *Manhattan*, *Time*, 30 April 1979

3.1 An Alternate Approach to Theory Building

Most contemporary communication researchers work within the traditions established by Paul Lazarsfeld and Robert Merton, believing that new and better methods of data collection and analysis will ultimately give rise to broad, useful theories to explain media effects. This view of theory building emphasizes empirical research data at the expense of all other sources, rejects speculation even when based on critical reasoning, and dismisses broad questions not easily answered by empirical data.

Our approach, by contrast, asks and tries to answer some fundamental questions about communication in general and mass communication in particular. This approach has its own limitations: It involves speculation that may not be easy to evaluate using existing scientific methods. Many of the concepts we discuss are too complex to be made operational and to be measured.

The answers that we offer will often be syntheses of existing theories—integrations of compatible ideas. In our attempt to speak to the fundamental questions, we risk being eclectic; we will cross and recross the lines of many academic disciplines. You must answer for yourselves whether our theory forms a useful whole or whether it simply brings together many potentially useful pieces in one place. Your answer will determine the way in which you read the chapters that follow. You can accept our broad theoretical framework and our eclectic approach, or you can merely select the pieces you find useful.

3.2 Eleven Fundamental Questions About Communication

In developing our theory of communication, we have sought the answers to eleven questions that are fundamental to our understanding of communication's role in society. These questions are much broader than the seven media-effects questions presented in chapter 1 and to which most mass communication researchers presently address themselves. Consider our answers carefully. What is your opinion of them? Can these questions initiate a meaningful consideration of communication, or are they too broad? Would you consider using them as a starting point for developing your own thinking about communication? Why or why not? We have offered some insight into our motivations for asking these questions; do you think our motivations have biased our choice of questions or influenced their wording in ways that are likely to reduce their usefulness?

The eleven questions are:

1. Why is all communication structured, and what are the consequences of this structure?

2. How can the structure of communication be analyzed?

3. How do we learn to structure communication?

4. How do we routinely engage in structured communication?

5. What purposes does structured communication serve?

6. How did public communication come to be created?

7. How is mass communication structured?

8. How are genres that structure mass communication created and used?

9. How do we learn to use structured mass communication?

10. How do we routinely use mass communication?

11. What are the consequences of our use of mass communication?

Why Is All Communication Structured, and What Are the Consequences of This Structure?

All communication is structured (i.e., follows certain rules) because without structure communication is impossible. Acts of communication are useful only because people agree on the performance and interpretation of these acts. If all of us spoke random nonsense syllables, for example, no communication would occur. But although some structuring of communication is always necessary, the nature and extent of this structuring may vary considerably.

High-Context and Low-Context Cultures

Edward Hall (1976) provided some useful insights into the degree and manner in which various societies structure communication. Specifically, he differentiated between *high-context cultures* and *low-context cultures.*

Some societies impose strong social constraints on communication acts. Several Eastern cultures, for example, permit only certain forms of communication in specific social situations. Even in social situations that we consider private, as within families, people are expected to control their communication carefully. In these societies, people who enter social situations have many firm expectations of the communication acts that will take place. They can rehearse easily or reflect upon their own actions before entering these situations and thus gain more control over them. Very effective and efficient communication occurs within the narrow limits imposed.

To Western observers, such communication is very subtle—the nod of a head, a few gestures, slightly varied voice tones, or a few vague phrases appear to communicate a great deal to people who can use the social context as a means of understanding what is going on. This communication is effective because the setting in which it occurs provides a means of interpretation. Those socially permissible acts of communication can easily be anticipated, attended to, interpreted, and acted upon. In these societies, a correlation exists between the constraints imposed on communication and the efficiency to be achieved in everyday communication. These are high-context cultures; there is high constraint and high efficiency.

Hall called societies like our own low-context cultures. We place fewer restrictions on the types of communication permitted in social situations. We sacrifice efficiency of communication but gain a greater diversity of communication. Hall's characterization of our society, however, may be too general. Although the public culture of our society permits greater freedom than in Eastern societies, communication is still rather narrowly constrained in the private lives of many people. Research on married couples, for example, suggests that as time passes spouses develop constrained but very efficient forms of communication between each other (Watzlawik, Weakland, and Fisch 1974). It is likely that whenever we communicate intensively with other people over a period of time, our communication acts will become constrained within ever narrower limits but will become more efficient. A glance from a spouse may communicate what it would take a stranger an hour to explain.

Those of us, by the same token, who live in families or cultural minorities that impose many constraints on everyday communication can anticipate and rehearse our participation in those high-context social situations. Teen-agers from restrictive homes tend to find public high schools and peer groups very troubling social environments. Most of us experience some sort of culture shock upon entering social situations where familiar constraints on communication are suddenly absent. For example, recently divorced people accustomed to the highly constrained but also highly efficient communication that develops between spouses often feel awkward in a low-context dating situation.

We live in a society composed of various high-context everyday cultures, but one that has developed a diverse low-context public culture. When we meet strangers, especially those who are not wearing a social uniform, we may find it difficult to anticipate how or what they will communicate and to interpret their communication acts unless they are using some formalized, conventional means of communicating in public.

Public communication, then, requires the development of formal rules that can structure communication between people in public places—people who may not share a high-context everyday culture. Public communication makes possible public action by people drawn from many different high-context everyday cultures. The objectives of public communication are limited: It does not usually seek to transform everyday culture or communication. Public communication is pragmatic communication between people united by their willingness to pursue a common set of conscious objectives. This communication serves to specify and define these objectives and to select or plan actions that can accomplish them.

Culture and Self-Development

The purpose of most everyday communication is likely to be different in societies that permit only high-context everyday cultures and have no well-developed low-context public cultures. High-context cultures greatly limit people's capacity to reflect upon themselves or the social environment. There is no need or purpose for intensive reflection; people simply take communication for granted. Reflection is largely a rehearsal of actions, anticipating what must be done. People do not question whether these actions are worth doing because their utility is obvious. In these high-context cultures, the sense of self that develops is likely to be very limited; people are likely to experience themselves only in terms of their capacity to act effectively in the social environment. If people can do what is expected of them, they are good—if not, they are bad. Self-evaluation is relatively simple, as is self-improvement: People must learn how to control their actions so that their performance meets standards considered acceptable by others.

Thus a relationship may exist between the rules that structure communication and the way in which individuals experience their daily lives and understand themselves. A high-context culture effectively integrates individuals into a traditional social order that they are expected to take for granted. Everyday communication serves as a means of learning, understanding, and obeying the rules governing social action.

Public communication, on the other hand, allows people to develop a public self that can be differentiated from the traditional self. Public selves are defined in terms of a limited range of arbitrary, pragmatic actions performed in public settings. Performance of these actions involves the acting out of a public role that need not be evaluated by the rules that govern action in high-context cultures. Newly divorced people, for example, may find it increasingly difficult to continue operating as spouses. The low-context communication situations they will encounter will demand new actions; they may even develop "swinging singles" selves to help them negotiate low-context situations.

How Can the Structure of Communication Be Analyzed?

All acts of communication are structured in two important ways. First, all communication involves a complex, highly organized sequence of actions that serve to create, transmit, and interpret sense stimuli. Second, all communication occurs within personal and social contexts; it occurs in an individual's mind, a social group, or both over a period of time. All communication has a past, a present, and a future. Public communication is possible because the structures that make it possible were created in human history. These structures permit a particular form of communication in the present that, in turn, shapes how communication will be conducted in the future. In this sense, public communication transcends time and opens us to both past and future.

We ordinarily take acts of communication for granted and fail to notice their complexity or the contexts in which they occur. All of us speak, read, and write at least one language. We easily make sense of sounds emanating from radios, images seen on television screens, densely printed letters on a newspaper page. The curious conventions of cartoons are no problem for us. Some acts of communication are so routine that we may not even notice them happening. When we greet friends, we routinely say "Hello" or "How are you?" without thinking; and we're disturbed only if they do not answer or if they reply, "I feel awful" instead of "Great, how are you?"

This simple example illustrates a most important feature of all communication acts: Rules govern all communication. Rules dictate the words to be used in greeting and the words to be used in response. Equally firm rules govern the appropriate accompanying gestures, facial expressions, and other forms of nonverbal communication going on at the same time. If all participants follow the rules, routine everyday communication takes place. But if improper greetings or responses are made, a much more complex form of communication follows.

Only when communication breaks down do we suddenly realize the complexity of the rules that govern it. Otherwise we are unaware of them because we learn them while conducting our everyday lives, from earliest childhood onward. Communication rules may vary greatly from one situation to another in our culture, but most of us have little difficulty in adjusting our communication as we move from situation to situation. We know that parents permit and expect certain forms of communication, whereas peers have very different expectations. We have learned the rules appropriate for these situations from our past communication experience in them.

Imagine the problems a friend would face if suddenly expected to live in your home or the difficulty one of your parents would have in "hanging out" with your friends. If you foresee only a few problems, you probably live in a high-context culture where communication is highly structured. In such a culture your friend could easily replace you because he or she would already know how to communicate in your home. Likewise your parent would know what to expect in your peer group. But if you foresee all kinds of problems, you probably live in a social environment that tolerates considerable diversity in everyday communication; that is, a low-context culture.

What are the likely consequences of these different rules for various everyday situations? Do you think of yourself as a different sort of person at home than with friends? Do you expect different things of yourself at home than with peers? What about your future? What role will your parents play in it? Your peers? We rarely stop to consider how our routine communication shapes our experience of ourselves and our expectations for the future. We rarely reflect on how our experience of ourselves, once developed through communication, can constrain our future communication. If you are what you eat, you are even more surely what (and how) you communicate. Not only what you are, but what you will become, is inherent in how you communicate.

Explicit and Implicit Coding Schemes

One of the most useful constructs for analyzing the rules that structure communication is communication *codes*. A communication code is a set of rules that structure an aspect of a message so that effective communication can take place. Several codes may be used to structure (encode) a message, while related coding schemes may be used to interpret (decode) this message.

We can divide codes into two basic types, *explicit* and *implicit,* according to whether they have been consciously or unconsciously developed and whether or not they have been arbitrarily represented by use of a second, more simplified coding scheme.

The standardized languages used in most developed nations are examples of explicit codes, with writing as the secondary coding scheme for representing them and dictionaries and grammatical handbooks to make their structural rules explicit. By contrast, the gestures and other nonverbal forms of communication that we use with our friends are an implicit code that has developed over the course of the friendship and may now give us a very effective means of communication. These codes may be consciously employed, but they are unconsciously developed. A smile and a subtle eye movement may communicate more than any number of spoken words, but there is no rulebook to refer to.

Elaborated and Restricted Codes

Basil Bernstein (1964) differentiated communication codes in another important way: according to their universality—or lack thereof—or, in other words, how widely they can be understood. *Restricted* codes can be understood only within the social or interpersonal context in which they were created. *Elaborated* codes can be understood by people living in very different kinds of everyday situations and even in different cultures. The reason why elaborated codes can be so widely understood is that they contain much information unnecessary to the message itself that people in different situations can use to decode and interpret specific messages. By comparison, messages based on restricted codes seem cryptic to people unfamiliar with them. These messages contain few cues to outsiders.

Bernstein found restricted codes operating in British working-class neighborhoods, for example. Often the utterances of insiders in these neighborhoods were unintelligible to outsiders—though both spoke English—because important cues required for interpretation were missing. A cockney lad's request for a "fag" is not an indication of his sexual preference; it represents his desire for a cigarette. A Soho teenager who "kips raw" simply sleeps without clothes. In addition, their sentences violated conventional grammatical rules, making it impossible to rely on such rules as a means of interpretation. Yet these restricted codes provided a useful and efficient means of communicating *within* the groups that used them. Their limitations became obvious only when group members were forced to communicate with outsiders.

Elaborated codes are meant to be understood in many different social or personal contexts. Added information, such as appropriate hand gestures and voice inflections, provides a context that enables any particular message to be widely understood. But the inclusion of this added information makes elaborated codes inefficient because so much redundant information must be provided in order to get the message across, and several different coding schemes may be necessary for communicating a simple message. Our cockney lad, once away from his neighborhood, will have a hard time satisfying his nicotine urge by approaching a stranger and asking, "Fag?" In his own restricted environment that might be enough, but outside of it, the more formal, inefficient "Pardon me, sir, may I have a cigarette?" accompanied by a deferential bow of the head might be necessary. Or consider what we do when we greet a stranger as opposed to a close friend: We are very careful to follow all the appropriate rules for greetings; we enunciate with extra care, keep our voice tone even, control our facial expressions and body gestures within an appropriate narrow range, and so on. In greeting friends, we may embrace them and use facial expressions and body gestures that express a variety of intense emotions. The friend quickly learns much more about us than the stranger.

Elaborated codes have a serious defect: They are easily *decontextualized*. They are easily taken from the social and personal contexts in which they are created and used for other purposes because they can be understood without reference to these personal and social contexts. For this reason, social or personal contexts that traditionally restricted communication cannot directly control the use of elaborated codes.

Imagine what it would be like to live in a society where no elaborated codes existed and where everyone lived in small, isolated communities in which only restricted codes were used. The restricted codes would provide an assumed, routine structure for everyday experience in these communities. Anyone who wanted to exercise power in this group would have to learn the restricted codes but, in doing so, would be learning much more—the unique perspective on existence underlying these codes. Effective rulers could not avoid knowing how community members view themselves and their social environment. Conversely, without this knowledge, rulers would be unable to use the restricted codes effectively and thus could not control others.

Now consider the power that is possible in complex societies where elaborated codes are widely used. These elaborated codes can be used to communicate commands understandable to people who live in many different social environments. Television advertisements, for example, communicate effectively to people who live in thousands of geographically and socially isolated communities. How is this possible? The language of television commercials is a universal language—action, color, music—a set of interrelated elaborated codes that can be decoded in many ways by viewers in differing everyday situations using differing implicit and explicit codes. Now consider how difficult it is for people living in those widely separated situations to control the influence of this advertising upon themselves and others around them. For example, even parents, who presumably exercise great influence, find it difficult to control the impact of advertising on their children.

Thus elaborated codes are both blessing and curse. They facilitate communication that can bind together and organize large, widely scattered populations; but they also reduce the ability of communities or publics to control the influence of communication on their lives. The tradition-bound folk community had an integrity that was guaranteed by its implicit restricted codes. Although the laws of distant lords might be harsh, complex and meaningful communication undisturbed by the elaborated codes used by elite groups could go on within the community (see Thomas and Znaniecki 1958, for example).

A Typology of Communication Codes

The concepts just discussed can be combined to generate a fourfold typology of codes (Figure I): implicit restricted codes, implicit elaborated codes, explicit restricted codes, and explicit elaborated codes. Two of the cells in this typology are easily explained.

Implicit restricted codes are best illustrated by the codes used in folk communities to structure most everyday communication. They are rarely represented by secondary coding schemes, but when they are (as when art is used to represent a religious ritual or symbol, for example), they cannot be decoded by people who have not engaged in everyday communication in the community over a long period of time. These codes enable the efficient, effective control of everyday actions.

Explicit elaborated codes are best illustrated by codes that underlie public communication. The most universal basic code used for public communication is a standardized language in which all words are represented by written symbols spelled in conventional ways. Grammatical rules provide a commonly accepted standard to be used in generating acceptable messages. There are also many less important codes of this type. Books of etiquette prescribe how certain public communications and actions are to be structured. Greetings should have a certain form, for example, and introductions should be performed in a certain way. Laws govern business transactions. We are protected from certain types of false or misleading advertising or sales tactics. For these codes to be truly explicit and elaborated, it is necessary that all people who are members of a public easily learn about them. Media for public education and information serve this purpose. Public school systems teach standardized languages and explain rules of etiquette and business communication.

These codes are modern social creations that require a long training period and active use if they are to serve as effective means of organizing large-scale social orders.

The remaining two types of codes are harder to explain. They result whenever public communication codes cease to be elaborated or explicit. One type is *explicit restricted codes*. For example, there is growing concern among educators that students' reading and mathematical skills are declining. If these skills are lost, standardized languages and arithmetic systems will cease to be elaborated codes; only elite groups that still possess them will be able to use them effectively. Everyday business transactions will be conducted according to a mysterious set of rules, and people who no longer know how to add or subtract numbers will be forced to trust the honesty of clerks who can easily overcharge them.

An example of a code that many believe should be elaborated, but

Figure I Typology of Communication Codes

	Implicit	*Explicit*
Restricted	*Codes used in folk communities* a) Unwritten, verbal language b) Religious rituals c) Rules used to determine how to cope with specific everyday situations	*Codes used by bureaucrats, technicians, and professionals* a) Legal language b) Medical language c) Scientific terminology d) Banking regulations
Elaborated	*Codes used to structure messages by means of mediated images* a) Specific types of television programming b) Television, radio, and print advertisements c) Film conventions d) Newpaper and magazine conventions e) Specific types of radio programming	*Codes used for public communication* a) Democratic discourse b) Public information c) Public entertainment

which has remained restricted, is the code used by lawyers. Most legal documents can be interpreted only by lawyers, but it can be argued that standardized language would serve just as well in these documents, thus eliminating need for the services of lawyers in simple transactions. Similarly many other professional groups have developed specialized (and therefore inherently restricted) codes. These codes generate communication every bit as mysterious to outsiders as the language of some ethnic neighborhoods. Physicians use a highly specialized vocabulary to make their communication about illness more efficient. Even loan agreements with banks rely on restricted codes. Our social order has many highly specialized vocabularies that are explicitly represented in textbooks on medicine, business, science, and technology; but their use is effectively restricted to those people permitted to complete long and, in some cases, difficult periods of training.

The use of explicit but restricted codes by bureaucrats, technicians, and professionals is usually defended with the argument that such codes provide an efficient form of communication that is necessary for effective control of the complex, important actions required in modern society. Standardized languages are said to be too ambiguous, lacking important terms for differentiating critical attributes of objects in the social or physical environment. Physicians would make mistakes in caring for patients if they used the same names used by lay people for diseases. More precisely, lay people use many different names for the same disease, and physicians who want to discuss the disease with other physicians want it always identified by the same name so they will make no mistake in transmitting information on remedies, case studies, and so on. Lawyers, too, would guard the interests of their clients poorly if they relied upon the standard language.

The most important feature of these explicit restricted codes is the creation of concepts that briefly summarize much information about social objects or actions. A physician needs only a few medical terms to summarize what might require paragraphs of detailed description in a standardized language. This use of language resembles the use of mathematical formulas by scientists. These formulas are a convenient, efficient means of summarizing vast amounts of information. Their only limitation is that one must be trained to use them, and this training is restricted. Outsiders who do not know these specialized codes are labeled as lay people, people who are unable to perform in a given situation as only insiders can be trusted to do.

In our social order, explicit restricted codes tend to be the languages of bureaucracies composed of professionals and technicians who use their codes to control the use of technology and skilled services. We must trust that these bureaucrats, the technologies they control, and the services they command will not be used to serve the interests of only a few.

There is no direct means of exercising control, however, because we cannot monitor and evaluate the specialized communication that bureaucrats use. Instead we must rely on other bureaucrats to monitor and evaluate it. Federal and state regulatory commissions are intended to ensure the honesty and integrity of the bureaucracies that deliver goods and services to us. But can the monitors be trusted? The dependence of our society upon explicit restricted codes has created many communication problems because public control and evaluation of these specialized languages has become increasingly difficult.

The fourth type of code is called *implicit elaborated codes*. Their creation has resulted from the invention of mass media technologies that facilitate cheap audio and visual representations, which quickly and efficiently become available to large numbers of people. Visual and audio images are easily structured in ways that can be widely understood and enjoyed. Cartoons, for example, can be viewed and enjoyed around the world with no need for words to interpret the actions and sounds being portrayed. "Tom and Jerry" and the "Road-runner" speak in a visually based language that is easily decoded by people everywhere. But the coding schemes used to structure visual and audio images for transmission by mass media are implicit. No commonly accepted means has yet been developed for representing them so that people can be systematically educated to create or decode these codes in a single "correct" way.

Creating messages by means of these coding schemes is said to be an art that cannot be taught and must be learned on the job. Researchers disagree about the possibility of ever developing a useful secondary code for representing the "language of film," for example. Many grammars of film have been proposed, but none has proved very useful. Similarly efforts are being made to educate people in visual communication, but these efforts are usually limited to specific types of images being used for specific purposes. For example, some schools are teaching children how television commercials are produced so that they will understand how very simple, poor-quality toys can be made to look interesting and useful. Are the languages of television and film inherently implicit or not? Methods are currently being developed to analyze media genres, and these methods may eventually make the implicit languages of mass media explicit. Already such genre studies have begun to provide useful insight into these codes.

Two Objectives for Communication Theory

We can now define two of our objectives for communication theory. Communication theory should serve as a means of elaborating and making explicit the communication codes used to control important social action so that publics can understand these codes. To accomplish this, communication theory should develop secondary coding schemes that can be used to represent implicit and restricted codes in ways that are useful to publics. The public should be better able to understand the communication of bureaucratic elites and media professionals who control the use of explicit restricted codes on the one hand and implicit elaborated codes on the other. Communication theory should provide a means of translating and usefully representing codes for publics so that these publics can become active evaluators of the most important forms of communication that occur in modern societies. Without the development of these secondary codes, publics cannot control the communication that serves to structure most of their important actions.

A second purpose for developing these secondary codes is to permit bureaucratic and mass media communicators themselves to evaluate the codes they use so that rules can be developed—rules that restrict harmful applications of codes and encourage the creation of messages most likely to benefit large numbers of people.

Much of the bureaucratic and mass media communication now produced is restricted by codes of ethics and operations. But such codes are based upon increasingly outmoded theories of communication. A theory that can usefully represent bureaucratic and mass communication codes can serve as a means of critically evaluating messages based upon these codes. This theory should be useful both to communication and to the publics whom it claims to serve.

Implicit in these two objectives for communication theory is a long-term goal—the creation of many active publics engaged in originating and exchanging various forms of public communication, both within and between specific publics. This is not a new goal. Americans have long assumed that active pluralistic interest groups were important to the creation of an innovative, heterogeneous, and stable social order (see Rose 1967). But any social and political power these groups have ever held has been steadily eroded by growing dependence upon bureaucrats and technicians, people who use explicit restricted and implicit elaborated codes for their own purposes.

How Do We Learn to Structure Communication?

We possess an amazing ability to learn how to use codes for structuring communication. By the age of three or four, children not only can decode a spoken language but most can use this language to encode complex statements obeying grammatical rules unknown to them. They have also learned the rules for properly expressing themselves in social situations. We learn to code communication so easily that we take this skill for granted.

Today's children learn to use communication codes in an incredibly complex communication environment, one that is further complicated by the invention of television. They learn a spoken language while communicating in a small, relatively homogeneous community centered around the nuclear family. In certain superficial ways, this community resembles the type of community in which language has been learned for centuries. But there are important differences. The standardized language that children learn today is homogeneous compared to the diverse dialects spoken only a few decades ago. They can use it to communicate with children across town or across the nation. Standardized language is now an elaborated code based on rules conventionalized through constant representation in writing and newspapers, on radio and television. Children can measure their speech against standards provided by the mass media.

Before the invention of modern electronic media technology, people had to be adults before they encountered and were permitted to use explicit elaborated codes. Literacy, not widespread, was an important and powerful skill that was often learned by a small minority of the population. Only people being educated for certain social roles in their communities were taught to read and write. They were usually taught a formal code (Latin) that was very different from the everyday language dialect they spoke at home. For several centuries, Latin served as an explicit elaborated code used by communication specialists serving the people who held social power.

Children now encounter sets of both explicit elaborated and implicit elaborated codes before they enter school. We take children's use of mass media for granted. Few parents think of stopping their children from watching television or listening to the radio, and few ever question what their children are experiencing when they use these mass media. We do not fully know the effects of children's early exposure to various codes. We know that these codes have great appeal for them, that they will spend hours watching television programs. When those programs end, however, they can tell us very little about what they have absorbed. Some describe a few powerful images in vague terms. Others recite jingles or list a few attributes of the characters they have seen. What does this mean? What is being communicated to them? How are they learning to control their experiences of themselves and others? What expectations are they forming of the larger social environment?

The communication that mass media bring to children is structured by an elite that lives in remote bureaucratic environments foreign to the living room. This elite is not bound by the codes that limit everyday communication in the child's home. Acts of violence are represented to children whose parents do not talk about such things. Much of the best and worst of human action is openly portrayed for children to see and possibly to use. They observe a baffling array of heterogeneous human actions that they have no basis for interpreting. Children do not know the dramatic conventions that adults can use to interpret television violence or comedy. They must learn about these conventions in the same way that children have always learned, by looking to others.

In a sense, the mass media present children with continued, easy access to what are essentially foreign languages, languages not spoken in the home. Parents do not explain these codes or provide the rules for interpreting them because they themselves are not aware of them—nor are they aware of the consequences of learning and using them.

One of the first uses that we make of communication as we mature is control of our senses. By structuring communication, we assume control over our capacities to experience feelings, see images, and conceptualize thoughts. Words exemplify how communication codes can be used to refer to feelings, images, or complex thoughts. They are said to objectify or reify essentially transient feelings, images, or thoughts. We can make feelings, images, or thoughts into objects by learning to speak the words that refer to them. Words become cues that we can use to call forth these feelings, images, or thoughts in ourselves and others. We can recreate experiences for ourselves by using words to reflect upon them. Those of us who keep diaries use the words written there to recall the past experiences that they represent.

But words are only one code that we can use to control feelings, images, or actions. What are children experiencing when they become excited in a supermarket while passing the cereal shelf? Have these bright boxes, with their elaborated visual images, recalled feelings, images, or thoughts first experienced in front of the television? How much control do children have over the messages conveyed by cereal boxes or toys that television attempts to link with important experiences?

How Do We Routinely Engage in Structured Communication?

All everyday communication occurs in situations, and different codes are used to structure communication in those different situations. The situation is the smallest unit of analysis that can be used for analyzing a specific set of messages, and message analysis requires a knowledge of the codes used in the situations where the messages occur. This knowledge may or may not be available for our conscious awareness and reflection. The task of understanding messages in a situation is complex if many codes, especially many implicit restricted codes, are used to structure the messages. But it is a relatively simple task if only a few explicit elaborated codes are used. Restricted codes will be much more confusing than elaborated codes to outsiders. People who enter a situation in which unknown restricted codes are used to structure communication are like anthropologists entering a tribal community whose language they do not speak and whose customs they do not understand. It will be hard for them to decide which attributes of the tribe are important, which gestures are to be watched, which vocal tones are to be ignored, or which vocalized syllables are important.

Imagine a social order in which only one language is spoken and a very simple form of nonverbal communication is used. A small number of different situations might exist—situations involving such things as food production, religious worship, food consumption, entertainment, political decision making, and rest. Spoken words and nonverbal gestures could serve to constrain actions within very narrow limits in these situations. People who misused these restricted and restrictive codes could be easily detected and punished or isolated from the community. In this society, few problems of communication would occur among adults because they could rely on their knowledge of codes to predict the actions of others accurately, and each could use the codes to control their own actions within prescribed limits. Only unexpected and uncontrollable events, such as storms or famine, would upset the routine of everyday life. Even then, religious rituals might be used to direct attention toward a future in which these events would be overcome.

We obviously do not live in this kind of social order. We face much different problems. Mass media have made possible the creation and use of many new elaborated codes that are unconstrained by the social situations in which messages based on these codes are consumed. The media transmit the spoken and written words of many competing groups. There is widespread use of the explicit elaborated language taught in the public schools. Only a few people in our society are able to cut themselves off from communication with the rest of society and create isolated communities in which a few restricted codes are used and the mass media are barred. How do we manage to live our lives amid the chaotic communication in our society? How do we manage to carry on a routine, everyday existence in which we can take important things for granted? How do we learn to make sense of the babble of codes in this everyday world?

The Concept of Frames

We can make sense of everyday situations because we have learned how to *frame* them. The concept of frames and framing is central to understanding communication. Frames are sets of cues that people use to organize experiences of situations. A frame can be derived from several codes—the cues (i.e., pieces of information) that make up the frame may be derived from such diverse codes as spoken words used in a family, public school language, television images, and religious concepts. Frames are social or personal definitions of situations that are used to organize actions in those situations.

Goffman (1974) wrote that frames can be either self-imposed, called into play by the situation in which the individual is operating, or both. When we frame a situation, we look for cues that direct our attention toward certain aspects or attributes of activity and away from others. Frames are the means by which we organize our perceptions of social events; through their use we are able to participate in

Frames and Framing

Framing is a communication activity that involves the application of many explicit and implicit, elaborated and restricted codes. It is the use of codes to control and guide sense perceptions so that social actions can be performed that will have specific consequences. We may or may not be consciously aware of the purposes that these actions have, and we may or may not be aware of the codes that we are using to frame an event in a situation. We may also be unaware of cues in the situation that lead us to impose a particular frame on an event, and we may or may not consciously cue ourselves to frame an event in a particular way. Framing is such a complex activity, in fact, that it is impossible to control more than a minor part of it consciously. Only when problems arise do we question the frame we have used to define a situation and the people in it.

Framing involves the applying of codes in specific situations. Therefore it is subject to restricted codes developed to control actions in situations. Framing uses codes to organize experience of situations, but this use is normally limited by cues present in the situations. Whenever we enter a social situation, we can expect to encounter only a narrow range of cues. Other people expect that we will use these cues to impose an appropriate frame and be able to control our experience in such a way that our actions will coordinate with theirs. If we fail to control our experience of situations adequately, we are expected to keep these feelings, images, and thoughts to ourselves. Expression of these irrelevant experiences might disrupt the social situation. For example, in most everyday situations we are expected to keep experiences of fear, sexual attraction, or anger under control. We are expected to ignore cues that might lead us to frame these situations as threatening, arousing, or frustrating. Behavior according to what such frames would suggest is appropriate—screaming, making sexual advances, or punching—is not usually accepted in our culture.

even quite complex social situations. As Hall (1976) noted, there are thousands of different frames that we can bring to the wide array of complex situations that we encounter daily.

What Purposes Does Structured Communication Serve?

Frames provide us with a means of quickly and easily imposing personally and socially useful meanings on events. They permit us to ignore irrelevant aspects of events that might otherwise distract our attention, arouse unnecessary emotions, divert our imagination, or confuse our thoughts. Frames are a highly efficient means of initiating and organizing our experience of social action. Their use is fundamental to our experience of ourselves as competent, rational beings who have some degree of control over our lives. Frames give rise to the impression that we live in an essentially ordered social world.

It must always be remembered, however, that frames are derived from and depend upon codes, and therefore that our experience of social reality is based on arbitrarily imposed limitations of which we are largely unaware. As long as frames enable us to maintain certain perceptions of everyday life, we rarely concern ourselves about the arbitrary structure that they impose on our actions or their consequences. We may buy and consume a product, for example, using the frame provided by its manufacturer in a commercial. As long as the product fits the frame, we will have little reason to question it. Only if it breaks down or causes an injury are we likely to question the frame we have of the product and criticize the manufacturer for misleading us. Only then do we become concerned about the codes used and the frame suggested by the manufacturer and begin to talk about deceptive advertising. As an example, for several years we were content to accept and use Ford Motor's framing of the Pinto automobile, which was small, inexpensive, and gas efficient. The cues offered in Ford commercials—attractive people who were also practical, upbeat music, pretty photography—directed our attention from other matters—safety, for example. When safety became an issue in our evaluation of the Pinto, most of us began to question Ford's arbitrary selection of various codes to communicate information about its car.

Frames can be used to limit and direct the social actions of others as well as our own. Upon entering social situations, we provide cues that we expect others to use in framing these situations. Ordinarily our cues fit with those provided by others so that all participants in the situation use and maintain the same frame. This is most likely to be true of routine events in situations that we participate in frequently. The actions of students and professors in classrooms are usually framed quickly and easily; professors provide cues suggesting that they expect to dominate communication and direct action in the classroom in certain ways; students respond by confining their communication and other actions within these narrow limits. The classroom instruction frame is thus cued, mobilized, and used to structure social action for the duration of the class period. As the end of the class period approaches, students do things that cue the instructor that they are no longer willing to use the classroom frame. They begin to close notebooks or put down pencils, cuing the instructor to search for a good way of concluding the lecture. In some schools a bell provides a recognized means of ending use of a frame so that participants can move on to another activity and a different frame.

Frame cues are a socially accepted means of inducing others to act as we want them to act. People who can express these cues quickly and easily, inducing others to frame social events in certain ways, tend to be regarded as leaders. Though these frames may be arbitrary, they serve to coordinate action in a situation. Leaders are said to give orders easily and to command the respect of followers naturally. In terms of this discussion, they induce their followers to frame situations as they, the leaders, do.

How Did Public Communication Come to Be Created?

It is impossible to trace the origins of high-context cultures that served to structure traditional forms of communication. These cultures can be found in every human society and appear to be a routinely created means of structuring social interaction between people who frequently communicate. Once created, they structure a wide range of everyday actions including much of the communication that takes place between individuals. They permit stable social orders to be created. These in turn permit groups to survive in relatively hostile environments in which structured, cooperative social action is necessary to provide food, shelter, and protection.

Rhetorical Theory and Public Discourse

The origin of various forms of public communication is somewhat obscure, but some important clues can be found in recorded history. Some of the earliest references occur in Greek history and philosophy. Aristotle provided the most elaborate and interesting description of public communication among the Greeks in his *rhetorical theory*. Rhetorical theory can be seen as a descriptive and prescriptive theory intended to explain and guide a unique form of public communication. Aristotle sought to understand the form of public communication that had been developed to facilitate democratic government in city-states like Athens. His rhetorical theory described the rules that could structure it. This type of communication can be called *public discourse* because it is structured according to consciously, explicitly formulated rules that can be publicly communicated, learned, and then applied by all people who are members of a public.

Public discourse was ideally suited to structuring public communication in city-states where a public—a small elite—collectively governed through face-to-face meetings of all its members. In these meetings, carefully structured public speeches and skill in debating issues were useful in influencing group decisions. People who had developed

---

Aristotle's Four Purposes of Rhetoric

But the art of Rhetoric has its value. It is valuable, first, because truth and justice are by nature more powerful than their opposites; so that, when decisions are not made as they should be, the speakers with right on their side have only themselves to thank for the outcome. . . . A proper knowledge and exercise of Rhetoric would prevent the triumph of fraud and injustice. . . .

Secondly, Rhetoric is valuable as a means of instruction. Even if our speaker had the most accurate scientific information, still there are persons whom he could not readily persuade with scientific arguments. True instruction, by the method of logic, is here impossible; the speaker must frame his proofs and arguments with the help of common knowledge and accepted opinions. . . .

Thirdly, in Rhetoric . . . we should be able to argue on either side of a question . . . in order that no aspect of the case escapes us, and that if our opponent makes unfair use of arguments, we may be able in turn to refute them.

Lastly, if it is a disgrace to a man when he cannot defend himself in a bodily way, it would be odd not to think him disgraced when he cannot defend himself with reason. . . .

From Cooper's (1960) translation of *The Rhetoric of Aristotle.*
Copyright 1932, renewed 1960.
Used by permission of Prentice-Hall.

---

skill in public discourse were highly respected because of their ability to influence these collective decisions. Skill in public discourse was thus a source of power in Greek society. The prescriptive rules of rhetorical theory were intended to ensure that this power would be used responsibly to serve the public interest, not for the pursuit of private gain. Aristotle defined how ethical communicators should act because skill in public discourse could easily be abused. Also, democratic publics needed to guard against unethical communicators who would violate rules. Two of the most fundamental of these rules were that communication should be limited to things that are true, and that it should serve the public interest.

Public Discourse and Democratic Government

Some useful insights into communication arise from rhetorical theory. The most important of these is the notion of public discourse as a collectively created medium of communication that must be respected by all who are given the right to communicate publicly and that can be undermined and corrupted by irresponsible communication. Furthermore, effective public discourse is possible only when every member of the public that uses it knows the rules and is willing and able to participate responsibly by listening to messages communicated publicly and then by acting appropriately in response to them.

Definitions of Public Communication, Publics, and Public Selves

A *public* is any group that creates and uses some form(s) of public communication to structure its actions. Publics use public communication to create low-context public cultures. Publics can be differentiated from folk communities that rely upon high-context traditional cultures to structure social action. They bring together people who use different high-context cultures to structure their private everyday lives.

The development of publics represents an important turning point in human history. Publics made possible democratic government, exchange of information, and creation of entertainment that could efficiently structure actions in large-scale, heterogeneous social orders. Publics enabled communication between people drawn from many different high-context everyday cultures.

For publics to serve as an effective means of social organization, all members must participate responsibly in public communication; and this requires the origination and evaluation of messages. When this does not occur, publics cease to exist as publics and become *masses* whose actions are structured by a culture they do not create or control.

Public communication is communication structured by use of consciously created, arbitrary rules that become conventionalized through acceptance and use by a public. These rules permit the public to achieve certain pragmatic objectives. Social roles, for example, are created by structuring public communication in specific ways. They involve presenting one's self in certain ways so that others will respond and act in desirable ways. Since social roles are recognized as human creations, we can reflect on them and consciously plan our actions in terms of them. This permits the development of *public selves,* which can be viewed as objects to be manipulated in certain ways to achieve desired objectives in public settings.

These definitions differ from the more popular meanings of these terms. A public must be a group *actively* engaged in applying communication to achieve collectively defined objectives. Excluded from this definition are forms of social organizations in which masses of individuals are passively governed by an elite even though this elite is elected by the masses. Masses passively respond to messages transmitted by elite groups via mass media; they do not actively engage in public communication. The content of messages is easily controlled by elite groups via mass media to serve their own interest.

We will later discuss additional ways of differentiating publics and masses and also public communication from mass communication. While most existing forms of mass communication are based upon earlier forms of public communication, significant differences occur when publics lose control over mass media content. Finally we will differentiate public selves from selves that arise through the use of mass communication.

If too many messages start to come from irresponsible communicators, the effectiveness of public discourse is likely to be impaired. Responsible members of the public are then forced to be more careful when communicating and evaluating communication. In time, public discourse may cease to provide an effective medium for organizing and democratically controlling the actions of members.

On the other hand, when public discourse is conducted according to the rules, it gives each member the opportunity to influence the actions of all other members. Every member has the right to speak out in the public interest and to be heard and respected by others. The actions of the public as a whole are governed democratically through the power of consciously structured public discourse.

For centuries after Aristotle wrote his rhetorical theory, successful publics were rare and short-lived. The Puritans, for example, had a relatively short history in England. Even in the Greek city-states, publics were a rare and very unstable form of government. And in the Christian-dominated world that followed the Romans, the notion that a group of people might democratically govern themselves was unthinkable; traditional authorities were believed to govern by divine providence. Publics were secular creations that threatened the natural, divinely created order of things. Not until the divinity of kings was openly questioned and challenged did the concept of publics again arouse interest and attention.

How Is Mass Communication Structured?

Implicit elaborated codes structure the sound and visual images in mass media messages. But how are these codes created, and what makes them so effective in communicating to mass audiences? They are created by simulating and exploiting the implicit restricted codes used to structure everyday communication. This simulation differs in one very important respect from the communication that it superficially resembles: It is no longer controlled by an isolated community of people who interact with each other daily but is purposely created by a distant community of mass communication professionals who use what they label artistic and business rules to control their use of these codes.

The messages that mass communication professionals create contain many ambiguous images, but they also contain much redundant information provided by implicit restricted codes that can be used to frame these images. Audience members who can interpret only a small part of the information are able to frame these messages and enjoy them. A good example is the information provided in many television situation comedies by the laugh track. A laugh track requires some elementary knowledge before it can be correctly interpreted, but this knowledge is easily gained from everyday communication with others. Children quickly learn that when others laugh something is supposed to be funny. Similarly, music present in sound tracks provides useful, easily understood cues for framing the visual images in a television program or a movie. Children learn to use these cues by observing their parents' reactions to music in everyday situations. Each of these sets of cues (laugh track, music) is a different implicit restricted code that we have learned to interpret during everyday communication with family and friends.

The everyday meanings of these codes are easily exploited by media professionals, who construct complex messages by combining many codes, thus creating ambiguous content that can be framed in many different but enjoyable ways by different audience members. In this way an implicit elaborated code is created from many everyday codes. Thus one audience member can enjoy the suspense created by the music and studio audience reactions during a quiz show, while another can imaginatively compete along with contestants; and someone else can imagine what it would be like to win the prizes that are described in such dramatic detail. Different sets of implicit restricted codes are present that can be used by each of these audience members to frame a quite different experience for themselves. Each might say that he or she has enjoyed the show, but none of them have an explicit coding scheme that they can use to reflect on their experience and analyze it.

The art of media professionals and the source of their power lie in their ability to take many otherwise implicit restricted codes and combine them to create an elaborated code that can be framed in appealing ways by many different people. This is a difficult task because some combinations of these codes might offend rather than entertain audiences. But once created, a successful combination of codes can be used over and over again. Certain silent-movie formulas are still used with great success by television producers, for example. Once a successful and perennially appealing combination of codes is found, media professionals feel little incentive to create new combinations.

Talk shows originated because radio made talk between people a commodity that was easy and cheap to transmit to mass audiences. The problem was how to broaden the appeal of this talk so that many people would tune in. An elaborated code was developed by presenting program hosts who possessed widely admired personal attributes that interested many different people living in very different social contexts. Once these star hosts were found, though initially by trial and error, their personal attributes and audience appeal could be analyzed, and similar people could be found in the future.

Rules quickly developed for radio talk-show stars that were designed to increase their appeal. Stars were always to speak in a friendly manner and never express anger, for example. The elaborated code implicit in talk shows exploits the desire of many people to frame program hosts as friends. These friends, however, would be quite boring by themselves because they could never talk about controversial things or titillate the imagination with descriptions of deviant actions. Thus the host needed a series of guests who, as one-timers, could say and do all of the deviant things that the hosts could not. Thus, as listeners or viewers of talk shows, we can tune in to be reassured and comforted by the consistently friendly host or to be titillated by the outrageous statements of guests. The program formats have evolved in an attempt to provide something for everyone—sets of implicit restricted codes that can be framed by viewers with very different purposes as they either consciously or unconsciously seek different experiences from media content.

One of the fundamental problems for users of the newer mass media (television, radio, and movies) is differentiating the media's simulated representations of everyday implicit restricted codes from the codes that users actually and routinely use in everyday life. In many cases, mass media professionals deliberately create this kind of confusion whereby, for example, viewers mistake television hosts for friends and sustain silent conversations with them day after day. Or perhaps some professionals naively believe that they are simply reflecting everyday codes to users.

Much of the misuse of mass media occurs because users cannot frame media content as simulated representations purposely created by media professionals. Instead, like the people who talk back to the talk shows, they frame it as reality. Children who see a new toy demonstrated on television, codes implying that the toy is highly entertaining, do not frame the demonstration as a hard sales pitch but perhaps as something their friend Captain Kangaroo wants them to know about so they can have more fun. Some viewers watch the evening newscasts, thinking that they are seeing the news "as it happens," but all news content is carefully structured and screened to create a product that is easy to frame as complete, objective, eye-witness reports of actual events.

The implicit elaborated codes that media professionals create from sets of implicit restricted codes can be called *genres*. A genre, as the term will be used here, is a fundamentally ambiguous code developed and used by media professionals to establish, increase, or maintain audiences for media-presented content, the ultimate purpose of which is commercial—the larger the audiences, the larger the profits for media professionals—but there may be many subpurposes that are less self-serving. Many media professionals claim to be artists or objective reporters. As such, they claim to use the genres of their media to enlighten, inform, or educate media users. In fact, however, these objectives are constantly subordinated to the necessity for profits; artists and reporters must keep their work within the confines of profit making genres or risk not being able to work at all.

The recurring revival of the Dracula horror genre in both film and television provides a useful example. Dracula is one proven profitable theme within the overall horror content genre. It is useful because the story can be represented by many different implicit restricted codes; the protagonist and his victims can be portrayed and therefore framed in many different ways. Fundamental to the story is the struggle between ultimate good and evil, but there are many important sub-plots. A 1979 television version of Dracula highlighted one of these by focusing on the sexual attractiveness of the vampire. In Dracula content, women behave as men sometimes fantasize them: meek, subordinate, easily controlled. This content could be framed in different ways by different viewers. Some female viewers might find Dracula attractive, whereas others might be repelled but titillated by his deviant actions; and still others might be disgusted by the sappy weakness of the women or angered by yet another form of violence against their sex. Some male viewers might admire Dracula's sexual prowess, whereas others could find his female cohorts more interesting. There is something here for everyone, or at least for a sizable segment of the potential viewing audience.

Another recurring genre is the Western that features the bar girl/prostitute with a heart of gold. Matt Dillon's Kitty in "Gunsmoke" could be framed either as the painted mistress of the Long Branch Saloon or as Marshal Dillon's dependable female companion—or even as a strong, independent businesswoman making a go of it in the Wild West.

To understand and use mass media properly, both as individuals and as a society, we must approach them as powerful technologies that facilitate the elaboration and commercialized representation of everyday codes. We should seek a useful understanding of the genres that have been developed by trying to understand the purposes they serve for audiences and the many unintended consequences that they have.

Media professionals often argue that the ambiguity of genres is a virtue. News reporters, for example, say that if conservatives can interpret the report of an event in one way and liberals in another, the report itself must be objective. Similarly many action/adventure shows are ambiguous because these genres use frequent deviant or puzzling actions to attract and hold the interest of viewers. Producers see this ambiguity as good because it affords the greatest amount of utility and pleasure to the largest number of people. Although deviance is routinely punished (criminals are almost always jailed and practical jokers always get their comeuppance), some media users can even choose to idolize deviants. Studies (Berkowitz, Parke, Leyens, and West 1974, for example) of aggressive teenagers indicate that they tend to identify with and emulate violent characters. In our terms, they frame these characters as interesting and attractive people. Such framing is possible because the program itself has been made deliberately ambiguous in the interest of attracting a larger audience.

Another defense offered for deliberate ambiguity is that reality itself is ambiguous, that media content simply reflects reality. In real life, criminals may have some attractive qualities—even Charles Manson or the Boston Strangler might have been kind to cats; therefore it is acceptable to represent these qualities on television. Most media professionals respond to any attack on their right to create ambiguous content with the argument that controlling such content would be censorship, which is counter to the interests of the total audience as well as a violation of free speech.

These questions are fundamental to the growing controversy over how mass media influence modern life. Should content be censored because a minority frames it unwisely? Should that minority be educated to use media content better? If so, who should educate—parents, teachers, peers, employers, religious leaders, or the federal government? How much right do media professionals have to introduce ambiguity into their content? These are questions that we hope our theory can address, and eventually answer, by developing a secondary coding scheme enabling media content to be represented, reflected upon, and analyzed.

How Are Genres That Structure Mass Communication Created and Used?

The codes of everyday life enable us to assume control over our experiences of ourselves and our social environment. We learn these codes by communicating in everyday situations, and we learn to use them to frame these situations effectively so that our action is meaningful and purposeful. Their usefulness is constantly tested during interaction with others in different situations. We gradually change codes and frames if they result in unsuccessful or painful actions in those everyday situations.

The genres used by media professionals are unrelated, however, to our own everyday codes and frames. They may simulate everyday codes and encourage us to impose everyday frames on media content, but media professionals have no direct knowledge of our own personal codes or frames. They can understand us only as audience segments, as types of media users who tend to use certain frames to interpret media content. But their own knowledge of implicit restricted codes and everyday framing is limited. Much of it is based on their own personal experience. It is not surprising that media professionals often make mistakes when they develop new or different genres, nor is it surprising that media characters use such simple, stylized codes. Media professionals have a very difficult task—they must represent many different forms of coding and facilitate many different forms of framing that they, as individuals, do not and cannot understand. For their work to succeed at all, they must rely on rather naive audiences of people eager for content structured by simple genres and who frame media content as they would frame everyday communication.

We often hear that program producers, particularly in television, use the LCD principle (Lowest Common Denominator) in designing media content. This means that they aim their program material at the lowest level of comprehension. The largest number of people, all using different, simple, and redundant codes, must be able to frame the message successfully in ways that they experience as enjoyable.

A genre is a formula for putting types of cues from many different codes into media content so that users impose certain frames and act as if they are receiving specific forms of everyday communication.

How Do We Learn to Use Structured Mass Communication?

Many of us never really learn to use mass communication. We use much of its content as though it actually is what it simulates—everyday communication based on implicit restricted codes. Most mass media professionals do little to discourage this use; in fact, they encourage it. They are merely producing realistic content, they say, that reflects what is going on in society. Even the producers of violent dramas argue that life is violent and that people are better off facing up to that harsh fact.

Television and film are often portrayed as magic windows through which we can watch the most interesting and important things going on around us. It is easy to forget that we are looking through camera lenses and gazing at staged events. These events contain cues that encourage us to use certain everyday codes and to frame them in routine ways. Most of us are so skilled at using these cues to impose routine frames on television and film events that we do so without any conscious thought. Only when an event is staged poorly or when the proper cues are badly presented do we become aware that we are watching images selected, created, and organized by media professionals.

We move through the world of television and film as we move through the world of everyday life, by taking communication for granted until it becomes a problem. So long as media content simulates well enough the codes learned in everyday communication, we take it for granted and easily frame and understand it. So long as this content seems to have the same consequences that everyday communication is expected to have (i.e., to inform and entertain us), we continue to use it without evaluating how well it serves us or what influences it might be having on our experiences.

How Do We Routinely Use Mass Communication?

During everyday communication involving other people or ourselves, we are both the creators or producers and the users of many implicit and explicit, restricted and elaborated codes that we routinely use to frame situations. To some degree, all of us are untutored but sophisticated folk artists who create experiences for ourselves out of the raw material available to us. Some of us are members of publics and are skilled in some form of public communication. The raw material we use in communicating is composed of the cues in situations provided by others and by our knowledge of various codes. To the extent that the codes we use are restricted and often controlled by others, our art may be very limited and limiting. We may frame a life that is limited to the community that taught us our codes, or we can rely on media genres to frame a fantasy life. Some codes, like standardized languages, enable us to understand and communicate with people in communities very different from those in which we grew up.

Our growing use of media content may be altering the restricted codes used to organize everyday experience. The folk art used to create everyday experience has become much more complicated and difficult. We experience many problems in controlling ourselves or in imposing order on everyday situations that people who communicate in folk communities do not encounter. But we have trouble admitting these problems to ourselves because that would mean we are not competent adults. Fortunately for us, the mass media give us easy access to many solutions for everyday problems.

Yet there is some irony to this situation. In many cases, our problems with framing everyday experience arise because we have allowed media content to alter our use of everyday codes. When we experience problems because of how we use these codes, we often turn to the creator of the problem—the media—for solutions. Ads tell us what toothpaste to use to whiten our teeth, for example, but it was those same ads that convinced us of the need to have white teeth.

81

Thus mass communication is the source both of problems and of solutions to problems. There is profit to be made in providing content that creates problems and profit to be made again in content that offers solutions.

When we gaze through the lenses of television and film cameras, we are looking at the artistic product of remote communities of content producers who are using commercial genres to generate their product. We have no direct control over those artistic communities or over the financial community that sponsors their work. Most of us have little insight into our own use of media content.

What Are the Consequences of Our Use of Mass Communication?

Our use of mass media can be both enriching and impoverishing. It can teach us new codes but may limit our effectiveness in using others. It shows us distant people, places, and things, but distracts us from the serious business of conducting our everyday lives. Use of media representations leads to increasing numbers of everyday problems; but, as earlier noted, these same representations offer solutions that appear to be useful. Mass media surround us with stories but reduce our ability to tell stories. One of the most important uses that we make of mass communication is to facilitate certain forms of communication play. Through communication play we can develop certain crucial skills that may in time compensate for the loss of communities using restricted codes.

It is relatively easy to criticize the mass media for disrupting and transforming the secure everyday experience that was possible in traditional communities. This criticism, however, fails to note that these folk communities were not necessarily ideal places in which to live humane lives. Existence within them was very restricted. Community members could develop only a very limited understanding of themselves and others. The routines of daily existence were structured by implicit restricted codes that, with no human awareness of them, could not be subject to conscious reflection. Efforts at reflection would only inhibit people's ability to perform as competent adults committed to the situations in which they lived.

In any case, we cannot return to these folk communities, no matter how dissatisfied we might be with modern society. Why? Because our use of explicit elaborated codes has enabled most of us to develop at least a limited capacity for introspection; we are simply too self-conscious to participate well in a folk community. We value our experience of ourselves too much.

If we cannot go back, where can we go? This book has offered some notions about public communication as a means of seeking an alternative. Participation in publics permits us to become self-examining people while we continue to engage in responsible social actions. Through our creation or choice of publics in which to act, we can participate with others in achieving important social objectives. Our participation in these publics can be a form of self-expression as well as a means of engaging in meaningful joint action with others.

For public communication to succeed in a media-dominated communication environment, we must develop new genres for structuring that communication. Public communication has been much neglected in the past century in favor of mass media genres. Many people now assume that mass media genres have made earlier forms of public communication obsolete because media simulations of public communication seem so much more efficient and effective. Why engage in community discussions when we can watch informed national leaders discuss public issues more articulately than we could? Why not simply let them do it all and learn from what they say? Why create publics when masses seem to do as well in maintaining a stable, productive social order? These are questions that we will address.

3.3   A Model of Everyday Communication

The fundamental task of human existence is to learn how to manage one's everyday life. This task has become much more difficult in modern society—and also much more important. What we make of ourselves is important not only to ourselves but also to our society. We must develop communication skills in order to be responsible participants in a social order that we can help create. We cannot rely on a traditional folk community to provide us with a secure existence and a limited sense of self. In the course of living our lives, we fulfill whatever potential we have as human beings; we express ourselves as people to others; we encounter problems that test our skills for organizing our experience; and most important, we choose purposes that let us plan a future that will determine what we can become. We cannot live responsible everyday lives without a critical knowledge of mass communication's role in our lives. Mass communication has transformed how we communicate. It can both help and hinder our efforts to realize our potential as human beings.

Figure II presents a model of the communication and framing process that illustrates and summarizes some of the points made in the preceding discussion or that will be made in the discussions that follow. This model emphasizes the continuity between everyday com-

Figure II Model of the Communication and Framing Process

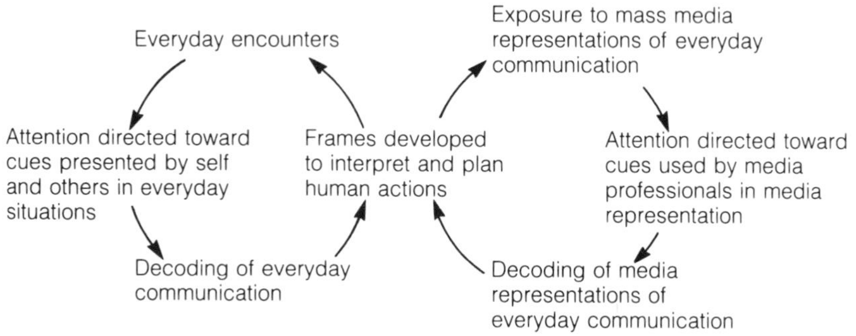

Everyday encounters

Exposure to mass media representations of everyday communication

Attention directed toward cues presented by self and others in everyday situations

Frames developed to interpret and plan human actions

Attention directed toward cues used by media professionals in media representation

Decoding of everyday communication

Decoding of media representations of everyday communication

munication with others and mass communication: We tend to develop and use the same set of frames to interpret both everyday encounters and mass media content. We are encouraged to do this by mass media content that simulates everyday communication. Also, because most of the framing that we do is unconscious, we tend to regard and use the cues present in mass media content as though such cues were present in everyday life.

Television is especially likely to be used in this way. It is a part of our home environment and is easily treated as a part of the family. Many of the cues that television producers use to help us frame their programs are taken from codes that we use in our everyday lives. Only rarely do we bother to refine our interpretation of television programs so that we can differentiate these programs from everyday communication. We know that the world of television is not real, but we find that what makes it artificial is hard to explain. We tend to be ambivalent about our evaluation of television, saying that it is both real and unreal, natural and artificial. But we continue using television and other mass media as routine forms of communication that we inevitably integrate into our everyday communication with consequences that are both good and bad.

The model shown in Figure II implies a very close relationship between everyday communication and mass communication. It suggests that the genres used by media professionals to structure how cues are presented in mass media messages can lead to decoding and framing that, in turn, has consequences for everyday life. Frames used in everyday communication can be imposed on media content, and vice versa. There are advantages and disadvantages to this linkage. Media professionals try to simulate everyday communication in ways that are attractive and interesting to large audiences. But when they are most successful, these representations necessarily influence the everyday communication that they simulate and represent.

The old radio and television comedy "Amos 'n' Andy" offers one example of the framing relationship between everyday and mass communication. This situation comedy aired on the CBS Television Network from June 1951 to June 1953. This was not a particularly strong period of racial or ethnic enlightenment in the United States. Segregation in schools, housing, the military, and most aspects of American life, in fact, was commonplace. Relatively few white people ever had any meaningful interaction with black people. The framing of situations in which white Americans dealt with black Americans, then, was not easy, and such encounters were either avoided or painfully enacted.

Imagine a married white couple exposed during that period to media representations of black people (in this example, Amos, Andy, the Kingfish, and Sapphire, not to mention the movies' Stepin Fetchit, assorted "Mammies," and others). Their attention might be directed by the program producers toward very specific cues: laziness, shiftlessness, conniving, and stupidity. Characterization of black people in this manner depended on standard cues that had been utilized for some time in the blackface comedy genre.

Once decoded, this information might become part of our imaginary white couple's store of frames. When they came into actual everyday contact with a black person, however, where would the information used to frame that encounter come from? Which cues would they attend to—those provided by the actual black person in the situation through his or her behavior, or those provided by Amos, Andy, and their friends? That choice would determine the framing and later decoding of this encounter; and it, in turn, would become part of the viewers' store of frames.

If our hypothetical viewers attended, in the actual encounter, to the Amos 'n' Andy–provided cues and framed the situation accordingly, they would behave in one way. But if they used the cues provided by the situation itself and the black person's behavior in it, they would probably behave differently—one hopes, more appropriately.

By the same token, should the encounter with the black person have been a positive one, our viewers, once that information becomes part of their collection of frames, might well start framing the "Amos 'n' Andy" program differently. No longer might it seem a harmless comedy about black people. Instead they might frame it as an unfunny, gross exaggeration of a destructive racial stereotype.

This example centers around a framing mistake—an error in interpretation of media content that might have arisen because of the way in which a given genre structured that content. Framing mistakes, analyzed individually, may seem fairly harmless, although the one just detailed does not. The long-term consequences of these errors, however, may be very serious.

3.4 Conclusion

Ours is a relatively low-context culture, one in which individuals need a good deal of immediate information to operate successfully. This information is provided in communication, from both the mass media and other people. A theory that helps us understand the role of communication in living our lives should answer some fundamental questions both about us and about our communication. The eleven questions that we proposed are:

1. Why is all communication structured, and what are the consequences of this structure?

2. How can the structure of communication be analyzed?

3. How do we learn to structure communication?

4. How do we routinely engage in structured communication?

5. What purposes does structured communication serve?

6. How did public communication come to be created?

7. How is mass communication structured?

8. How are the genres that structure mass communication created and used?

9. How do we learn to use structured mass communication?

10. How do we routinely use mass communication?

11. What are the consequences of our use of mass communication?

Structure shows itself in the type of culture we create. High-context cultures have very narrow limits within which their members can communicate and act. Low-context cultures place fewer restrictions on the communication allowed in social situations. As such, their members often find that appropriate behavior and communication are not easy tasks.

The structure of communication in different cultures can be analyzed by using codes. A code is a set of communication rules that structures an aspect of a message so that effective communication can take place. Codes with rules that are more or less explicitly established are explicit codes. Codes that have developed without the aid of explicit rules are implicit codes.

Explicit and implicit codes can be either restricted (if they are understood only within the social context in which they occur) or elaborated (if they can be understood by people in a variety of different situations). Our society has developed various types of codes, each with different purposes and consequences.

We use these various codes to frame or interpret social situations. These frames are social or personal definitions of situations that we use to organize our actions in them. The codes found in everyday life and in mass communication help us develop our store of frames so that we can successfully perform in a wide variety of situations.

Problems sometimes occur, however, when mass media use implicit elaborated codes to simulate implicit restricted codes. We structure much of our lives by using implicit restricted codes, and we have a good deal of control over them; but we have no control over the media professionals' use of implicit elaborated codes. When we mistakenly use media-provided frames to evaluate everyday situations, we may have trouble behaving appropriately.

Genres are sets of cues taken from implicit elaborated codes that media professionals use to simulate our everyday implicit restricted codes. They are created and developed for the building and maintenance of mass audiences, not necessarily for individuals' personal control over their lives. Our ability to act and reflect on our actions in different situations—our public communication—may be influenced by framing based on codes that are out of our control and designed for purposes other than the ones we might have wanted for ourselves.

The next five chapters offer a systematic critical introduction to the role of mass communication in our lives and society. It is centered around the concept of framing mistakes: using media-created frames to interpret everyday life and using everyday frames to interpret media representations. In the next chapter, we will explain how these mistakes occur; and in the following four chapters, we will consider their long- and short-term consequences.

References

Berkowitz, L.; Parke, R. D.; Leyens, J. P.; and West, S. 1974. Reaction of juvenile delinquents to "justified" and "less justified" movie violence. *J. Res. Crime Delinq.* 11: 16–24.

Bernstein, B. 1964. Elaborated and restricted codes: their social origins and some consequences. *Am. Anthropol.* 66: 55–69.

Cooper, L., trans. 1960. *The rhetoric of Aristotle.* Englewood Cliffs, N.J.: Prentice-Hall.

Goffman, E. 1974. *Frame analysis: an essay on the organization of experience.* Cambridge: Harvard Univ. Press.

Hall, E. T. 1976. *Beyond culture.* Garden City, N.Y.: Anchor Press.

Rose, A. M. 1967. *The power structure: political process in American society.* New York: Oxford Univ. Press.

Thomas, W. I., and Znaniecki, F. 1958. *The Polish peasant in Europe and America.* New York: Dover.

Watzlawik, P.; Weakland, J.; and Fisch, R. 1974. *Change: principles of problem formation and problem resolution.* New York: Norton.

Additional Readings

Public Communication and Rhetorical Theory

Borden, G. A.; Gregg, R. N.; and Grove, T. G. 1969. *Speech behavior and human interaction.* Englewood Cliffs, N.J.: Prentice-Hall.

Sennet, R. 1978. *The fall of public man: on the social psychology of capitalism.* New York: Random House.

Structured Communication

Cicourel, A. V. 1972. Basic and normative rules in the negotiation of status and role. In *Studies in interaction,* ed. D. Sudnow, pp. 229–58. New York: Free Press.

Luckman, T. 1975. *Sociology of language.* Indianapolis: Bobbs-Merrill.

Miller, J. G. 1965. Living systems: basic concepts. *Behav. Sci.* 10: 193–411.

Genres

Cawelti, J. G. 1976. *Adventure, mystery, and romance.* Chicago: Univ. of Chicago Press.

Douglas, M. 1975. *Implicit meanings.* London: Routledge & Kegan Paul.

Peterson, R. A. 1976. *Production of culture.* Beverly Hills, Calif.: Sage.

Chapter 4

Framing Media Representations as Everyday Communication

We are not like the movies—
merchants of dreams, salesmen of
escape. We deal primarily with reality.

Sylvester Weaver, former NBC
president, *Look*, 7 September 1971

Soupy Sales, then a popular
children's TV entertainer with an
early-morning program for moppets,
looked his fans right in the eye and in
a low and conspiratorial voice asked:
"Is Daddy asleep? He is? Good! Find
his wallet and slip out some of those
funny green pieces of paper with all
those nice pictures of George
Washington, Abraham Lincoln and
Alexander Hamilton and send them
along to your old pal, Soupy, care of
WNEW, New York." The next day the
mail began to pour in. . . .

From a report on children's television
advertising by the Federal Trade
Commission, March 1978

4.1 Introduction

This is a chapter about mistakes—mistakes we make when we use mass media.

One specific mistake is that when we confront media representations, we use the codes of everyday communication to frame them.

89

Then, as social psychologist W. J. Thomas has argued (Volkhart 1951), they become real in their consequences. We often ignore these consequences, which we neither anticipate nor understand; and we deny the power of media representations, telling ourselves that we are merely entertaining ourselves, playing games in our minds.

Most of us, however, are more attracted by and involved in media use than we will admit. To some extent, all of us live in the world of mass media; we inadvertently become serious in our use of them and unconsciously frame their content as real. We pass through the looking glass in the blink of an eye—suddenly the characters of the mass media become actual for us, not just electronic blips or celluloid reflections. They are people, and we are in their presence. We can identify with them, laugh with them, cry with them, fear for them, love them, and despise them. We can be concerned about their futures, try to solve their problems for them, and see them as living the life we would live if only we had the ambition, luck, or courage to do so.

Most media consumers frame at least some of their encounters with media representations as everyday communication. We know that children are fond of having breakfast *with* Captain Kangaroo and that they may fret when they see Santa Claus on television on Christmas Eve. "How can he deliver all the children's toys if he's with me?" Grown-ups, too, sometimes confuse everyday communication and mass media representations. It is now soap opera legend that one devoted viewer bought a new dress in order to "attend" the television wedding of her favorite soap opera character and then became justifiably upset when the ceremony was canceled at the last moment. It seems that the almost-bride's pregnant half sister by her mother's marriage to the drunken oral surgeon from City Hospital confessed that she was carrying the unborn child of the groom-to-be, an obviously unfaithful though marvelously handsome criminal lawyer from one of Center City's finest families.

Other soap opera fans have been known to send get-well cards and home remedies to ailing characters. An actress who played a soap opera shrew was actually assaulted on a New York City street by a woman who resented her shabby treatment of her video husband and lover.

There are many other examples of people using media representations as everyday communication. We have all seen viewers scream at television sporting events and boo video referees. In fact, the media representations of sporting events have become so real for many fans that when they actually attend an event in person, they seem to be constantly looking for the instant replay; when it doesn't come, they feel cheated. "Shoulda stayed home and watched on TV" is almost as common a stadium refrain as "We're number one!" Many sports teams have gone so far as to install giant video screens in an attempt to satisfy the expectations created by the fans' television habit.

One final example of people defining media representations of communication as everyday communication is the famous Halloween "War of the Worlds" broadcast of 1938. People literally fled into the hills from the radio-reported advance of warlike Martian invaders. The producers of this radio drama used a news format, with on-the-spot reports and program interruptions. These techniques cued thousands of listeners to frame the alien attack as real. We might reasonably respond that we are too sophisticated as media consumers to fall for something like that today. But the media industries have matured as well. The sources of our daily mass media messages have reached such a high level of sophistication in the creation of various genres that it is often difficult to avoid confusing mass media content with everyday communication. Moreover, these same media industries and other entities within our society intentionally design and present media representations to encourage such substitution.

4.2   How Children Use Media Representations as Everyday Communication

This chapter's opening quotations include an account of the "Soupy Sales incident," in which that television performer asked his youthful friends to take money from their parents' wallets and purses and send it to him. Some did. For these children, the Soupy Sales television program was not just a television program; their friend Soupy asked them for a favor and what was a friend to do but comply?

Later in this chapter we will discuss how media representations are created to simulate everyday communication. In the case of children, this would seem to be a particularly important issue. Parental concern can be seen in the pointed questioning by a spokeswoman for Action for Children's Television aimed at Senator John Pastore, who at the time (1972) was chairing U.S. Senate hearings on television's effects: "Would you allow a salesman in your living room to sell something to a five-year-old?" she asked the Senator. When he said no, she continued, "Well then, why do you let him sell to five-year-olds on television?"

Indeed, children are prodigious consumers of the mass media, particularly television. American children aged three to five watch more than fifty-four hours of television per week—nearly 65 percent of their waking hours. Each year in this country, children and adolescents watch more than 90 billion hours of television, with some children averaging six to seven hours a day. And there is a good deal of logic behind the assertion that these youthful viewers are more susceptible to the impact of this viewing than adults. In our society, the playgrounds are getting bigger and the backyards smaller. Ever since World War II, with its rapid industrialization and urbanization of our formerly rural nation, the nature of families and the socialization of their children have changed. More and more mothers are taking to the job market. More and more parents find themselves with a greater number of available leisure activities than ever before; and, with increased income, they are taking advantage of those choices. As a result, parents are less involved than ever before in the growing up of their children. As sociologist Urie Bronfenbrenner (1970) put it, "Whereas American children used to spend much of their time with their parents and other grown-ups, more and more of their waking hours are now lived out in the world of peers and of the television screen."

Clearly, children would seem most likely to frame media representations as everyday communication. From the moment babies are born, they begin to learn from their environment. At first they learn what to expect from their new world by chance interactions with their surroundings. This is the reason why very young children see the world as self-centered; it exists only insofar as it affects and is affected by them. We often see young children hide their eyes from some offending agent in their environment. If they cannot see it, according to their logic, it does not exist. But with increasing age, children come to understand that a world exists apart from themselves, a world that must be understood in terms of newly formed images; that is, implicit codes. Where do those codes come from?

Parents are a child's primary socializing agent; they define the child's world as well as creating and defining its symbols. At about age two, however, a change occurs. The child enters what is known as the *operational stage* (Flavell 1977), a period of psychological development that continues until about age twelve. In this period of maturation, children tend to accept experiences at face value. They do not have the cognitive ability to test new information or experiences against existing information and experiences. They cannot question the usefulness of the implicit codes they have learned. Moreover, these young children do not have a wide store of frames against which to measure and define new situations. When they enter the stage of *cognitive thought* (somewhere around twelve or thirteen years old), they may come to see new information or experiences as problematic— as propositions or hypotheses to be tested and framed in alternative ways. Until then, however, the reality of any situation is defined without reflection by the children themselves by means of implicit codes. Contemporary thought on psychological development recognizes that these stages are really only rough approximations of when certain skills appear; their order, however, is accepted as accurate.

In a detailed look at how young children decode and use media representations as everyday communication, one researcher (Hawkins 1976) identified four ways in which children judge the reality of television. There was a *magic window reality* where children can interpret the representations either as merely drama or as real people presented by television. He identified a *social expectation reality* where children evaluate how similar the representations are to those things they encounter in the real world. A third reality was a *usefulness reality*— how useful do children find television representations in helping themselves understand their own real-world situations? Finally he identified an *actuality reality* where children do not see representations at all but actual events—not real people and things on television, just real people and things.

What Hawkins discovered is that young children tend to see television as a magic window—the people in it and their encounters with them are real. Equally important was the finding that these young children were likely to use the information provided by these real people in the television set to help them deal with their own everyday situations; that is, they experienced a higher usefulness reality than older children. They were using information derived from genres representing everyday communication to structure their own actual everyday communication.

As children mature, however, their cognitive abilities grow, and they can create and use many different frames. They can consciously reflect upon how mass media representations of situations compare to those from their everyday life. This has been called *adult discount;* that is, the possible impact of the child's use of media representations is reduced, or discounted, by potential comparisons with everyday situations and frames learned through communication on the road to adulthood. Those of us who grew up watching Walt Disney movies faced the day when we finally had to admit to ourselves that dogs and deer do not talk.

Much as that inevitable December experience of seeing parents putting gifts under the Christmas tree alters a child's expectations about Santa Claus, seeing actual cops and real teachers and an expanding everyday world can add to and alter the maturing child's store of frames. What we cannot know is how much these frames are altered, how the use of media representations has influenced individual children's personalities and development, or how their definitions of the growing number of everyday situations they enter are influenced by those years of taking the reality of media representations for granted.

4.3 Making Media Representations Seem Like Everyday Communication

Although children often do not have the cognitive ability to discern the difference between media representations and everyday situations, we presume that most adults have this ability. All of us, however, sometimes find ourselves imposing everyday communication codes on media representations. Why? One reason may well be that we want to. The exciting experience of media representations can often be more satisfying or "real" than much of our own dull everyday experience.

Another reason that we adults may experience media representations as real encounters is that the mass media industries and their clients use ambiguous genres that can best be defined by using everyday codes. Mass communication industries—newspapers and broadcasters, for example—advertisers, and politicians all benefit from the mistakes we make when we define media representations as everyday communication. We will look at four areas in which media content producers consciously create and apply inherently misleading genres: television and movie entertainment, news, advertising campaigns, and political campaigns and politics.

Entertainment Fare

We have already described televised sports, which offer us a seat "at ringside" or "at the fifty-yard line." So successful, in fact, were television producers in convincing fans to define media representations of the events as real and to substitute television for stadium viewing that some leagues and teams (those in the National Football League, for example) were forced to institute television blackouts. To draw fans back into the ball parks and stadiums, the leagues prohibited access to the media representations by forbidding local broadcasts of games that did not sell out.

But the mass communication entertainment industries use their reality-creating skills in areas other than sports. When we enter a movie theater, for example, we are exposed to cues that encourage us to enter a state of *willing suspension of disbelief;* that is, we are asked to frame the filmmaker's celluloid conventions as everyday communication. A cut from one scene to another usually tells us that the action in the two scenes is occurring simultaneously. We know that in everyday life we cannot be transported from one place to another instantaneously, but we suspend our disbelief for the duration of the film. A dissolve from one scene to another tells us that some period of time has passed. Again, we have not yet mastered travel into the future,

94

but we ignore this disbelief and trust the filmmaker's cues. We frame the film representation as though it were everyday communication. Imposition of these frames commits us to sitting and watching; it also adds to our enjoyment of that particular media use.

When we read a novel, though, we are constantly reminded that it is not everyday communication because we are forced at somewhat regular intervals to make concessions to this medium: We must interrupt the communication to turn pages or even stop reading altogether. We prefer to be viewers who impose everyday codes on films. Sometimes we are so engaged in this imposed frame that we become irate with talkative seatmates or distressed at glimpsing a boom microphone or the wires that help the hero fly, or some other production device.

The producers of television entertainment use different conventions in their efforts to present their wares as everyday communication. They cannot depend on viewers being seated in isolated darkness for an uninterrupted extended period of time. Television programming enters a distraction-filled environment (the home) through a distraction-filled medium (commercial television).

To create the impression that the upcoming thirty- or sixty-minute media encounter is indeed everyday communication, contemporary programs generally open with an establishing sequence of film. "All in the Family" opens with a long shot that moves down a real Queens, New York, street, and this look at an actual neighborhood ends with a tight shot of an actual housefront. Through a dissolve, we are invited into the Archie Bunker household, where we see two ordinary people playing the piano. To strengthen the credibility of the situation, one of the performers announces at either the beginning or end of the program that the show (or the communication) was taped before a *live* audience.

This method of establishing the realness of the characters and the ensuing situations is standard for virtually all contemporary entertainment programming. Compare this, however, to a few years ago when programs were introduced by titles and credits rolling over cartoon caricatures of the stars ("My Three Sons" and "Bewitched" are two good examples).

Television producers and programmers have discovered that if they can encourage intimacy and identification with the characters— if, in other words, they can build audience involvement through the imposition of certain frames—they can increase the loyalty, commitment, and of course numbers of viewers. When the medium exposes itself by intruding at commercial time, the viewers could leave. But when they are engaged in interesting everyday communication with mediated but apparently real people, they are more likely to stay tuned in and even look forward to the next meeting.

Skeptical? Ask any friend to name his or her favorite entertainment program. Ask that friend to recount the action. More than likely you will get answers like "Fonzie did this" or "McGarrett did that," not "Henry Winkler as Fonzie acted out a humorous skit in which he took two girls to the same dance," or "Jack Lord, who plays McGarrett, was involved in a dramatic performance in which he and the other actors who play the officers of the Hawaii 5-0 police were called on to apprehend two actors posing as vengeful, demented assassins." Jean Stapleton, for one, often complains that she must constantly tell people that she is *not* Edith Bunker.

We do suspend disbelief, we do approach and frame many media representations as if they were everyday communication. As adults, we can supposedly discern reality from fantasy. Or can we? How much of what we learn or assimilate during our media use is ultimately added to our store of frames? We can consciously reflect and separate everyday from mass media communication, but the dispensers of the media representations encourage us (and in many cases we are more than willing) not to reflect. And even when we consciously view a media representation as just that and only frame it as everyday communication for the duration of our media use, what do we take back to the everyday world and what do we leave behind in media land?

News

Ever since he became anchorman on the CBS Evening News in 1962, Walter Cronkite's trademark had been the closing of his news show with "And that's the way it is, (plug in the appropriate date)." But despite his well-deserved credibility, Mr. Cronkite was wrong. That was not the way it was.

Almost every media market in this country has at least one local station that calls itself "Eyewitness News." The intent is to convey the impression of reality; that is, through their station with its "Mini-Cams," "Action-Cams," and "City-Cams" bringing on-the-spot news, you see the real events; you participate in important everyday situations all over town. As with the national news, however, we are not eyewitnesses nor are we offered an opportunity to know the way it is. We are merely given the necessary visual material to feel as if we were participating and to frame the news events as if we were actually present. We are persuaded to see the news media representations of events as the event itself in all its complexity. Perhaps worse, we are led to believe that the events presented are the only important events for that day. The banner motto for the *New York Times*, for example, is "All the news that's fit to print," a slogan no nearer the truth than Mr. Cronkite's "And that's the way it is."

Our society has grown so large and developed so dramatically in this century that all of us depend on the mass media for our experience of the day's events, local, national, and international. Most of us do not receive news by word of mouth but from the mass media. Virtually all of our experience with the day's important happenings is mediated by mass media representations (unless, of course, we are lucky—or unlucky—enough to be part of a news story).

A Roper Organization poll (1979) asked people, "Where do you usually get most of your news about what's going on in the world today?" The respondents could offer more than one answer. Sixty-seven percent named television, 49 percent said newspapers, 20 percent responded radio, and 5 percent said magazines. Only 5 percent responded that they got their news from other people. That same analysis showed that 47 percent of the respondents felt that television was the most credible source of news information, and 23 percent thought newspapers were most believable.

This dependence on and trust in the mass media news dispensers is somewhat warranted. The television network news companies do a remarkable job of collecting, categorizing, condensing, and presenting representations of events. The local television news organizations do a conscientious job of highlighting important events, given the self-imposed limitations of short program length, time for sports and weather, interludes for friendly chatter among newspeople, and so on. Our print journalists, too, and their newspapers are almost without equal in the world for providing news as they define it. The presenters of the news perform tasks with apparent responsibility, but their representations are not everyday communication of unmediated experience. The media industries present the news to us as unmediated events, but because of the way news is collected and distributed, the news can never be more than a superficial but commercially useful representation of actual events.

From all of the day's known happenings in the world (see Epstein 1973), the three commercial television networks *choose the day's topics* (usually between twenty and thirty stories for the three networks in an evening). They *choose the parts* of those happenings to relay to us. They *choose how to present* those chosen portions (how to edit the story, what the voice-over copy will say, how much film to use, and so on).

Take an average day on Capitol Hill, for example. Of all the committee meetings and sittings of both House and Senate, a network may choose one subcommittee hearing that it feels will interest most of its viewers. It may choose to cover only the chairperson's opening remarks, the questioning of a witness by a committee member, or a witness's response. Finally it may film the give-and-take between committee members and witnesses, editing the film so that the answer follows the question. It may air only the opening remarks and then have a reporter stand in the now empty meeting room and do a verbal report on the day's activities. It might choose to show no film and simply have the anchorperson read a brief report.

Local news programs make similar collection and presentation judgments, as do newspapers. Thus what are presented as unmediated events are actually representations that have been shaped and defined by various *gatekeepers*. These gatekeepers change events in many ways as these events pass from the everyday world to newsroom to media representation. For example, the reporter covers the story in a certain way; the cameraperson films it according to a set of professional, technical, and personal criteria; a writer works out the copy for the anchorperson and the voice-over announcer; a film editor edits the story based on available film and shot selection; the news director decides how much time the story should get and where it is placed in the news program; and so on.

The problem arises not so much in the presence and functioning of these interpreters or gatekeepers—because they are necessary and skilled actors in the news-gathering and dissemination process—but in the representation of their product as "eyewitness," "on the spot," "the way it is," that is, not to be questioned. With large numbers of Americans using these media representations and coding their simplifications of events as real, the risk exists that people will later use the frames they have developed while using these representations to define their own everyday communication. Many big-city mayors, for example, have complained that viewers take the news reports of city crime as actual everyday happenings and thus stop going into the city at night.

Although not alone in his warning, historian Daniel J. Boorstin (1978, p. 14) predicted one plausible consequence of this mistake:

> Millions of Americans . . . [sit] placidly before the tube when they might be participants in the stream that was once reality. . . . [this behavior] expresses itself in an overshadowing mood of helplessness. We are tempted to become spectators, not only of what is on the tube, but of all experience. We see so much, every day on the screen, of catastrophes that we can do nothing about—floods, fires, terrorist attacks, kidnappings, starvation and corruption—that we make these the very prototypes of experience. A world to be looked at, to be entertained by (or alarmed or shocked by). But not a world to act in.

The development of the newspaper industry in our country offers a useful illustration of how media organizations discover and use genres and how these representations come to replace everyday communication. The penny press was the first mass newspaper published in the United States. Its commercial success was due in part to the low-cost, high-volume printing permitted by the steam-driven printing press. But it was also partly due to the news genre developed by

Benjamin Day. Before 1835, most of the news printed in newspapers was of little interest to most newly literate readers. News consisted of long, complex political and economic essays based on public communication genres. The political news was read only by the upper-middle-class members of political parties who supported the newspapers that printed it; the economic news was read only by merchants.

Day proposed to broaden the audience for news by changing the definition of news. The new genre that he proposed was based on the everyday gossip that circulated freely in large urban centers. Day filled his newspaper with accounts of current local events, structured like stories told by one friend to another. These accounts, however, were only representations of gossip and, as such, were very different from the actuality. Real gossip circulates within a community of people and tends to use restricted codes, which provide people with a means of easily and usefully encoding and decoding gossip. Gossip circulates because it serves purposes of the community, and it is structured by and limited to that community.

While the penny press news simulated gossip, it was not bound by the same community rules. Newspapers circulate freely through many different types of communities. They can do this because they use elaborated codes that superficially resemble restricted codes. One of the ways in which Day made elaborated codes resemble restricted codes was by ordering his writers to use popular adjectives and sentences that sounded like everyday speech. This writing style produced representations much more likely to be mistaken for everyday speech than the very formal styles used by old-fashioned journalists like Benjamin Franklin or Thomas Paine.

In time, news stories replaced community gossip; that is, the genre succeeded in displacing the everyday communication that it was patterned after. Shibutani (1966) has argued that there is a close relationship between the flow of rumor, which he labeled informal news, and the flow of news within modern societies. When news flow is reduced, the circulation of rumors increases; and when news flow is adequate, the circulation of rumors declines. Shibutani's work suggests how Day's news genre could displace gossip as a source of news. Newspapers provided efficient, thorough coverage of events that people were curious about. If they read the newspaper, they had little need to seek out neighborhood gossip for accounts of events.

As the newspaper industry developed, the news story genre evolved. During the yellow journalism era of the late nineteenth century, the genre was broadened to include pseudoevents staged by newspapers and news sources for the purpose of creating copy. This allowed the proliferation of fictional accounts of events that were later revealed to be hoaxes. When Henry M. Stanley found Dr. Livingstone in Africa, Stanley was not on a humanitarian mission; he was a news reporter creating a pseudoevent. The yellow journalism news genre fused gossip and fantasy into a powerful, attractive formula for creating news stories.

The motivation to develop this genre was created by intense competition between large urban newspapers like those of Joseph Pulitzer and William Randolph Hearst in New York City. These men used the news genres they created to build large newspaper organizations and, in the case of Hearst, an empire that stretched from coast to coast. These great personal editors (as they were later labeled) were willing to twist the news genre to produce whatever content people were willing to buy, no matter how distorted or false. Such abuse was possible and even easy because readers interpreted news stories by using everyday codes without insight into the formulas that shaped these stories. Newspapers told exciting, attractive stories that could be substituted for gossip and other forms of everyday communication. Exaggeration and falsehood were of limited concern to readers primarily interested in making these stories substitute for certain forms of everyday communication.

Today local television news programs offer a format that is not so different from the penny press news genre. Local television newspeople claim to be "eyewitnesses" and implicitly assure us that getting news from them is like "hearing it from a friend." The informal or happy news format assures us that newscasters are friendly people, that the news genre simulates everyday communication. This local news genre is especially attractive to those viewers who want to frame the news as they would frame gossip. It assures them that they are getting the news straight from trustworthy friends, not from professional newspeople working for a remote media bureaucracy.

This example illustrates the relationship between the genres of the mass media industries and the codes used in everyday life. Media genres are initially based on everyday codes. They are successful in drawing audiences to media because they give people easy access to communication that in everyday life may be more difficult to engage in. They are touted as a replacement for inefficient everyday communication. After all, who would argue that news stories are not an improvement over neighborhood gossip?

Media genres, then, generate a product that is superior in certain respects to the everyday communication they replace, but this product is not always a completely acceptable substitute. Gossip did more than simply transmit information. By engaging in gossip, people learned implicit restricted codes that helped them organize their lives within the confines of a relatively isolated community. The codes learned in reading news stories are not so useful in organizing one's own experience. They give a less clear picture of a specific community's values, for example. News reporters using various news genres employ elaborated codes, and they are intentionally ambiguous (they would say objective) in the construction of their messages. These elaborated codes and the stories they tell may raise as many questions about experience as they answer. Take the big-city mayor's complaint again: What do the twenty seconds of film and subsequent half-minute of reporting devoted to a shooting in a downtown bar tell people about the community in which they live? Is it unsafe? Are their fellow people animals? Is this an isolated example of stupidity?

Advertising Campaigns

What is "halitosis"? The dictionary and we define it as bad breath. But halitosis is nothing more than a medical-sounding word coined long ago by an advertising copywriter for a mouthwash advertising campaign. All of us and our friends have occasionally suffered from the "blahs," "ring-around-the-collar," "Big Mac Attacks," or at least the "frizzies." Our everyday lives are filled with a myriad of maladies that, except for media attention, would have gone unnamed and probably unfelt.

Advertisers, like the mass communication industries themselves, encourage us to experience their purposive media representations as everyday communication. Two primary components of any persuasive attempt lie in (a) using everyday codes to (b) convince the targets that they have an actual need. In some cases, like talking a friend into going to the movies, for example, those tasks are simple enough. Create the need: "We need a study break." Use coding that he or she can easily decode: "Let's go to the movies." But advertisers face a more formidable situation; they must reach large and diverse numbers of people with one or a few simple, short messages. These persuasive attempts are limited by a host of legal, social, and media-related factors (such as space and placement on the page or the need to fit the ad into a twenty-second spot). And once disseminated, they are unalterable. Faced with these problems, advertisers choose the best genre for producing consumer needs by creating representations that are easily mistaken for everyday communication. They hope we will frame their media representations of these needs as we would frame needs suggested by everyday communication.

A clever and fascinating 1977 film, "The 30-Second Dream," identified four realities or types of experiences that advertisers try to lure us into creating for ourselves:

Intimacy. We are invited into the most personal of moments, the couple becoming engaged or the two women walking and quietly discussing feminine deodorants. The advertiser invites us into these private situations. We feel privileged and we empathize because we too desire such intimacy. Americans greatly dislike loneliness. We join the "Pepsi People" or we use the soap "for people who like people."

Family. Christmas dinner, Thanksgiving Day, wedding day—we are invited to them all, and more often than not the camera angle through which we attend is a family member's eye view. We rarely look on the family at the table from the outside. We are present when problems arise (water spots on the crystal, leftovers again), and we are party to solutions that preserve the sanctity of the family (a new dishwashing liquid, a special dessert).

Vitality. We are taken on boat rides, glider flights, water and snow skis, polo ponies. The perspective is usually that of the "subjective camera"; that is, we see the action as if we were participants. The wind whistles, the snow sprays and chills our faces, and a hand thrusts a beer or soft drink in our direction. We have taken part in a lively physical activity with a group of young, attractive people, and the product is as much a part of the situation as we are.

Success. We are taken from boardroom to private jet to waiting luxury car. We are offered encounters with successful people, and we learn that this car is a sign of success, that this broker can add to our wealth. Then comes a knock at the door. It opens, and two well-dressed attractive couples raise their already-filled glasses of wine and toast, "To the good life!"

In all of these "realities," we are cued to frame ourselves as participants, to perceive these representations as everyday communication. Performers talk directly, frankly, and seemingly individually to each of us: "My mother-in-law is coming and I'm so nervous"; "I can't believe I ate the whole thing." What better means of creating the impression of a need than to involve targets of the ad in the situation where the need is experienced? And what better way to create a familiar code than having them participate?

Several contemporary familiar trends lend credence to the proposition that advertisers encourage people to use their media representations as everyday communication. One trend is the demise of the pitchman. Our everyday experiences with salespeople have taught us that they will inevitably try to sell us something. Therefore when we are confronted by them, we frame them negatively, put up our guard and resist the sales effort. Rarely do we see these pitchmen in contemporary advertising. Instead we are offered ordinary people in routine everyday life or in humorous soft-sell situations. When a pitchman is used, he or she is usually someone we know from another environment: an actor, athlete, famous person. They are not salespeople hawking someone's wares but respected individuals offering testimonial.

A second trend is the use of hidden-camera and "on-the-street" interviews. We are introduced to ordinary people in routine situations—the laundromat, the supermarket—who ostensibly tell us their actual feelings about the product.

The rise of the unglamorous or plain-looking actor is another trend. We now meet real-looking people in commercials. Gone are the days of the impeccably dressed, lovely housewife not sweating over the kitchen stove. In fact, several talent agencies now deal only in real-looking people.

One such campaign, the 1972 Alka-Seltzer "Try it you'll like it— I can't believe I ate the whole thing" series, was so successful that fully 85 percent of the people interviewed by a market research firm could identify the ads and the product. At least one woman wrote to the ad agency responsible for the campaign and claimed that, although she did not use the product, she was so enamored of that poor man who ate the whole thing at the waiter's behest that she bought Alka-Seltzer and flushed it down the toilet!

Finally there is the advent of "personification" campaigns. No longer is it enough simply to buy the product; we are asked to *be* the product. We are fortunate, however, that if we cannot join the "Pepsi People" and be part of the "Pepsi Generation," we have the option of becoming a "Pepper." The U.S. Army wants you to "join the people who've joined the Army."

Political Campaigns and Politics

Few of us will ever actually have the opportunity to meet a major (or even minor) political candidate. As they hustle from speech to meeting, meeting to stumping, they have little time to do more than offer us a quick glimpse, creating images by which we can identify them. All of us have ample opportunity, however, to encounter those images through the mass media in a number of different settings, settings that the candidates hope we will accept as everyday communication.

Very few voters will, or even can, consistently follow a political campaign, checking out and evaluating the candidates, assessing their stands on the various issues. But all voters can, and most do, learn to frame candidates based on their mediated communication with them. Over 80 million people, for example, watched at least one of the 1960 Kennedy-Nixon television debates. Those who listened to them on the radio tended to think that Richard Nixon had outdone the youthful, inexperienced John F. Kennedy. The Republican's words carried more weight. Those who watched on television, however, proclaimed Kennedy the winner. His words were less important than his warmth, his sincerity, his willingness to talk one-to-one to voters and look them in the eye. All of these qualities came across on television (Kraus 1962). Voters' communication with this "real" man went far toward winning him the presidency and creating what we now see happening in political campaigns.

For example, since television there has been a movement away from reliance on paid political commercials. Candidates no longer hire only Madison Avenue advertising agencies to assist them in their campaigns; they hire media consultants, experts who can make the best use of all media to present the candidate to the people. Many of their tactics are designed to encourage voters to accept their mediated communication with the candidate as everyday communication. These tactics include the following:

1. Make news, not just commercials. News is framed as an actual event. The voters become eyewitnesses to the candidate's activities, meeting the candidate in the everyday world, not in a world mediated by an ad person. Together with the candidate they open new supermarkets, meet with newspaper editors, visit schools.

2. Set the candidate's media pitch in nonpolitical settings. To present a candidate talking at fundraising dinners is to offer the voter a "politician." To present that same candidate in a nursing home talking with elderly patients is to offer the voter an opportunity to eavesdrop on a real person at work.

3. Design campaign television spots to look like news stories. Broadcasters have taken great pains to make the news seem real; candidates should and do take advantage of those efforts.

4. Have the candidate appear on as many television and radio interview and talk shows as possible. Even create these programs for the candidate if necessary. Interview and call-in programs offer the voter a chance to frame the candidate as an actual person, a friend, not a packaged politician. They give the impression of spontaneity, immediacy, and intimacy.

One influence that the mass media have had on politics involves the transformation of public communication between people and their leaders. Just as mass media simulated and replaced gossip and many forms of folk and public entertainment, they also simulated and gradually replaced public communication about politics. The eighteenth and nineteenth centuries were eras of great orators—people skilled in articulating the objectives of the communities in which they lived and capable of motivating public actions to accomplish those objectives. These orators learned the objectives of their communities through routine everyday communication. Their talent lay in being able to consciously reflect on these objectives and make them explicit in public communication. In the eighteenth and nineteenth centuries, political parties still served as publics in which the skills of discourse could be learned and the products of that communication could be prepared and consumed.

Political parties were, in certain respects, communication organizations with the same functions as modern mass media. They recruited public speakers, trained them, and gave them opportunities for reflection about public action. When these orators were prepared to communicate, the parties gave them platforms on which to speak. Political parties provided a context for public communication as well as the social and personal rules that prevented it from becoming too irresponsible. Public communication used elaborated codes, but their use was grounded in political parties and remained explicit for the publics that they served. Any particular orator could only be as irresponsible as the party allowed.

The development of mass media—first, mass newspapers, then radio, and subsequently television—greatly reduced the control of political parties over public communication. Mass media professionals found they could attract audiences by simulating that communication using various genres. Political campaigns had developed as an important means of engaging people in public communication, so the media developed genres for representing these campaigns to their audiences. Various types of campaign news stories were developed. Romantic stories glorified particular candidates as political heroes; ironic stories revealed that even heroes had feet of clay. Campaigns were described as horse races with first one candidate ahead, then another. Daily event reports were necessary to ascertain who was leading at any given moment.

In the process of using genres to represent campaigns and attract audiences, the media intruded into and disrupted public communication, reducing its power to structure political communication. In time, candidates realized that media coverage was more important than the platforms provided by their political parties. Political television could be used to compensate for a lack of support by party members. Candidates no longer needed to construct their messages according to party rules. They could say or do anything that would attract and persuade mass audiences. Participation in public communication had given them skills in using explicit elaborated codes that could now be used to structure messages designed to be transmitted by the mass media.

The disruption of political parties and the political process that they controlled is only one example of how mass media may have transformed public communication. Most of us mistake watching communication for being involved in it, mistake the media genre representations of communication for communication itself. Lazarsfeld and Merton (1960, p. 502) referred to this phenomenon as the *narcotizing dysfunction.* "Exposure to this flood of [mass communication] information may serve to narcotize rather than to energize the average reader or listener," they wrote. "As an increasing [amount] of time is devoted to [mass media], a decreasing share is available for organized action."

We sometimes think that, by watching candidates on television, we can responsibly participate in politics. We think that we can get to know candidates by watching political advertisements. Our naiveté encourages politicians to use media genres as a means of appealing to us. They begin to play the role of television characters because they know that we want to elect the kinds of people we see attractively presented on television, not the party hacks our parents elected to office. They know we want to see them express attractive images, not bore us with long-winded lectures. But when we participate in politics in this way, we are acting as members of a mass audience created by mass media through the use of genres. We are not acting as responsible members of a public committed to certain specific objectives that serve its interests; nor are we acting as members of a restricted folk community voting in its own best interests. We are voting for characters in a local, state, or national drama. We are electing people to act out news stories for us, not people who will make decisions constrained by the public that elected them. Our political representatives were once bound by rules created by publics, but today they find their rules in media genres and the organizations that use these genres.

It can be argued that media organizations and their professionals are the last remaining public that retains influence over the political process. But this is a very unusual public, a public skilled in the process of communicating but lacking explicit purposes or objectives beyond communicating. In fact, it is a public that questions the need for moral purpose as part of the communication process. Media professionals argue that communication can be objective, morally neutral, without long-term purpose. The mass audience will impose whatever purpose it chooses.

This unique media public, however, does have one short-term purpose: It tries to attract and hold audiences. The creation and transmission of objective news stories interesting to and trusted by many people is the purpose of these media professionals, who thus make money for their employers and themselves. What rules does this public establish for political leaders? They must perform according to standards set by news reporters. They must serve as good and useful sources of news. They must provide easy access to any information that reporters might need in constructing appealing stories. They must treat reporters with respect and acknowledge the power of the media organizations. They must beware of acting like villains, must perform in public like heroes. They must smile for the camera and wave to the crowd of invisible spectators.

Closely related to our use of media representations as real en-counters with candidates is our framing of media representations of candidates once they are elected. Political leaders often encourage us to substitute media representations of our government for direct en-counters in its workings. Our nation is so large and the seats of power are so far removed from most of us that our participation in our government—something that is encouraged from our first days in school—has become largely symbolic. Elections offer us some oppor-tunity to participate, but the daily operation of our government occurs apart from our active participation.

What we know of that world of politics comes largely through the mass media; politics has become a spectator sport. Political scientist Murry Edelman (1967, p. 5) wrote:

> For most [people] most of the time politics is a series of pictures in the mind, placed there by television news, newspapers, magazines, and discussions. The pictures create a moving panorama taking place in a world the mass public never quite touches, yet one its members come to fear or cheer, often with passion and sometimes with action. They are told of legislatures passing laws, foreign political figures threatening or offering trade agreements, wars starting and ending, candidates for public office losing or winning, decisions made to spend unimaginable sums of money to go to the moon.
>
> There is, on the other hand, the immediate world in which people make and do things that have directly observable conse-quences. In these activities [people] can check their acts and as-sumptions against the consequences and correct errors. There is feed-back. Some [people], relatively few, are involved in politics in this direct way.
>
> Politics is for most of us a passing parade of abstract symbols.

Yet we are taught and encouraged to participate *directly*. Accord-ingly, our leaders structure our media encounters with them and their workings to simulate everyday communication. Jimmy Carter, wear-ing a sweater and taking phone calls from everyday Americans, talks to us over television and radio from a fireside. We become his advisers and confidants. We travel with Richard Nixon for ten hours a day as he visits Red China. We see our government work, and we seem to be part of the decision-making process.

4.4   Conclusion

This chapter dealt with the mistakes we make when we frame media representations as everyday communication. Our fundamental criti-cism of contemporary mass media genres is that they simulate every-

107

day communication in ways that result in framing mistakes. These mistakes may have consequences not intended by either the producers of media content or their audiences.

Much of the fault lies with us. It is easy to trust the skillfully told stories of the media professionals, and it is often difficult to replace these stories with forms of communication that may have more long-term usefulness for us. In addition, the media professionals often encourage us to accept their representations as everyday communication.

All mass communication, however, should be based on more explicit codes. Its users should understand the codes used to structure it, and they should be able to create their own codes for evaluating it. Contemporary implicit elaborated codes are easily used by communication professionals to serve the interests of particular segments of society rather than society as a whole. Elaborating existing media codes through analyzing and understanding the genres based on them can help us establish forms of communication to replace these genres. Surely it is possible to develop forms of communication that do not exploit framing mistakes but instead encourage and facilitate broad participation in the creation, use, and evaluation of media messages.

In this chapter we discussed the problems that children face in differentiating the media's implicit codes from those in their everyday lives, as well as the problems that adults face in being encouraged to use media representations as everyday communication.

In entertainment fare, specific genres are created that demand our willing suspension of disbelief. Our involvement in and enjoyment of the media message depends on our acceptance of its codes as everyday codes.

News genres have come to replace community gossip for some people and participation in the day's events for others. Inasmuch as we are "eyewitnesses" and we know "the way it is," there is little need for increased real-world involvement.

In their attempt to persuade us to purchase their products, advertisers involve us personally in the content of their ads. Persuasion depends on the creation of needs and the use of easily decoded codes to explain how those needs can be met. Leading the television viewer, for example, to see the commercial as everyday communication simplifies these tasks for the advertiser.

By replacing public communication about politics with media representations of politics, we can feel as if we are participating in our government, something that we are told is good. That participation, however, is mediated, not actual, involvement.

These framing mistakes may have significant consequences for our lives. Adulthood, however, involves developing our ability to make conscious, rational choices about what we will and will not accept and believe. Understanding media genres and their codes can help us reduce these framing mistakes and may make those choices easier.

References

Boorstin, D. J. 1978. The road to diplopia. *TV Guide* 26:13–14.

Bronfenbrenner, U. 1970. *Two worlds of childhood: U.S. and U.S.S.R.* New York: Russel Sage Foundation.

Edelman, M. 1967. *The symbolic uses of politics.* Urbana: Univ. of Illinois Press.

Epstein, E. J. 1973. *News from nowhere: television and the news.* New York: Random House.

Flavell, J. H. 1977. *Cognitive development.* Englewood Cliffs, N. J.: Prentice-Hall.

Hawkins, R. P. 1976. The dimensional structure of children's perceptions of television reality. Paper presented to International Communication Association, April 1976, at Portland, Oregon.

Kraus, S. 1962. *The great debates: background, perspective, effects.* Bloomington: Indiana Univ. Press.

Lawrence-Branden-Seidel Films. 1977. *The 30-second dream.* Baltimore: Mass Media Ministries.

Lazarsfeld, P. F., and Merton, R. K. 1960. Mass communication, popular taste and organized social action. In *Mass Communication,* ed. W. Schramm, pp. 492–512. Urbana: Univ. of Illinois Press.

Roper Organization, Inc. 1979. *Changing public attitudes toward television and other mass media, a twenty year review 1959–1978.* New York: Television Information Office.

Shibutani, T. 1966. *Improvised news.* Indianapolis: Bobbs-Merrill.

Volkhart, E. H. 1951. *Social behavior and personality; contributions of W. I. Thomas to theory and social research.* New York: Social Science Research Council.

Additional Readings

Entertainment Genres

Booth, W. C. 1961. *The rhetoric of fiction.* Chicago: Univ. of Chicago Press.

Miller, M., and Rhodes, E. 1964. *Only you, Dick Daring.* New York: Sloan.

Morson, G. S. 1979. *The war of the Well(e)s.* J. Comm. 29: 10–20.

Shanks, B. 1977. *The cool fire: how to make it in television.* New York: Vintage.

News Genres

Cirino, R. 1972. *Don't blame the people.* New York: Random House.

———. 1974. *Power to persuade; mass media and the news.* New York: Bantam.

Crouse, T. 1974. *The boys on the bus.* New York: Ballantine.

Diamond, E. 1978. *Good news, bad news.* Cambridge: Massachusetts Inst. of Technology Press.

Efron, E. 1971. *The news twisters.* Los Angeles: Nash.

Gans, H. J. 1979. *Deciding what's news.* New York: Free Press.

Powers, R. 1977. Eyewitless news. *Columbia Journalism Rev.* 16: 17–24.

Schlesinger, P. 1978. *Putting reality together: B.B.C. News.* London: Constable.

Schudson, M. 1978. *Discovering the news: a social history of American newspapers.* New York: Basic Books.

Tuchman, G. 1978. *Making news: a study in the construction of reality.* New York: Free Press.

Campaign and Political Genres

Barrett, M. 1973. *The politics of broadcasting.* New York: Crowell.

Chester, E. W. 1969. *Radio, television, and American politics.* New York: Sheed & Ward.

Kraus, S., and Davis, D. K. 1976. *The effects of mass communication on political behavior.* University Park: Pennsylvania State Univ. Press.

Nimmo, D. 1970. *The political persuaders: the techniques of modern election campaigns.* Englewood Cliffs, N.J.: Prentice-Hall.

Advertising Genres

Brower, C. 1974. *Me and other advertising geniuses.* Garden City, N.Y.: Doubleday.

Buxton, E. 1972. *Promise them anything.* New York: Stein & Day.

Della Femina, J. 1970. *From those wonderful folks who gave you Pearl Harbor.* New York: Simon & Schuster.

Polykoff, S. 1975. *Does she . . . or doesn't she?* Garden City, N.Y.: Doubleday.

Chapter 5

Mass Entertainment and Everyday Life

We have triumphantly invented, perfected, and distributed to the humblest cottage . . . one of the greatest technical marvels in history, television, and have used it for what? To bring Coney Island into every home. It is as though movable type had been devoted exclusively since Gutenberg's time to the publication of comic books.

> Robert M. Hutchins, former Chairman of the Center for the Study of Democratic Institutions, *Look*, 7 September 1971

In the education of the American people I am Recess.

> Garry Marshall; creator of television's *Laverne and Shirley, Happy Days, Mork and Mindy* and others; *TV Guide*, 19 May 1979

5.1 Introduction

There is an interesting aspect to recess. Most of us have learned as much valuable information in the schoolyard as in the schoolroom. We learned how to get along, how to make friends, how to make believe, how to play different games, how to sneak out for a cigarette and not get caught. Recess did not get us into college, but it helped us negotiate the sometimes difficult personal and social situations that we would encounter in college. And yet we often discount recess. Play is somehow less socially worthy than work. Recess is seen as somehow less meaningful than school.

Fantasy and Reality

If people have a difficult time understanding the value of play, they seem to find that coming to grips with fantasy is equally hard. Because of the constant presence of the mass media, we are forced to confront and try to answer an age-old philosophical question: "Where does reality stop and fantasy begin?" Equally troublesome too is the question of the relationship between reality and fantasy. Mass media technology transmits elaborate representations of everyday communication. In an important sense, these media representations are not real; yet they may well depict what we willingly frame as reality. We make them real for ourselves by imposing everyday codes on them, and once defined as real, these messages have real consequences.

Elite critics of the mass media have long argued that, because people use the media primarily for entertainment, the media would inevitably subvert our society and transform us into zombies who live in a world of fantasy. Life should be 'ived seriously, life involves hard work if it is to be successful, these critics argue, and mass media encourage us to play too much. Media content distracts us from things that demand our full attention.

Media industry defenders, on the other hand, have charged that these critics are biased by their moral beliefs. It is not immoral to watch television; in fact, they claim, it may be a very healthy means of recreation. Life is not all work; we cannot take things seriously all the time. The American way of life is to work hard and play hard. People demand top quality entertainment and refuse to be satisfied by neighborhood comedians or traveling minstrel shows. They want the best that show business can offer brought into their homes. Both critics and industry defenders have good arguments, but both tend to carry them to clearly mistaken conclusions. We are not being transformed into zombies nor are we being entertained in the best manner possible.

Harold Mendelsohn on Mass Entertainment

In his book *Mass Entertainment* (1966), Harold Mendelsohn discussed many of the questions that have proved divisive in the debate over the effects of mass entertainment. When we view entertaining content, are we only escaping from reality or are we preparing ourselves in some way to better face the real world? Are we capable of regularly creating childlike fantasy experiences for ourselves with no changes in our adult experience? What is the relationship between the simple fantasies in which we indulge when we view a typical mass entertainment program and the all too real rules we use to structure serious activities? How does traditional cultural content relate to media fantasies and to serious rules? If we preferred and used traditional cultural content as the elite critics say we should, would we be better able to cope with serious situations?

Mendelsohn's answers to these questions tended to support the Practicus position, that of the media professionals. He argued that escape is not bad because normal adults use fantasy purposely, and this use does not interfere with their ability for serious work. While traditional culture is good, it would not necessarily be any more useful than mass entertainment fantasy in serving largely uneducated mass audiences. Traditional culture would be uplifting if people could learn to understand and appreciate it, but it might fail to serve some of the useful purposes served by fantasy. Mendelsohn substantiated his arguments with a review of psychological and social psychological research. But while his answers seemed plausible, subsequent research has been inconclusive in documenting the positive purposes served by mass entertainment, and some negative influences have been found.

Mendelsohn would probably agree with this limited effects summary of his position: Mass entertainment will normally have positive and desirable effects for most individuals who make normal use of this content. Negative effects may occur under unusual conditions or when individuals misuse this content. This view of mass entertainment effects is widely held among mass media researchers. Consequently research has focused on examining situations in which negative effects are thought most likely to occur. Children have been intensively studied because they lack the ability to differentiate between fantasy and reality and thus may confuse the two and be misled by entertainment content (see Hawkins 1976, for example). Heavy users of mass entertainment content have also been studied because they are thought to be abusing this content and may show acute effects (see Jackson-Beeck and Sobol 1979, for example). Normal adults, therefore, have been ignored because they are thought to be immune from negative influence.

Communication Play as Defined by William Stephenson

An even more optimistic view of mass entertainment has been advanced by William Stephenson (1967). His *play theory of mass communication* presented answers to the same questions addressed by Mendelsohn. He argued that our use of mass entertainment content should not be defined as mere escape or diversion, that play is important because we use the media content to engage in *convergent selectivity*. Stephenson saw this as a very positive use of mass communication. It is the audience members' freedom to choose (select) from a wide variety of products, items, fads, and so on that are brought together (converged) before them. It involves making choices among many interesting, attractive, and appealing alternatives. Through our use of mass communication, we learn how to express ourselves in meaningful ways through the choices we make. And through this nonserious use of communication—*communication play*— we learn to equate ourselves with our unique pattern of choices. Stephenson noted that this form of self-expression is possible only in modern societies where individuals are permitted to make choices concerning friends, family, work, home, consumption, and communication. These choices were denied to individuals in older, traditional societies.

Thus communication play is characteristic of life in modern societies. It is through this pleasant use of mass communication that we become prepared to make the choices expected of us. We learn to value these choices and to understand ourselves in terms of them.

Stephenson's ideas are closely related to those of the motivation researchers in advertising. Advertising encourages and assists our communication play by enhancing our appreciation of the consumption choices available to us. We more fully enjoy buying a car, for example, because we have read the advertising. Through the use of ad messages, we are able to transform what might otherwise be trivial, mundane purchases into fantasy experiences as we titillate ourselves with attractive choices. Do we want to express ourselves as the bold, romantic owner of a new Cordoba, or do we want people to know that we are thrifty and practical Chevette buyers? Which choice best expresses us?

While communication play is an integral part of modern life, Stephenson also suggested that it is important only for individuals and that it has limited societal importance. Communication play improves the life of individuals by giving them a means of self-expression that is not socially disruptive and is easily constrained within acceptable social limits. From the societal perspective, communication play is important because it assures a stable social order in which the desires of individuals are being created, expressed, and fulfilled. Stephenson argued, however, that communication play does not permit *social control* through direct influence on the beliefs and values (implicit restricted codes) that social groups use to structure group life. In other words, the mass media have little impact on important facets of our lives.

Stephenson's discussion of communication play suggests that people can engage in this form of communication without any impact on other forms of everyday communication. Play will not interfere with work; instead it enhances everyday life by facilitating self-expression and may actually improve people's capacity to work efficiently. Play does not affect the serious activities controlled by social groups nor do the choices promoted by communication play interfere with these serious activities. Communication based on implicit restricted codes is one thing, and communication play is quite another. These forms of communication complement one another and do not compete.

Stephenson could cite much of the early research on persuasion to substantiate his position. This research found that persuasive mass media messages rarely influenced beliefs or values that were strongly held by individuals. Media messages simply reinforced existing attitudes or led to the creation of new attitudes only if there were no preexisting attitudes (Klapper 1960). Therefore play theory concluded that mass communication has only the power to influence and enhance the most unimportant choices that are not already structured by implicit restricted codes learned in groups. Our concern with mass communication, then, should concentrate on how it helps us engage in convergent selectivity.

But Stephenson's play theory of mass communication differentiates communication play from everyday communication in ways that may be inappropriate. Individuals do not easily distinguish between these forms of communication, and an important competition exists between mass entertainment on the one hand and serious forms of group communication on the other. The debate over the effects of mass entertainment centers around this question: whether communication play can be engaged in as a personal luxury permitted by modern life without any long-term consequences to the individual or the social order. Mendelsohn and Stephenson tell us, based on their theories and reviews of current knowledge about communication effects, that there is little need for concern. There is, however, an alternate position that raises doubts about the central assumptions of their arguments.

5.2   Goffman's Definitions of Play and Keyings

Erving Goffman offered a different view of play that links it much more closely with serious action (Goffman 1974, pp. 41–47). He argued that play is best viewed as a simulation of serious action. Both play and serious action must be framed, and the frames for play are usually simple variations of the frames used for serious action. We can fight seriously with someone; or, by altering a few rules in the serious frame, we can play at fighting.

Goffman differentiated two types of frames. Frames that we use to structure serious actions are defined as *primary frames*. Frames that structure play are called *play frames* (or *keyings*). Goffman called the serious frames "primary" because he felt that all play frames are derived from serious or primary frames. His definition of play emphasizes the relationship between play and serious action. Play simulates more serious forms of action and, when we learn play frames (or keyings of serious frames), we are learning something about the primary frames from which they were derived. Play imitates serious action and, by engaging in it, we can alter how we engage in serious action.

The concept of play frames or keyings is especially useful because it emphasizes the continuity that exists between play and serious action. Goffman derived the term "keying" to explain play frames from the notion of musical keys. The same song can be played in different keys, some higher and some lower. The same song played in different keys sounds similar, yet each playing is clearly different. It is possible to conceive of ourselves as actors capable of playing out our actions in different keys. Our choice of which particular keying to use in a different situation may depend on many different factors. We may be forced to use a certain keying by societal authorities—no matter how foolish the police officer writing out a traffic ticket for us may look, we cannot laugh; we must use a serious keying. Other people may negotiate the use of a certain keying—a professor sets the range of possible keyings for the classroom with his or her manner, attire, tone of voice, use of humor, rate of speech. We can impose a certain keying as the only possible way of framing a situation, or we can alternate between several different keyings (or variations of an appropriate primary frame) while we are in a situation—we can be serious when the officer or professor is looking and playful when we are unobserved.

Serious and Nonserious Action

Goffman's definition of play calls attention to several important things that we take for granted about everyday life. We tend to categorize our everyday actions into two general modes, serious actions and nonserious actions. We shift keyings to alternate between them, and we differentiate these two types of actions in several ways.

Serious actions require concentration; we must be careful to perform them with skills that we have learned. When we are acting seriously, there is little time to think about what we are doing or to question why we are doing it. Serious action demands focused attention on the present—there is no time for reflection on the past or anticipation of the future. We are performing on stage; rehearsals are over. We must do the job as best and efficiently as we can. There will be time for reflection later.

When we act seriously, we do not question the frame we are using to organize our experience of our actions. We take our experiences for granted—

they are a natural, expected part of our actions. It is important that we keep our experiences under control, and we cannot afford to let inappropriate emotions intrude into serious situations. Imagine the consequences of expressing hostility toward friends while they are helping us perform a serious task. Our anger would interfere with the job, so we will ordinarily keep it under control and talk about it later. Similarly we cannot daydream or allow our thoughts to wander in serious situations. These actions would betray a lack of commitment, purpose, or seriousness. Most importantly, we see serious actions as those that will have significant long-term consequences for ourselves and others. Our seriousness is a recognition that these actions can alter the conditions of our lives in positive and negative ways.

Nonserious actions, on the other hand, do not require full concentration. We can be less careful about our actions. If we do something wrong, the consequences will be limited. If a trainee pilot crashes a flight simulator, for example, no one will be killed. When we act nonseriously, we are often backstage, engaged in rehearsing for serious actions. It is possible to be reflective about what we are doing, to analyze past actions and plan future ones. We can stop taking our experiences for granted and raise questions about them. Are we controlling our emotions properly in serious situations? Do we feel certain things enough but not too much? The frames for nonserious action usually allow us to express a wider range of feelings, images, or ideas. It may be possible to communicate things about ourselves in nonserious situations that we cannot communicate in serious ones.

Sitting with a group of friends in the student union coffee shop, for example, we would probably be unwilling to be serious and say, "Listen, folks, I cannot for the life of me get a date. I just don't know what's wrong with me." The risk of ostracism or of an unpleasant, hurtful response is too great. We would be much more likely to choose a less serious keying and say something like, "I'm so darn good looking that I intimidate people. They're afraid to go out with me because they just know they won't be able to control themselves." Those in the group who can accurately read the keying will probably respond sympathetically; there is reduced danger that someone will reply with a serious discussion of our faults.

Our ability to change keyings while acting in situations gives us great flexibility in performing actions. It is a skill that is important in ambiguous situations where we may need to try out several similar frames of varying seriousness to determine which is most useful. We can change keyings in an effort to reduce the seriousness of an oppressive situation, for example, or we can change keyings to increase the seriousness of actions in other situations.

Through the use of keyings, we can easily introduce play into much of our everyday action and, in doing so, change the purpose that that action serves for ourselves and others. If we are skilled at changing keyings in situations, we possess a very important means of controlling ourselves and others. College, for example, would be a tremendous bore if we always employed the societally mandated, serious student framing of college life. The person who can tell a joke and put others at ease in situations (change the keyings they use to structure their actions) exerts a very useful form of control. Similarly, someone who can quickly cue others to impose a more serious keying is also exercising an important form of power over a situation. Such people can dictate the frame that will be used in the situation and thus can control that situation. Some of the most important negotiation of framing that takes place in everyday life concerns the keying that will be used to structure the action of participants in situations. People who cannot participate in this negotiation must either accept keyings selected by others or persist in acting in deviant ways that others find difficult to understand.

If you doubt the importance of keying, consider the way in which your own peer groups go about structuring action. Consider the range of keyings imposed in conducting even a rather simple group discussion. Someone may tell a joke and, for a few minutes, very casual conversation and laughter may occur. Suddenly someone may speak in a very serious tone of voice and cue the group to pay close attention while that person describes a personal problem. Someone who resents this effort to impose a serious keying may joke about the problem. Cues exchanged by group members may quickly determine which keying the group will use. Group conversations are a fairly complex, participatory form of communication play. Our ability to participate in them and help create them is an important skill that involves negotiating keyings.

Serious and Nonserious Situations

The two modes of action, serious and nonserious, are found in social situations considered appropriate for them. Some situations are said to demand serious action, and others are said to demand nonserious action. We can be nonserious when we are "hanging out" with an old friend of the same sex, but we may be quite serious on a first date with a member of the opposite sex. We can be nonserious watching television with a group of peers, but we must be very serious when we attend church with parents. Very serious situations are structured by primary frames that are understood by all participants. These situations demand that situation participants act in certain ways and control their experiences within certain ranges. Nonserious situations are structured by keyings that are similar to primary frames, but these keyings are more flexible, allowing for a wider range of actions and more variation in the experience of the participants.

Situations tend to be defined as serious by societal authorities; that is, by people who exercise power. Power can be defined as the ability to define situations as serious and to dictate the use of particular primary frames to structure experience and action by all participants in those situations. Laws, for example, force us to frame situations as serious. Serious situations serve to organize and constrain our actions within rather narrow limits. They increase our ability to act productively by forcing us to concentrate completely on what we are doing. The order from someone else to take something seriously is a very subtle command. It tells us to impose a simple, unambiguous frame on a situation and to organize our experience in terms of it. Parents often exhort their children to grow up and act like adults. What they usually mean is that the children should control their actions within rather narrow ranges and hide whatever emotions they experience that are irrelevant to given situations.

Purposes of Play

We take for granted the usefulness of serious situations, but we forget that play can serve equally important objectives. Nonserious actions serve many purposes, of which five are most significant:

1. Play provides an opportunity to learn about primary frames so that we can be serious later. Children at play are learning to be adults, learning to engage in serious actions that will have important consequences. Serious actions are learned by imitating adult actions in serious situations. In play, children can make mistakes without suffering tragic consequences. They can make mistakes without appearing to be uncommitted or lacking purpose. Through imitation of various serious actions, they gradually acquire the skill to be serious. For example, a child will first learn to play at running before actually trying to enter a serious race in which there is the chance of losing. Races, in turn, are less serious than running to escape being injured.

2. Nonserious keyings can provide people with a resting place during serious situations. In many serious situations, for example, rest periods are established to provide less serious interludes in these situations. It is possible for a participant to declare "time out," to stop the serious action momentarily and cue others to impose a less serious keying. This may be accomplished quite easily by telling a joke or by signaling exhaustion with a long sigh. In other situations, we can use excuses or disclaimers to explain that we no longer want to be taken so seriously, that we do not want to be held responsible for our actions.

119

3. Nonserious keyings provide opportunities for self-expression, but this self-expression goes far beyond the choices discussed by Stephenson. The actions that we take in serious situations are no longer considered to provide sufficient opportunities for self-expression. Performance of a social role is simply evidence of our skill as a social actor. This skill may be one important aspect of our self, but usually other dimensions also exist that are thought to be important. We usually say that, when we are using less serious keyings, we are free to "be ourselves," "let our hair down," "let it all hang out." When we use less serious keyings, we can display our capacity to feel and express certain emotions; we can exercise our ability to perceive and express images, to conceive and express thoughts. These are capacities that mark us as unique human beings, people worthy of attention and respect as individuals. In nonserious keyings, then, our most important human capacities can be developed, nurtured, and expressed. Some of these capacities will later be used when primary frames are imposed, while other capacities may have little or no societal utility.

4. Nonserious keyings provide amusement. We amuse ourselves by imposing keyings on situations that we know permit amusement. One of the terms we use for this is "kidding around." "Putting people on" is another. When we kid around, we pretend to believe something and act as if certain things are true that we know are not. Amusement permits self-expression, but its major purpose seems to be pretending for the sake of pretending, or to see what will happen if one acts as if something is true. We amuse ourselves to satisfy our curiosity—to find out what will happen if we impose a less serious frame.

5. Nonserious keyings allow critical reflection or discussion about how to frame situations. Such reflection and discussion are impossible during serious action but may be carried on before or after such action. We can act much like the director or choreographer of a theatrical production: We can consider what we should do on stage, where we should stand, what tone of voice to use, what makeup to wear, what movements to make, or what lighting to use. Reflection and discussion about framing are among the most important activities that we engage in. Although we often negotiate frames unconsciously, there are times when conscious thought becomes important. Through reflection, then, we can gain conscious awareness of how we are framing situations; and through discussion, we may be able to negotiate framing with others consciously and bring about changes in framing that are mutually desirable.

5.3 Communication Play and Everyday Life

It is misleading to view our use of mass communication as free simply because societal authorities do not directly control the situations in which it occurs. Control need not be direct to be effective.

Communication Play

All forms of play use keyings that are simple imitations of the primary frames used to structure serious action. But some keyings are more conventionalized than others. Some of them require knowledge of only a few simple rules for action, while others are much more complex. The rules for some keyings are expressed in explicit elaborated codes, while rules for other types of keyings are communicated by implicit restricted codes. The game of tag exemplifies a game based on a keying with conventionalized simple rules. By contrast, use of even a simple mass entertainment program requires a much more complex keying. The program contains many cues that must be used to create the keying. Genre cues aid users in imposing the appropriate genre keying. Correct interpretation and use of the content requires continuing close attention to the cues being communicated.

It is possible to regard use of a mass entertainment program as a type of play, in which many rules must be given to participants while they are playing. Even though each program creates a relatively unique keying situation, this creation and its use are based on conventionalized and elaborated rules (genre cues). The term "communication play" refers to those forms of play in which much continued communication about rules is necessary for keyings to be developed and imposed. Tag requires little communication about rules, while use of a mass entertainment television program requires decoding of a continuous stream of cues—the visual, musical, temporal, and story cues of both program and commercials.

Americans have long assumed that their system of mass communication is much freer than forms of communication used in other social orders. But it can be argued that earlier types of social control over communication—such as censorship or the use of restricted codes like Latin—have been replaced by a new form of control that we are unaware of because we do not understand the genres used to structure mass media content or reflect on the frames we use to decode it. We readily accept genre cues when they are supplied by program producers because their use allows us to create personal experiences that we enjoy.

The subtle form of control exercised by media professionals when they offer us content that must be framed in certain ways to be understood and enjoyed is clearly effective in controlling the nonserious communication of the ever-growing mass audience. If it was not, we would not continue to attend movies, read newspapers and magazines, listen to radio, or watch television. But how does this control influence everyday action? Is Mendelsohn right? Do media professionals control only the fantasies of most Americans, or does this control extend into everyday actions that are seemingly insulated from influence? Goffman's definition of play implies important links between play and serious action.

Two Forms of Communication Play

Communication play can be differentiated. In *participatory communication play*, negotiation of framing rules occurs. People engaged in such play are free to offer framing cues to each other. The keying that is created is a collective product. Each participant can strive to create a keying in which personally important objectives can be achieved. Those individuals who possess better communication skills will be more likely to dominate participatory play, but their dominance is subject to the criticism of others. Frequent participation in this play can improve communication skills and enable individuals to gain greater control over play situations. Such play is public when the codes used are explicit and elaborated so they can be learned and used by many people from differing everyday contexts. Participatory communication play can be used to develop frames for serious as well as nonserious actions.

Children playing "doctor," for example, can negotiate many different frames: doctor, nurse, patient, parent, ambulance driver, ambulance chaser. The experiences acquired through the use of these keyings may well be important for developing fuller primary frames about health, doctors, medical care, dealing with people in need, dealing with professionals on whom they might someday depend, and so on.

The second form of communication play is essentially passive. In *elite dominated communication play*, framing rules are created and communicated by a small number of people who alone possess the skill necessary to encode these rules. The keying that is created is more or less the direct product of the elite community that develops and transmits the framing rules. These keyings can serve only a limited range of objectives for media users. The only control that nonelite people can exercise is through their choice of communication content to use for play. They can seek out those types of content that offer more potential to satisfy personally important objectives. But some of the purposes that can be served by play cannot be served by elite dominated communication play. Frequent participation in this play does not increase skill in controlling the play; rather, it increases the ease with which elite keyings can be imposed so that they are taken for granted and not questioned. The codes used in elite dominated communication are implicit (there are no books on how to interpret a filmmaker's visual cues), and control over them is easily retained by the elite community that created them (there is no negotiation with the public on which codes will be used in a forthcoming film, for example).

The development of mass communication and its subsequent routinization of elite dominated communication play have altered some of our most important forms of communication play. They have brought with them important consequences for serious action.

Social Conversation

Perhaps the most common form of communication play is *social conversation*. Conversation can be used to serve the five purposes of play. It can serve to rehearse our serious actions; we can talk to others about what we are doing right and wrong. We can tell others our plans and obtain their advice. Discussions of serious actions with others can help us reflect on those actions. Others may frame serious actions differently than we do, and we can think about those differences.

Conversations also provide an opportunity for rest. Some types of conversations are so routinized, so well-structured by informal codes, that we do not even have to think while we engage in them. "Hi." "How are you?" "Good." "I'm doing great, too." "Weather's great, isn't it?" "Sure didn't expect that rain on Saturday." "What're you doing this weekend?" "That sounds interesting." "I ought to try that sometime." We can engage in such social chatter for hours if we choose to. It is a relaxing, pleasant way of spending time with someone else. Usually many opportunities for amusement occur during a conversation. We can "put someone on" by adopting an opinion that we know the person will find unacceptable, or we can purposefully disrupt social chatter with a contrived distressing announcement. Friends may put each other down and tell jokes about each other as a form of amusement, knowing that none of it is intended seriously. Conversations also permit self-expression. We can communicate things about ourselves that gain the attention, respect, and involvement of others in the conversation.

How do you engage in social conversation? You probably play it with different rules and different degrees of seriousness with different types of people. With co-workers, most of us tend to engage in social chatter to create nonserious spaces in serious work situations. We have a few acquaintances that we like to "clown around with"— people that we find amusing even if we find it hard to talk to them seriously. We also have a few close friends with whom we converse in very special ways according to rules unknown to anyone else. It is in these conversations that the potential for self-expression and self-development is greatest, because the frames that govern them are very much subject to our control. We can usually count on friends to cooperate with us in altering rules so that new forms of self-expression and self-development become possible.

We tend to take social conversation for granted as a routine part of everyday life. We expect to talk to certain people each day, and we can often accurately predict the content of these conversations. Even though the rules of the social conversation game are very flexible, we tend to develop rules for ourselves that structure our conversations in certain ways.

It is important to note that social conversations are ordinarily limited to people who are social equals or who agree to converse with each other as though they were equals. Power of one conversationalist over another can easily subvert and disrupt conversation, transforming it into a serious activity in which participants act out their constrained social roles dictated by the primary frames demanded by serious situations. Social conversation is played by social equals who respect each other's rights to improvise rules. It is a game that can become a most powerful means of linking two or more people together into a social unit, an entity that uses the frames developed in social conversation to structure serious action.

Disruption of Social Conversation

Richard Sennett (1977, pp. 261–64) provided a plausible argument concerning the way in which mass communication disrupts social conversation. He argued that as mass communication has become predominant, people have become increasingly unwilling to express themselves to others—particularly to unfamiliar others or others in public situations—through conversation. They would rather passively watch the performances of skilled communicators. The consequences for social conversation have been sad; conversations with others are conducted defensively or not at all, and people have become unwilling to play at conversation. Sennett argued that as public communication has declined, individuals have become increasingly anxious about expressing and understanding themselves through private social con-

124

versations. This places a heavy burden on a rather fragile form of communication play.

When we seek only a serious understanding of ourselves through conversation, we transform something that is most effective when nonserious into an activity that is too serious. Social conversation is most useful to us when we employ it to develop and impose various keyings, when we experiment with expressing ourselves in different ways, and—most importantly—when we take the opportunity to reflect on what we are doing. The danger of transforming social conversation into a serious activity is that it deprives us of a crucial opportunity for play. If we cannot engage in communication play among friends and family and if mass communication and social roles dominate public situations, few opportunities remain for participatory communication play. Sennett linked many modern problems to this overburdening of social conversation. Conversation becomes a threat to individuals rather than an opportunity to enjoy each other creatively and help each other achieve less serious short-term objectives that must be met before long-term objectives can be accomplished. If communication between people breaks down, individuals are left to create a self-centered understanding of themselves.

There is another, less extreme way in which mass communication has altered social communication. Keyings learned in viewing mass entertainment programs may be easily imposed on social conversations. The use of these frames can conventionalize conversation so that participants know what to expect from each other. Teen-agers are often especially anxious about what they should or should not say in conversations with others, and conversations with the opposite sex are especially troublesome. Television programs, however, provide many examples of how these conversations should proceed, what topics should be discussed, how one should present oneself, who should seek to control the conversation, what purposes the conversation should serve, and so on. But to the extent that they rely on these keyings, individuals give up control over their own social conversation. Conversation ceases to be participatory play and inadvertantly becomes elite dominated.

When mass communication intrudes on our ability to engage in social conversation, it deprives us of a potentially important means of developing control over our lives and of participating in publics. Cooperation with others established through social conversation can later serve many purposes. If we cannot establish communication based on conversation, we may resort to manipulation of others. We may seek ways of gaining social power so that we can force others to frame situations as we want.

Social conversation permits us to learn very useful communication skills that can enable us to communicate effectively in public situations. If it is disrupted, we may be unable to participate in public communication and may accept elite control as the only practical alternative. The skills required to engage in participatory communication play can only be learned when this form of play is valued for what it can accomplish and when we avoid transforming it to make it serve purposes that media genres imply it should serve.

Storytelling

This form of communication play is no longer as popular as it once was. Mass media simulations of *storytelling* may have gradually encouraged us to depend upon media for our stories. Stories, however, are much more important to us than they may appear. Stories purport to reveal certain basic mysteries of human existence. They are a means of objectifying human action, putting it into words that explain it. We fundamentally depend on stories for our conceptions of what human existence is all about. Our ability to understand (frame) them determines how deep our understanding of life will be, and our ability to create stories determines in large part how much of our own life we will be able to make sense of and express to others.

Every story told about action implies much more about that action than the plot of the story reveals. To be understood, stories must be framed; and in the process of framing, we come to take for granted the perspective on action that is implicit in the story. Stories explain how actions are linked to each other. They reveal the *social connectedness* of human actions. Social connectedness is an arbitrary relationship between actions that is created by people acting according to the informal or formal coding schemes prevalent in their social order.

How do stories communicate about social connectedness? Stories concern events that involve sequences of actions carried out by people or actors meant to represent people (for example, animals are sometimes used to represent people in fairy tales). Stories reveal things about actions that are hidden in everyday life. They tell us about the unobservable feelings, perceptions, and thoughts of characters as they commit observable actions. One of the most important things that stories tell us about characters is their motivations—the unique set of feelings, perceptions, and thoughts that are linked to their actions. In everyday life, we cannot read the minds of other people; we can only guess at what is motivating their actions. We often cannot reflect on what is going through our own mind as we act. The more serious the situation we are acting in, the more likely we are to act first and only later attempt to reconstruct what we did and why.

Stories can be viewed as a means of analyzing and investigating everyday mysteries. But storytelling is a form of play, not a science. As play, it is structured according to certain rules constraining the types of stories that will be generated. Earlier we discussed how news story genres constrain the work of news reporters. The rules for coding stories in everyday life constrain storytellers in similar ways, but these codes are the implicit restricted codes of particular communities of people, not the elaborated codes of a media bureaucracy. Though no such rule is inscribed in any book in the library, for example, most storytellers know not to tell a traveling-salesman–farmer's-daughter joke to their grandmother.

The rules that structure storytelling in a particular community reveal much about how people in that community are expected to experience their social environment. These rules determine such things as: *(a)* certain actions that must always precede certain other actions (e.g., must prayer precede serious action?); *(b)* the limited range of feelings, perceptions, and thoughts that can be experienced by people acting in certain ways; *(c)* the motives that are appropriate for actions and those that are inappropriate; and *(d)* the amount of control and responsibility that human beings have over their actions. In religious communities, for example, stories tend to emphasize the role that divine beings play in human existence. When the gods control or influence actions, human beings do not have much responsibility for what they do. Only the grace of gods permits people to experience life in certain appropriate ways, and divine punishment forces people to experience evil feelings, perceptions, or thoughts.

Most of us tell secularized stories about ourselves that imitate stories we hear. We attribute motives to ourselves that we know are appropriate. We use a vocabulary of motives, a dictionary of reasons why people do things, to explain to ourselves and others why we act in certain ways. Unless we are members of religious communities, we do not mention God in our stories. We attribute responsibility to ourselves, or we say that we were forced to do something by other people. Imagine how differently a deeply religious Irish Catholic grandfather and his grandson, a marijuana devotee living on an Oregon commune, might relate the events surrounding an electrical storm in which the residence of each was struck by lightning.

Like social conversations, storytelling is a form of play that we can frame more or less seriously. We can tell jokes about ourselves, or we can provide very serious explanations of our actions. We can listen to others with great concern about how they are living their lives, or we can treat their stories as social chatter. Like social conversations, storytelling has the potential for becoming a very powerful means of linking people together in a social unit. When we tell stories about ourselves, we can merely amuse or relax ourselves and others; or we can reflect on serious actions, rehearse for serious situations, or engage in useful self-expression. There are many easily learned conventions for storytelling that we can use if we want to avoid being serious.

Storytelling is likely to be most participatory when it occurs among social equals. We are much more likely to tell conventional stories to social superiors or inferiors. Superiors have the power to punish us for inappropriate feelings, perceptions, or thoughts. How likely is it that students will admit to a professor that they wrote a term paper just because it was a course requirement but found it to be a meaningless, trivial task? Such confessions will be told only to friends. On the other hand, most of us feel that we should put on a show for social inferiors. Inferiors have no right to know what we actually feel, see, or think. The story we tell them about ourselves is likely to be quite conventional.

Storytelling among social equals can become a flexible participatory means of exploring the mysteries of everyday life. These stories are still constrained by available coding schemes, but it is no longer necessary to depict motives conventionally. Discrepancies in social connectedness can be noted. Consider storytelling between a husband and wife who feel free to tell stories that deviate markedly from the conventional stories told about the social roles they occupy. The wife will be free to explain that she dislikes what she is doing even though she may continue to do it. Both husband and wife can construct stories that allow them to understand each other better as unique people rather than as social actors occupying certain social roles. A woman who is a highly successful banker, for example, is much freer to express her job insecurities to her husband than to her male co-workers.

Disruption of Storytelling

Has mass communication disrupted everyday storytelling? There is growing evidence that it has. For example, the codes used by mass media to represent stories are much more powerful than those available to us in our daily lives. We cannot tell stories about ourselves using wide-angle lenses or stereophonic sound. We cannot hire attractive performers to play our part and portray us more dramatically than we actually are. Our efforts to describe our experiences seem so simple and boring by comparison. Also, when we do talk about ourselves, it is easy for us to use keyings from media genres to describe or evaluate ourselves. This is especially likely to happen if we identify with television or movie characters and view their lives as similar to or better than our own. We can see aspects of ourselves in the attributes of Mary Tyler Moore or Laverne and Shirley or James Bond, or we can see personal characteristics that we wish we could express. These characters' attributes may seem so much more important, and therefore more real, than any description of ourselves. We may begin to use them as an implicit or even explicit reference point in telling stories about ourselves.

In addition, most people look to the mass media for stories. We no longer turn to friends as often as did earlier generations. We know that if we push the button on a television set, pick up a newspaper, or go to a movie, we will find stories that are more exciting and absorbing than stories told by others. We have come to expect that stories will entertain us in certain ways, and everyday stories usually fail to do this.

Another way in which storytelling has been disrupted is that when we do tell stories, we tend to borrow our plots from the mass media. We describe our motives in terms used on television programs and in films. We see our actions as having the same consequences of similar actions in media content, especially when actual observation of those consequences is difficult. We ascribe to other people the roles we see portrayed in the mass media. Media representations of how actions and events are linked have become the standard for judging reality. We are best able to frame our own actions by imposing the keyings found in media content.

Like social conversation, storytelling is a potentially enriching form of participatory communication play. We can be creative in communicating to others about ourselves and the social connectedness that we experience. But to be able to engage in storytelling, we need to develop certain communication skills. These skills will not develop as long as we are awed and dominated by the stories we receive through mass media.

Everyday Drama

Another form of play that can be differentiated is *everyday drama*. This is the rehearsal—either mental or physical—of actions in which we are about to, or usually do, engage. Like storytelling, everyday drama has been strongly influenced by media simulations. Some observers, for example, argue that many forms of everyday drama occur because we are imitating what we see in the media. But everyday drama seems to precede mass media simulations of it, and it performs many functions that media simulations cannot.

This drama is apparent among children engaging in pretended actions. Children attempt to act out social roles, seeking to behave as if those role situations were actual. They act as if they were adults doing important things. But do adults also engage in such playacting?

Do they rehearse serious situations and act out social roles? In *The Presentation of Self in Everyday Life* (1959), Erving Goffman argued that adults do engage in much everyday drama. The very serious situations in life are too important to enter without some conscious preparation. Everyday drama occurs whenever we consciously act out a sequence of actions outside the context in which they are appropriate. As a rehearsal for serious action, it occurs backstage. Serious action is not drama; it is reality. We can playact a serious part backstage with the knowledge that others will not take our actions seriously and that they may participate and help us develop our performance skill. How many times have we asked friends to listen to our "approach" for getting a date, or asked our spouses to listen to us recite the speech that we must deliver? When we do these things, we know that others will take them as rehearsals and help us refine them.

Everyday dramas are acted out in nonserious situations using keyings and can serve any of the five purposes of play. We can engage in everyday drama as a form of relaxation. When we mimic someone or speak with an ethnic accent, for example, we are engaging in everyday drama. Whenever we go beyond telling a joke to act it out, we are engaging in a simple form of everyday drama. The practical joke can be regarded as another simple form in which the joker fabricates a situation designed to embarrass or mildly shock another person. These jokes are an amusing everyday drama. The joker puts on an act that purposefully disrupts what someone else is doing.

Everyday drama, however, can be used for more serious purposes as well. We have already noted that it is very well-suited for rehearsing important and serious everyday situations. A commonly used term from the Watergate era was "scenario." President Nixon and his cohorts frequently engaged in lengthy sessions of everyday drama to rehearse various parts that they might play in future situations. One part that President Nixon always rehearsed at length was his role at press conferences—the answers he would give to anticipated questions.

Everyday drama also permits self-expression and allows for reflection. When we act out a part backstage, we can view ourselves as the authors of our actions. We can see these actions as a creative expression of ourselves and can explore ways of developing innovative social roles for ourselves. In some cases, we alone will be aware of how we have elaborated a social role to make it more meaningful to us. Others will still use the primary frames appropriate to serious situations to predict and interpret our actions. They will fail to notice minor innovation in our actions. But we will notice these embellishments, and our creative additions can create a keying that may make even our most serious social roles more personally meaningful. Acting out a social part backstage gives us the opportunity to reflect on that part. The person who rehearses a speech before a mirror may ask, "Do I really want to say that?" Acting out a social part objectifies it for us; we are better able to see what we are doing and ask ourselves questions about it.

Everyday drama is play that can be used as a powerful medium of communication between social equals. Equals do not feel compelled to play fixed parts for each other. They do not have to act out real-life roles. They are free to improvise and to act out parts that satirize social roles (create keyings) that they play in serious situations. The banker is free to act the pompous bureaucrat for his friends, just as the college professor can demonstrate to colleagues how she "wows" her students. Such acting out of serious parts can be useful to groups of people intent upon understanding themselves better.

Disruption of Everyday Drama

Like social conversation and storytelling, everyday drama has also been disrupted by mass entertainment and in many of the same ways. Some of us take everyday drama too seriously and are reluctant to engage in it, even among friends. There are few public places that we consider as backstage and more suitable for rehearsals than actual performances. Some of us question the display of everyday drama and demean people who seem unable to take life seriously and insist on playacting silly roles in public places.

Media content tends to perpetuate a myth about public places that encourages development of these demeaning views about everyday drama. It carefully delineates backstage and onstage situations. Most public situations are depicted as being onstage. Many comedy programs feature characters who constantly make mistakes because they fail to realize that they are onstage. They engage in backstage playacting in front of strangers who laugh at their mistakes. Mork from Ork behaves in public the way someone should behave backstage, and this makes rather ordinary actions suddenly very funny because of the incredulous or offended reactions of strangers.

Media dramas rarely show us much everyday drama; but when performed, it tends to be flawless. Content producers do not want to bore us by showing an inept performance that might disrupt a primary frame they are cuing us to impose. Imagine an Alfred Hitchcock movie in which we are shown a killer ineptly rehearsing a murder, or an episode of "Kojak" in which we see Kojak practicing how to jump from a speeding car.

Media genres tell us that if an action occurs in public, it must be serious. Everyday drama is not to be conducted in public; and when it is conducted privately, it should be skillfully performed. This implies that the only appropriate place for everyday drama is behind closed doors with only ourselves as an audience. As such, it cannot be participatory. It does not involve strangers in a form of action that would serve important purposes for them. Instead it serves to heighten an individual's sense of ineptitude and may increase that person's reluctance to attempt everyday drama in front of others.

This view of the decline of everyday drama is closely related to an argument advanced by Richard Sennett (1977, pp. 205–13). Sennett maintained that the displacement of public communication by mass communication is accompanied by a growing public reverence for great performers. These performers are respected for their ability to express themselves publicly in ways that no ordinary person would dare to attempt. Great performers can play musical instruments, perform plays, and articulate political arguments that compel the attention of masses. Their greatness is self-defined. Because they are performers in the media, they must of necessity be great.

Sennett attributed our reluctance to perform everyday drama in public to a fear that we would inadvertently express things about ourselves that are best kept hidden from public view. But our fear may not be based on concern about revealing an evil side of ourselves so much as about looking foolish in front of strangers or even friends.

This perspective on everyday drama may account for why we seem to have such mixed feelings about the great performers who provide us with the mass entertainment that we so avidly consume. We admire these people, but we also envy and fear them. How did they manage to learn how to perform in public? Why are they so talented and we so inept? Are we seeking to learn their secret as we read their life stories in fan magazines? Are we reassured that our fear of public performance is correct when we read about an actress's divorce or the death of a rock singer in mysterious circumstances? Does skill at everyday drama require making a pact with the devil, or can it be learned by everyone who can overcome barriers created by a passive dependence upon mass entertainment?

5.4 Conclusion

This chapter concerned play, something that we often dismiss as unimportant. Two influential mass communication theorists, Harold Mendelsohn and William Stephenson, have argued that our play with the mass media is a good form of play in the sense that it allows us to relax and be entertained, while it offers no harmful or socially important effects. Stephenson offered his idea of convergent selectivity as evidence. He argued that through its use, we can make many choices among a great variety of interesting, attractive, and appealing alternatives. Through these choices, he continued, we can come to define and better understand ourselves. The mass media, he argued, serve us personally in this way, but they have little or no influence on important social or societal matters.

There may, however, be another way to look at communication play through the mass media. Erving Goffman wrote that two basic types of frames exist: primary frames used to structure action in serious situations, and secondary frames (or keyings) used to structure action in nonserious situations. Serious action demands concentration and allows only a narrow range of action. Nonserious action allows us much more freedom; we can "be ourselves."

We tend to take the usefulness of serious action for granted. It feeds us, provides us with our social role, and so on. But play, too, serves valuable functions. Through nonserious action, we learn the primary frames on which the keyings that we use are based, and these frames can be used in later serious action. We can use play or keyings as rest in serious action. It offers us opportunity for self-expression, it provides amusement, and it allows critical reflection and discussion about how to frame serious situations that we may later meet.

Our play can be either participatory (when negotiation of appropriate frames occurs), or it can be elite dominated (when the framing is created and communicated by a small number of people who alone possess the skill necessary to encode those structures). The growth of the mass media has encouraged our dependence on elite dominated communication play.

Elite dominated communication play has altered our basic forms of communication play and thus our serious action.

People engage in social conversation; but, as the media have become predominant, people are less likely to express themselves in this way. Also, keyings found in mass entertainment come to be used for framing social conversation.

Media simulations of stories have come to replace storytelling as a common form of communication play. We depend on the media for our stories. We traditionally used stories to explicate social connectedness, how things in the world are related. Elite dominated mass communication now provides this picture of connectedness for us.

When we consciously act out a sequence of actions outside the context in which they are usually appropriate, we are engaging in a form of communication play called everyday drama. The mass media have influenced it by providing frames for the appropriate use of everyday drama, frames that we might not have developed for ourselves. In addition, media representations of everyday drama are usually flawless, inhibiting our use of it because we fear failure.

Play can be fun, but it can also have serious consequences. We ignore the power of play in our lives because we tend to see only its short-term, nonserious consequences. In some respects, we are right; much of the play we engage in is for relaxation and amusement. But it does have serious uses. Through communication play, we can develop necessary human capacities and learn how to live more meaningful lives.

References

Goffman, E. 1959. *The presentation of self in everyday life*. New York: Doubleday.

————. 1974. *Frame analysis: an essay on the organization of experience*. Cambridge: Harvard Univ. Press.

Hawkins, R. P. 1976. The dimensional structure of children's perceptions of television reality. Paper presented to International Communication Association, April 1976, at Portland, Oregon.

Jackson-Beeck, M., and Sobol, J. 1979. Television viewers, nonviewers, and heavy viewers. Paper presented to Association for Education in Journalism, August 1979, at Houston, Texas.

Klapper, J. 1960. *The effects of mass communication*. New York: Free Press.

Mendelsohn, H. 1966. *Mass entertainment*. New Haven: College and Univ. Press.

Sennett, R. 1977. *The fall of public man*. New York: Knopf.

Stephenson, W. 1967. *The play theory of mass communication*. Chicago: Univ. of Chicago Press.

Additional Readings on Mass Entertainment and Everyday Life

Booth, C. W. 1961. *The rhetoric of fiction*. Chicago: Univ. of Chicago Press.

Casty, A. 1973. *Mass media and mass man*. New York: Holt, Rinehart & Winston.

Real, M. R. 1977. *Mass-mediated culture*. Englewood Cliffs, N.J.: Prentice-Hall.

Skornia, H. J. 1965. *Television and society*. New York: McGraw-Hill.

Stein, B. 1979. *The view from Sunset Boulevard: America as brought to you by the people who make television*. New York: Basic Books.

Chapter 6

Mass Communication, Self, and Society

Television series represent genres of artistic performance. They structure a viewer's way of perceiving, of making connections, and of following a story line. Try, for example, to bring to consciousness the difference between the experience of watching television and the experience of learning through reading, argument, the advice of elders, lectures in school, or other forms of structuring perception. The conventions of the various sorts of television series re-create different sorts of "worlds." These "worlds" raise questions—and, to some extent, illuminate certain features of experience that we notice in ourselves and around us as we watch.

From Michael Novak's "Television Shapes the Soul," in *Mass Media Issues*, edited by L. L. Sellars and W. L. Rivers (Englewood Cliffs, N.J.: Prentice-Hall, 1977)

6.1 Introduction

To what extent does our understanding of ourselves depend on mass media genres? Although we can only speculate about our reliance on and use of media genres for self-understanding, we may well depend to some degree on the frames that we use to interpret these genres to interpret ourselves.

The model of the communication and framing process presented in chapter 3 depicted the interrelationship between media use and everyday communication. Frames developed during both types of communication can be and are imposed on all future communication, both mass mediated and everyday. One consequence is that media professionals are able to create attractive media content by simulating everyday communication. When these simulations are made more accessible and easier to engage in than the everyday communication they simulate, they gradually tend to displace everyday communication. An imbalance begins to develop as media content becomes defined as real, creating new frames to be used in everyday life.

Chapter 4 illustrated how this simulation and replacement occurs, how it creates some occasional short-term problems as well as the potential for much more serious long-term ones.

Chapter 5 examined the dynamics of the framing process and found that communication play has an essential role in it. Through communication play, we are temporarily able to escape the restrictions we impose on ourselves through primary frames and can relax, learn, and reflect. In this way, those forms of everyday communication that provide opportunities for communication play are quite vital to us. Without these interludes, there exists the danger that we will become prisoners of the primary frames that societal authorities and media professionals lead us to impose on everyday and mass communication.

What happens when mass-mediated communication play displaces everyday communication play? Is mass-mediated play likely to be as useful in providing frames for everyday action and, more importantly, in freeing ourselves from the constraints inherent in certain primary frames? Chapter 5 implied that mass-mediated play was not as useful, and Figure III illustrates this view.

Exposure to media simulations of everyday communication is increasing as those simulations continue to displace everyday communication. Our routine way of framing them is to rely on genre cues to create an interesting, attractive experience for ourselves. Even moderately skilled media users have learned many genre cues and routinely use them to determine how to frame media content. Such cues constitute an implicit elaborated code that can sometimes be inappropriately used to guide framing in everyday life. This results in less useful framing of everyday life and can have serious consequences for understanding ourselves, our daily problems, and our social order.

The self is not a static entity that we can easily analyze and interpret; nor is it the sum created by the simple interaction of rather static parts. The self is best viewed as a dynamic system that develops from our experience of and communication in the social environment. It gradually permits us to impose organization on our experience and

Figure III Model of the Communication Play Process

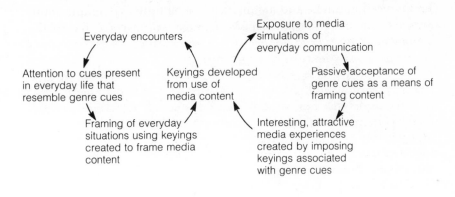

communication. The self is an agent of stability in our lives, but it is a dynamic, ever-changing source of stability. What happens, however, to this agent of stability when it encounters increasing amounts of ambiguous mass communication content that it must structure and interpret?

6.2 The Self System

Self system refers to the way in which our everyday sense of our self is created and organized. The term implies that the self is made up of several parts that are dynamically interrelated with each other.

This view of how the self system develops was originally proposed by Herbert Mead (1934), one of the first to define the self as a dynamic entity that involved parts linked to each other by communication. He sees the self as arising through communication and as something that becomes known to us only through an internal dialogue (*intra*personal communication). The fundamental ways in which changes in the self can occur are (*a*) through changes in the forms of communication routinely encountered and used in the social environment, or (*b*) through changes in the use of communication made possible by re-flection using communication play. Another way of saying this is that the self system can change when the social environment facilitates or forces changes in communication, or when communication play alters self-knowledge.

When children leave home and begin school, for example, entirely new demands are made of them. They are ordinarily required to sit in classroom seats for prolonged periods of time and speak only when spoken to. Informal conversations with friends can occur only during certain time periods. Children are required to learn that school is a serious place where certain forms of communication are restricted and where their experiences must be controlled.

Some situations in school are more serious than others. In time, children learn when it is appropriate to be serious and when they can play. How do children make these adjustments? How do they learn to take themselves seriously in some school situations and not in others? How are these changes in the self system made possible? Two types of learning must occur. Children must learn the frame for these serious situations, and they must learn how to impose it on themselves so that they can organize their experiences and actions.

Intrapersonal Communication and Framing Styles

The self system is a social process that involves *intrapersonal communication* between two parts of the self (see Meltzer 1967): the *I* (which we experience as the source of personally meaningful intentions of actions), and the *Me* (which consists of the frames that we have learned). The I raises the question of what to do, and the Me determines what is appropriate in a given social situation. This dialogue occurs between the part of ourselves that is fundamentally idiosyncratic and personal and the part of ourselves that is a social product. The only conscious awareness that we can have of this self system consists of the intrapersonal communication between these two parts of the self. Intrapersonal communication must be structured, just as any form of communication must be structured. Its structure is especially crucial, however, because it determines how we use and impose frames on everyday situations—it becomes our *framing style.*

Either the I or the Me can dominate intrapersonal communication. In the first case, the individual will engage in action that appears to others as impulsive, badly organized, and socially inappropriate. In the second, the individual will appear to be socially inhibited, unable to act in idiosyncratic ways.

As individuals mature, they can develop increasingly complex forms of intrapersonal communication so that the dialogue between the I and Me can give rise to unique experiences of oneself.

Fundamental to the development of unique framing styles are the various forms of play, especially communication play. Through play, various keyings for the same situation can be learned and imposed (without the necessity of assuming responsibility for actions or suffering their consequences). Play can quickly expand the number and variety of frames that an individual has available for use, enriching the opportunities for the I/Me dialogue.

Four Styles of Framing Situations

Four basic framing styles fundamentally differ in their consequences for the people who adopt them. They are: (*a*) the social learning style, (*b*) the looking-glass–self style, (*c*) the generalized-other style, and (*d*) the reflective-self style. They are differentiated according to their consequences and the nature of the internal dialogue that they permit during framing. Thus each is ultimately linked to certain forms of communication play that are used to structure this internal dialogue, and each is influenced by our use of mass media.

The *social learning style* is the simplest of the four. It is the acceptance of environmentally provided cues for framing situations. The essential purpose of this style is adjustment to various social situations, a very reasonable purpose for relatively egocentric young children to have. They must learn how to control their experiences and structure their actions in ways acceptable to others. They do this by learning the frames appropriate for various situations. Once these are learned, they can be imposed on experience whenever similar situations are entered. To determine what frames to impose, children watch for cues in the situation, then impose the frames suggested by them.

Adult life, however, is not as easy to frame. As we mature, we discover that there are usually several socially acceptable ways of acting in certain situations, especially in less serious ones. Parents may teach us one frame, while peers teach us another, and a schoolteacher provides us with a third. If we persist in the social learning style, we will be forced to learn how to frame similar situations differently, depending on who is present in the situation; the same situation may be experienced quite differently depending upon whether parents or friends are present. A grade of D on an exam may be a joke with friends but deadly serious business with parents.

We live in a relatively heterogeneous society in which many different frames are used by different individuals. Is it always necessary to frame our experience differently depending on who is present? If we strictly adhere to the social learning style, it would be. But we can adopt an alternate style—the *looking-glass–self style*. The concept of a looking-glass self was first discussed by Cooley (1970, p. 380). He argued that we develop our understanding of ourselves by imagining how we look to certain people:

> A self-idea of this sort seems to have three principal elements: the imagination of our appearance to the other person; the imagination of his judgment of that appearance, and some sort of self-feeling, such as pride or mortification. The comparison with a looking-glass hardly suggests the second element, the imagined judgment which is essential . . . [but] we are ashamed to seem evasive in the presence of a straightforward man, cowardly in the presence of a brave one, gross in the eyes of a refined one, and so on.

In the looking-glass–self style, we look at ourselves through the eyes of others, which become the mirror in which we see ourselves. But not everyone's eyes become our mirror. What sharply differentiates this style of framing from the social learning style is that we value some people more than others. We care more what some people think of us. These more important people are *reference others,* and we view ourselves through their eyes when we adopt the looking-glass–self style; these reference others become the important mirrors for evaluating ourselves.

How does this affect framing? Quite simply. We will try to frame situations and our experience in ways that are most acceptable to reference others. We will even use these frames when reference others are not present, even when we know that their use may have short-term disadvantages and are apparently inappropriate, if we think that reference others would be pleased to see us acting in certain ways.

Children who limit their reference others to their parents will act as though their parents are present even when playing with friends or attending school. Friends will find it difficult to get them to do what they consider appropriate in a play situation. Children with parents as reference others may say, "My mommy wouldn't like me to do that," or "Daddy told me it wasn't nice to do things like that." If we use the looking-glass–self style, we live for and through others; we live in the presence of unseen reference others. The looking-glass–self style introduces some consistency into our framing. It provides us with points of reference, but they are points of reference outside ourselves that may be controlled by other people.

The *generalized-other style* can be viewed as a variant of the looking-glass–self strategy. The looking-glass–self style may be difficult to maintain, especially if one has chosen reference others who encourage the use of very divergent codes and frames. This results in framing problems. How should a specific situation be framed—through the eyes of mother or the eyes of a close friend? Whose presence is to be used as a reference point in a situation? In the generalized-other style, this ambiguity is resolved by creating an idealized other—a reference point that is consistent and permanent because it is not part of everyday experience. An ideal other is created, and action is framed in terms of the perceived frames of this generalized other.

The generalized-other style is appealing because it allows us to frame our actions easily and consistently. Consequently our power to act is greatly increased, and we act more efficiently and effectively, especially when we use a generalized other learned in our job or other important social group. But we also act with less reflection, less consideration of alternate frames. The generalized other demands that action be framed in one way—the right way. We consider other frames at our own peril.

The final strategy is the *reflective-self style*. It is the development and application of frames that are the product of experience, thought, and reflection. It depends on the development of reflective skills through communication play. By using this style, people can develop capacities for framing their actions without direct reference to things or people outside themselves.

To employ the reflective-self style effectively, individuals must use reason, that intellectual faculty of sound judgment and good sense— or in other words, the capacity for reflection on frames and framing. It is this ability that enables individuals to develop and impose frames based on explicit elaborated codes. Reason is possible only when a reflective-self style is used to frame situations and structure experience. We typically associate reason with seriousness, however, and this may be misleading. The capacity for reason arises in large part out of communication play because that play can generate the variety of keyings that make reasoned reflection and choice possible. Moreover, it is through communication play that the capacity for flexible (rather than primary frame-dominated) self-evaluation can arise.

Using Framing Styles for Identification

How are these four framing styles used in everyday life? Perhaps the most plausible answer is that we each tend to use each style to varying degrees. Most adults have learned how to use all four styles but may tend to allow one to dominate because it has proven useful in the past. Some people routinely rely on cues in their immediate social environment; others tend to view the world through the eyes of reference others. Some lean on a generalized other for their perspective, while still others engage in self-reflection using personally meaningful values. In certain situations, we may alter our style and switch from one to another; we may also switch styles as we move from one situation to another.

One task of everyday life is to present ourselves in situations so that other people will recognize and respect us as social actors and so that we will know who we are and what we are doing in the situation. We seek to be *identified* by others in a particular way—as a person occupying a certain social position, enjoying certain affective relationships, and experiencing certain moods (Stone 1977, pp. 4–7). One of the most important things that framing styles permit us to do in everyday life is to determine how to present ourselves so that others can identify us as we want to be identified. When we do this, we create a social object, a personal identity located in the situation in which it is created. An identity is a concrete expression of our self system—a manifestation of the self system in the social environment.

The task of being desirably identified in situations requires the performance of actions that can be defined as a *social role*. Performance of the role is made possible by framing the situation in specific ways to determine what actions will produce the desired identification by others. In serious situations, a rather specific primary frame must be used, while nonserious situations may permit a variety of keyings. In the classroom, for example, your professors will usually use a serious primary frame, that of professor. But at a student/faculty softball game, they may use a less serious framing (a keying). In both situations, your professors are professors, but they may choose different frames to personify themselves in the different situations.

Stone (1977, pp. 8–9) pointed out that we are not equally committed to all roles that we enact. Some roles are viewed as more important than others. We take some roles more seriously than others because they are part of a primary frame. Stone used the term *role distance* to specify how committed people are to a certain role that they enact. Role distance is a function of the frames used to frame the situation. If primary frames are used, we will tend to be committed to our role; if keyings are used, we will have less commitment.

The preceding discussion may seem unduly abstract and unrelated to understanding mass communication. But one of the fundamental questions regarding use of mass communication involves self-identification with mass media content. It has long been assumed that content will have greater effect if users identify with it. But definitions of identification have been imprecise and vague. To understand how we identify with mass communication content, we must understand how we try to be identified by others in everyday life. A similar process operates when we choose to suspend disbelief and use primary frames to interpret media content. We can choose to regard the actions of a character in a media representation as though they were our own actions. In doing this, we commit ourselves to these actions, and we can vicariously enjoy the social identity that they call forth from other characters. It is through this process of identification that we become the hero or heroine of a film or television drama. We need not totally identify with the characters, but if we remain too distant from the roles they are enacting, we will be "only entertained"; thus many of us choose close identification to ensure a more meaningful or exciting media experience.

Using Framing Styles for Personification

Another important task of everyday life is *personification;* that is, assessing the identities of other people in the situations we enter. We make our assessments of them as they are making their assessments of us. We must determine the social position of others, assess our feelings for them and the feelings of others for them, and appraise their social value and their mood. This personification of others occurs at the same time that we are seeking to personify ourselves and express our identities to them. In most situations, people cooperate in helping one another engage in personification of themselves and others. This is called *negotiation of identity*. I will take you seriously or playfully as a certain type of person if you will take me seriously or playfully. In *Gender Displays* (1979), Erving Goffman argued that conversations in which personification is negotiated make much use of *social displays*. These displays are framing cues that serve to set the tone and direction for the negotiations that occur. One important function of these displays is to signal the social status or mood of participants.

When you enter a situation, for example, you may immediately shake hands with a man, address him as "sir," bow your head and avert your eyes slightly, and use a respectful tone of voice. This display signals your recognition that you are in the presence of a social superior whose attention and respect you are anxious to solicit. You could use very different displays. You could simply walk in very boldly, address him by his first name, gaze straight into his eyes, and use a sarcastic tone of voice. We often use the term "first impressions" when referring to the initial social displays that precede our conversations with others. These displays are said to "get conversations off on the right foot" or to "give off bad vibes."

Social displays are very important and useful to our everyday lives, but how do we learn them? Goffman argued that we learn them as children growing up in a society dominated by adults. As children, we learn how to display subordination, and during play we learn to imitate adult superiority. Children are serious in acting as subordinates, and they play at being superiors; in other words, they learn social displays by using social learning strategies. These displays are among the most important cues in social situations. Children quickly learn to note and imitate them. But displays learned as children continue to be used throughout our adult life. They can be defined as an essential everyday code that enables personification to proceed efficiently in most everyday situations. We are quickly and accurately able to personify other people if we know how to use and interpret social displays.

Social displays tend to be most important when people are strangers or communicate only infrequently. In fact, one of the most important functions of social displays is to help us personify media characters. Our interpretation of their social displays gives us the impression of knowing them as people.

Using Framing Styles to Determine Seriousness

Social displays are also useful in performing a third task of everyday communication. We must negotiate with others to determine the *seriousness* of a situation. In some situations, such negotiation is unnecessary. When we enter a church, for example, we know that the situation is to be taken seriously, and we can expect others to use a primary frame. Similarly when we attend a football game, we know that we are free to impose many different keyings. We can play at being spectators, we can be loyal fans and scream insults at the referees, or we can be discreet, somewhat cynical observers who bet on the opposing team. The greater the ambiguity of a situation in terms of its seriousness, the more necessary it becomes to negotiate how to frame it. Social displays become useful in signaling our intent to take a situation seriously or nonseriously.

One final point about social displays is that they serve as a means of increasing the effectiveness with which power is exercised by social authorities. Social displays allow people who possess power to be identified quickly and taken seriously (if they so intend). Social displays can be used to encourage subordinates to impose primary frames on situations and to constrain their experiences within the limits of those frames. This is an important source of power in our low-context public culture. Social displays are one of the most useful and subtle codes that make up this public culture. They can be understood by people who grow up in very different regions of the nation and in very different social situations. Mass communication is important because it serves to teach all of us the same social displays. Although social displays have always existed, television content in particular has elaborated and homogenized the codes used for them because they are an essential part of those codes used to create genre products.

6.3   Styles of Media Use

The personal style that people develop for use in negotiating everyday situations is likely to be related to the style they use for negotiating situations they encounter in media representations of everyday life.

The Social Learning Style

People who use the social learning style are likely to be passive, uncritical media users. They look to media content for the cues that will allow them to frame that content. They have no confidence in their own ability to provide a useful frame and do not perceive any need to impose personally chosen keyings. The media professionals who create the content are assumed to be experts who know what they are doing. They have put certain cues into the content that they intend to be interpreted in certain ways—such cues are to be located, interpreted, and used as the professional intended.

Two basic types of social learning–style users can be differentiated. The first type is totally unself-conscious. This user is like the child who regards media representations as real, raising no question concerning the reality of media content. Framing cues provided by the content are used as though they were present in everyday life. These media users can very easily "lose themselves" in media content. When they turn on a television program, they are walking into an everyday situation, adopting the perspective of a character. If the program producer and director have used one main character to provide the reference point for the program, such viewers will quickly identify with this character, view his or her actions as though they were their own, and accept the personification of themselves given them by other characters in situations.

This unself-conscious involvement in media content is most likely to occur among young children who have not learned to use reference others or generalized others as reference points for their actions; but it may also occur among adults. People who find their everyday life to be troublesome, who cannot find any meaningful reference point from which to frame their actions, tend to be unself-conscious users of media content. This use permits them to escape their problematic everyday lives where they must struggle to impose primary frames. The world of media content simulates everyday life but is different in one very important respect. Most media content has at least one built-in or implicit reference point from which the content is intended to be framed. Moreover, many redundant cues are provided to assist users in imposing frames. Interpretation of the content is rather simple when compared with the problems of negotiating everyday situations because none of the frames is wrong if it permits the user to experience content in personally meaningful ways.

The world of television is ideally suited to the viewer who uses a social learning style. Such viewers can quickly determine which characters to identify with and what personification to attribute to themselves and others. Cues constantly aid them in maintaining the frames intended by the program producer. Viewers who do not use the social learning style may find television content too redundant, too predictable, too easy to interpret, or too likely to provide cues that interfere with the way in which they want to interpret the content.

Much of the program planning done by television professionals seems to have social learning–guided viewers in mind. Program producers think in terms of specific audiences with certain demographic characteristics who respond to certain cues, and who can be easily induced to frame a show in ways they will find pleasant and that will ultimately prove profitable to the program producers.

The second type of social learning media user possesses more self-consciousness. They can never lose themselves completely in media content. They know that the content is not to be taken seriously from a societal point of view, that they are only viewing a media simulation of everyday communication. But they have also learned how to suspend their disbelief and act as if these nonserious situations are serious. They have learned how to involve themselves in play. In fact, these users may be sophisticated media users. They know the game that media professionals are playing; they know that cues are intended to induce them to frame content in certain ways. They tend to play along with media professionals. They will appreciate a professional who does an especially good job of encouraging them to suspend their disbelief and impose primary frames on media representations. They will disdain media producers who fail in their representations and create something that is merely amusing rather than believable.

These social learning media users use media content as a means of simulating an everyday experience for themselves. If the simulation is competently done but does not induce strong involvement, they will label it entertaining but not realistic. If the representation is highly involving, if it temporarily permits them to suspend disbelief and to frame the content as they would frame everyday communication, the content is judged meaningful and worthwhile. For these media users, the experience itself is what makes media use worthwhile. There is no need for this experience to add up to anything or to contribute anything personally useful. The experience becomes an end in itself, just as living through everyday events can become an end in itself.

Most of these users do not expect to learn anything from media use; it is a means of passing time, of using up experience. For them, media use becomes the ultimate consumer product, a product that packages experience and permits the individual to consume life in pleasant bits and pieces. For this second type of social learning viewer, a television show is like a prefabricated house or a paint-by-numbers picture; all the instructions for creating an experience are provided. Users only need to fit the precut pieces together to build the experience for themselves, need only use the indicated colors to paint their experience into something meaningful. Once the house is completed or the picture painted, it can be discarded and a new experience can be constructed.

Consequences of the Social Learning Style

What consequences may result from widespread use of the social learning style to frame media content? When we learn the cues that help us create prefabricated experiences for ourselves, we are learning an elaborated code that can be used in everyday life. Goffman (1979) suggested one way in which these elaborated codes can subtly influence our lives. He argued, for example, that advertising constantly displays women in stylized ways, consistently showing them in nonserious situations and playing subordinate roles. Social displays permit advertisers to portray women easily in roles that encourage their audiences to frame them and the advertisements in certain ways. Advertising has come a long way since a woman in a bikini was propped up next to the advertiser's product in the hope that she would catch a male reader's eye. Today the use of women in magazine advertisements can be compared to background music. The picture of a female model displayed in a certain way cues us to frame the advertisement in a certain way—to take it less seriously, to be entertained by it, to learn about the product without involvement.

But when social displays are used to sell products in this way or when women are portrayed in certain nonserious roles on television simply to draw audiences for programs, what are the consequences for society? This is an important question that can only be answered with speculation. Does media content that displays women in nonserious roles make it more difficult for women to personify themselves as serious people in everyday life? It is likely that if men have learned these social displays, they may often pick up extraneous cues about women in everyday situations and frame them as nonserious and subordinate.

Goffman points out that people who are not taken seriously can never act responsibly in ways that will produce personal consequences. They are saved from seriousness by others who act as benign protectors. Ultimately, however, people who are saved from being serious must pay the price. Their right to act is restricted; they are protected from themselves.

The subtle power exerted by media representations of minorities may lie in the suggestion that people with certain racial, sexual, or ethnic attributes should not be taken seriously and should not take themselves seriously. If these representations are treated seriously by many people, and especially if they are accepted seriously by minorities themselves, the consequences are likely to be harmful. People who have surrendered responsibility for their actions have effectively surrendered their capacity to be human. To develop as human beings, people must strive to assume responsibility for their actions, knowing that they will often make mistakes and that often the consequences of some actions are tragic. When we are saved from ourselves, we forever remain children living in a secure paradise, but we lack the power to act seriously. We lack the power to do things that may have consequences.

The Looking-Glass–Self Style

There are two different ways of using the looking-glass–self style to organize our experience of media content: We can bring our reference other with us to the media encounter, or we can find our reference other in that situation. The consequences of these two ways are likely to be different. When we bring our reference others with us, it is as though they are reading over our shoulder or sitting next to us while we view a movie or television. We are constantly wondering how this content looks to our reference other—what does my friend think, how would my mother define this, what would my teacher say? Most of us do this to some extent when the reference other is physically present, but some of us do it all the time. The reference other aids us in framing the content. We can reject content that we think would be offensive to the reference other and actively seek out content that we think would be pleasing to the reference other.

The second way of using the looking-glass–self style involves finding the reference other in the media content. Horton and Wohl (1956) have referred to this way of using media content as *parasocial interaction*. In this interaction, the media user employs cues provided by a media character to create a personification for the character. The user suspends disbelief and acts as if the media character is an actual person. In some instances, when the media situation containing the character is defined by the viewer as socially serious (as might occur with television news), the character may be defined as an important person whom the viewer or reader is fortunate to know.

Through the magic of the media, it is possible for each of us to discover people whom we can admire and respect. But even when these characters appear to us in content defined as real and serious (i.e., news), we must remind ourselves that we are observing characters, not people. The distinction is a very important one. Characters perform for cameras in public places arranged for the convenience of media professionals and must use elaborated coding schemes to communicate to us about themselves. Friends meet in private places, perform for each other, and tend to use less elaborated, more restricted coding schemes to communicate. Horton and Wohl (1956, p. 216) described the nature of the relationship that can develop between people and television characters:

> The persona (character) offers, above all, a continuing relationship. His appearance is a regular and dependable event, to be counted on, planned for, and integrated into the routines of daily life. His devotees "live with him" and share the small episodes of his public life—and to some extent his private life away from the show. . . . In time, the devotee—the "fan"—comes to believe he "knows" the persona more intimately and profoundly than others do; that he "understands" his character and appreciates his values and motives.

Media characters are attractive reference others for some people because they provide very stable reference points. The immediate purpose that they serve is to help the media user make sense of the mediated situation in which they appear. Talk-show hosts make it clear which guests they like and which guests they find offensive. Quiz-show hosts are remarkable for their unfailing enthusiasm and excitement, suggesting to viewers that everything and everybody on the show is important and worth viewing. National news-show anchorpersons provide a similar definition for their content but do so by using very sober tones of voice and calm, reassuring mannerisms. By contrast, local news-show hosts are more likely to portray themselves as friendly neighbors who are appropriately serious when reading serious news and break into smiles when reading nonserious stories.

Consequences of the Looking-Glass–Self Style

Media characters provide useful social displays that aid our framing efforts. We can use the social learning style to interpret them or we can use the looking-glass style to personify characters and believe they are communicating to us as people. People who become fans of a certain character will probably begin to use him or her as a means of defining everyday events. Walter Cronkite may look over their shoulder when they read a newspaper, and Johnny Carson may be present when they tell a joke or story about themselves. The sparkling conversationalists that appear to us on television may sit beside us when we converse and pass judgment when we stumble over sentences or experience a loss for words.

Television is a powerful source of characters that all of us, to some extent, use as reference points. They are not confined to the media world in which they are created. When we suspend disbelief, we enter the media world; and when we leave that world, the characters we have met are likely to come home with us. Sometimes they come as welcome friends whose presence we solicit and enjoy. Sometimes they come as somber judges or authoritative critics whose advice we may not like but find hard to refute. When we turn to characters for advice on framing our everyday lives, we cannot control the consequences for ourselves.

The Generalized-Other Style

American mass media content often is not very useful to people who seek to use a generalized-other style. Why? Because most content is purposely ambiguous and objective. It is designed to be framed in several different ways and lacks cues that would enable it to be consistently defined in only one way. Genres are successful because they are attractive to people who frame their content differently. This does not mean that such content is difficult to frame; it means that media users must learn to watch for the sets of cues that are intended for them and will enable them to frame the content.

In our society, generalized others tend to be created by social groups and serve as a means of recruiting members, helping them organize their experiences into congruence with those of other group members. Generalized others are created by religious, military, political, business, and professional organizations. These organizations offer explicit restricted codes that can be used to organize experience. Much of the communication that they use to recruit and maintain members is based on public information genres. Read the code of ethics for any professional organization; typically such codes are lists of actions that members should or should not do. Violation of the codes will be punished by excommunication from the group. These codes serve as a means of directing group members toward objectives deemed important by the group. To nonmembers, they are often boring to read and needlessly filled with technical jargon; but to serious members, they are a highly condensed, explicit summarization of the codes essential to group membership. Each word is meaningful, and the structure of each sentence is important.

Consequences of the Generalized-Other Style

An inherent tension exists between the social organizations in our society that retain control over specific serious situations and the media industries that demand great freedom in creating ambiguous content. The tension arises because media professionals often produce content that represents the serious situations controlled by social organizations. The mass media present doctors, lawyers, businesspeople, clergy, and many other people who are committed members of social organizations. But the actions of media characters are determined by content genres, not by the codes of professional organizations. Sometimes this results in a very favorable representation of professionals, as in the television show "Marcus Welby"; and sometimes the representations are less favorable, as in the book and movie "Coma."

Social organizations compete with the media industries for control over how we organize our experience of certain serious situations. Traditional professions like medicine, law, or business have succeeded in creating many popular myths about how people should act in the situations that they control. In the traditional patient role, we are expected to transform ourselves into objects for the physician and permit ourselves to be manipulated like machines in need of repair. But medical programs on television tell us that physicians make mistakes and often have ulterior motives or are unconcerned about the welfare of their patients. Why do media professionals tell us these stories when they know that they may shake our faith in members of traditional professions?

Research on program producers suggests that they are unconcerned about matters of faith (see Cantor 1971). They are concerned about building audiences, and they believe that dramatic action occasionally requires a bad character who can be opposed and overcome by a hero or heroine. The heroine in "Coma" is able to engage in important, interesting action only because an evil hospital administrator is engaged in a lucrative plot to sell body parts. The producer probably had no vendetta against hospital administrators and would probably argue that the positive portrayal of the heroine as a female physician will actually increase public trust of the medical profession. Perhaps and perhaps not.

We are entertained by watching people at work, and we suspend disbelief to watch them at play. Only a few years ago, a situation comedy based upon the serious situations involved in police work or the work of senators or physicians would have seemed improbable. But now we can laugh at everybody's work; we can even laugh at a flying nun.

Media portrayals of social organizations have the potential to weaken the primary frames that these organizations impose. These portrayals are inevitably heretical and challenge the authority of the generalized others that are created by the most serious social organizations in our society. Social organizations create generalized others based on explicit restricted codes. When media portrayals mock group members and their commitment to generalized others, they implicitly raise doubts about the codes on which social organizations are based. These codes are being replaced by content genres, elaborated coding schemes created to make profits by attracting audiences.

The Reflective-Self Style

People seeking to use a reflective-self style to frame many forms of media content will encounter quite predictable frustrations. Media representations are at best superficially moral, at worst amoral. They do not portray keyings useful for reflection. Content genres are used to create audiences, not to explore and elucidate human values. Vampires, for example, can serve as a means of appealing to the middle-aged female frustrated by a less-than-thrilling marriage bed, not as a means of assessing the nature of evil. News reporters proudly announce that they are totally objective in their reports of events; they say that they give us only the facts and do not evaluate events. But they do make evaluations; they repackage the events into news stories, then edit the stories into a television show or newspaper front page. These repackaged events are meant to be interesting and enjoyable to viewers or readers who want to be guided toward certain brief experiences by the social displays and other cues provided by the content producers and anchor characters.

People who have developed a variety of keyings to aid them in reflecting how they frame experiences will tend to find this media content either trivial or offensive. If you have developed a strong personal ethic against aggression and violence, for example, much television and movie drama will disturb you. Every time a hero or heroine unnecessarily draws a gun or smashes an enemy into submission, the frame implied by the producer is one that you might find unacceptable. Similarly, if you believe that sexual relations are ideally found only within the context of a long-term relationship with another person, much of the sexual innuendo and not-so-subtle bed hopping alluded to in much media content should distress you. It may not matter if the hero and heroine are nice people who seem to be genuinely enjoying their brief sexual interlude; your values would tell you that this is nonsense—this should not happen.

6.4 Framing Styles: Some Alternative Concepts

The existence of framing styles implies that most individuals develop routinized ways of coping with everyday situations and media content. These styles are not consciously chosen strategies for framing situations or content but develop over time as individuals are forced to make sense of situations or content and structure their experiences of them. One may learn to use different styles in different situations without an awareness of changing how one goes about framing. Framing styles are developed and persist because they have proven effective in framing certain past situations. So long as they enable unproblematic framing, they are likely to be routinely used in similar situations.

This conception of framing styles can be contrasted with one of the most widely applied concepts used to study mass communication—*selectivity*. In its simplest form, selectivity implies that individuals tend to expose themselves only to messages with which they agree (selective exposure); tend to distort messages to fit their preexisting beliefs (selective perception); and tend to remember only those parts of messages with which they agree (selective retention).

Research findings on selectivity have been very inconsistent (see Sears and Freedman 1967). Some studies show that it operates, some conclude that it does not. Some research claiming to demonstrate that selectivity does operate shows that it either increases or decreases media impact. One reason for this inconsistency of results may be that people with differing framing styles display different patterns of exposure, perception, and retention. People using the looking-glass–self or generalized-other styles would probably act in a manner consistent with the notion of selectivity; but people using social learning or reflective-self styles might be less predictable. If the social learning style, for example, has become an individual's preferred style of media use because it is the most useful for enjoying genre-structured content, selectivity may offer little toward understanding that use—the individual may forego selectivity in favor of content-provided cues.

The concept of framing styles can be contrasted with another popular notion for interpreting media use—*uses and gratification* (see Blumler and Katz 1974). The uses and gratification approach has focused on the consciously developed reasons that people can give for their use of mass media. Individuals are questioned to determine whether they use media content to achieve certain personal purposes. In fact, however, it may be impossible for people to determine their conscious uses for media content, and they may not be accurately able to assess the gratifications they get from that use (see Anderson and Meyer 1974).

People are usually vague about their reasons for using media. They say they turn to media for entertainment, for news, or to relax. Examination of framing styles might provide a fuller understanding of people's uses and gratifications. This analysis could go beyond assessing the consciously held motives for media use; it could probe how frames are imposed on different types of content. The experiences that individuals create for themselves could be analyzed in greater depth.

The uses and gratifications approach has been important in recentering research attention on situations of media use and in arguing that media audiences can be active as well as passive. The explanatory power of this framework, however, has proven to be limited. A framing style analysis suggests why. Uses and gratifications may help us understand the media use of people who use a generalized-other or reflective-self style (both of which require or encourage some conscious awareness of media use); but they may be much less helpful in understanding media use that is structured by the looking-glass–self style (especially if the reference other is in the media content) and the social learning style. The social learning style produces media use that is passive and cannot be predicted by consciously understood gratifications.

Both of these concepts—selectivity and uses and gratifications—are middle-range theories and illustrate the strengths and limitations of such theories. Both concepts are easily operationalized in terms of questionnaire items and communication experiments. And both have produced some explanations of media effects. But both concepts have generated contradictory findings, and neither has permitted the development of consistent, powerful explanations of what will happen when media content is used. Both are based on rather simple conceptions of how humans perceive and experience things, and both make many assumptions about perception and experience so that researchers can proceed with scientific observations. The hope is that more meaningful empirical findings will justify these assumptions, but in the absence of such findings, the concepts of uses and gratification and selectivity can be easily challenged (see Sears and Freedman 1967 and Elliott 1974 for criticisms of these concepts).

6.5 Conclusion

Our exposure to media representations of everyday communication seems to be increasing. As this happens, it displaces the actual everyday communication that it simulates. What happens to our understandings of ourselves, then, when this happens? The self that we develop and present is a function of our communication in and with our environment. Alterations in how we communicate, therefore, are bound to alter our selves.

The way in which our everyday sense of ourselves is created and organized is called our self system. It results from the internal dialogue between our idiosyncratic and personal selves and our social selves. We can change our conception of ourselves by altering this dialogue. This can happen when the environment forces or facilitates that change or when we engage in self-reflective communication play.

The maintenance of the self system, then, relies on our framing of situations in the environment and the communication that takes place in them. To do this, we develop routinized ways of coping with situations and media content. These are not consciously chosen strategies or styles; they develop over time as we are forced to make sense of situations and content and structure our experiences of them. They are developed and persist because they prove effective.

Four framing styles can be differentiated. Individuals who use the social learning style seek cues in the social situation or media content and frame them as those cues demand. Those who use the looking-glass–self style frame situations and content as they think various important reference others would want.

People who use the generalized-other framing style use a constant reference point for framing, an idealized other. Finally, those who use the reflective-self style depend on the reflective skills they develop through communication play to aid their framing of situations and content.

We use each style to some degree, and although we learn all four styles, we tend to allow one to dominate. The style we use in a given situation or encounter with the media allows us to be identified as we want by others; allows us to personify or assess the identity of others; and allows us to determine the seriousness or keyings to impose on situations and people.

Different framing styles may result in different consequences from media use. Media consumers who use the social learning style depend on cues provided by the content producers and thus may learn these elaborated codes and carry them over into everyday communication. People who use the looking-glass–self style risk transforming media characters into reference others for framing everyday life.

Individuals who depend on the generalized-other style may find that the media representations of those others do not conform to their everyday experience. Media portray various generalized others and their societal groups by using genre cues, not necessarily the cues of the groups themselves. Thus the primary frames used by societal organizations to structure the serious actions of their members may be weakened.

People who use the reflective-self style to frame media content are usually frustrated in their framing attempts because media content is intentionally created to be amoral. Its simplicity and dependence on easily understood genre cues make reflection unnecessary and most often unrewarding.

References

Anderson, J. A., and Meyer, T. P. 1974. *Man and communication.* Washington: College and Univ. Press.

Blumler, J. G., and Katz, E. 1974. *The uses of mass communication.* Beverly Hills, Calif.: Sage.

Cantor, M. G. 1971. *The Hollywood TV producer: his work and his audience.* New York: Basic Books.

Cooley, C. H. 1970. Human nature and the social order. In *Social psychology through symbolic interaction,* ed. G. P. Stone and H. A. Faberman, pp. 377–82. Waltham, Mass.: Ginn-Blaisdell.

Elliott, P. 1974. Uses and gratification research: a critique and a sociological alternative. In *The uses of mass communication,* ed. J. G. Blumler and E. Katz, pp. 249–68. Beverly Hills, Calif.: Sage.

Goffman, E. 1979. *Gender displays.* New York: Holt, Rinehart & Winston.

Horton, D., and Wohl, R. R. 1956. Mass communication and para-social interaction: observation on intimacy at a distance. *Psychiatry* 19: 215–29.

Mead, G. H. 1934. *Mind, self, and society.* Chicago: Univ. of Chicago Press.

Meltzer, B. N. 1967. Mead's social psychology. In *Symbolic interactionism,* ed. J. G. Manis and B. N. Meltzer, pp. 5–24. Boston: Allyn & Bacon.

Sears, D. O., and Freedman, J. L. 1967. Selective exposure to information: a critical review. *Pub. Opinion Q.* 31: 194–213.

Stone, G. P. 1977. Personal acts. *Symbolic Interaction:* 1: 2–19.

Additional Readings

The Self System

Cardwell, J. D. 1971. *Social psychology, a symbolic interaction perspective.* Philadelphia: Davis.

White, R. W. 1972. *The enterprise of living.* New York: Holt, Rinehart & Winston.

Selectivity

Cannell, C. F., and MacDonald, J. C. 1956. The impact of health news on attitudes and behavior. *Journalism Q.* 33: 315–23.

Freedman, J. L., and Sears, D. O. 1965. Selective exposure. In *Advances in experimental social psychology, vol. 2,* ed. L. Berkowitz, pp. 58–97. New York: Academic Press.

Schramm, W., and Carter, R. F. 1959. Effectiveness of a political telethon. *Pub. Opinion Q.* 23: 121–26.

Zimmerman, C., and Bauer, R. A. 1956. The effect of an audience upon what is remembered. *Pub. Opinion Q.* 20: 238–48.

Uses and Gratifications

Katz, E.; Blumler, J. G.; and Gurevitch, M. 1974. Utilization of mass communication by the individual. In *The uses of mass communication,* ed. J. G. Blumler and E. Katz, pp. 19–34. Beverly Hills, Calif.: Sage.

Nordenstreng, K. 1970. Comments on "gratifications research" in broadcasting. *Pub. Opinion Q.* 34: 130–32.

Chapter 7

Mass Communication and Everyday Problems

Detroit (AP)—A Detroit newspaper thought it had an offer few could reject—$500 if a family agreed to turn off its television set for one month. The *Detroit Free Press* approached 120 families with the offer. And 93 turned it down.

From an Associated Press wire story that appeared in the Austin (Texas) *American Statesman*, 31 October 1977

7.1 Introduction

The 26 September 1978 *National Enquirer* offered its readers this headline: "Top University Studies Show How to Use TV to Live Longer." "Actual medical studies, done separately at Stanford University and the University of California," the accompanying story reported, proved that "good TV can be good medicine. You'll help yourself live longer by wisely using television." The story quoted a Stanford professor as saying, "When you watch Laverne and Shirley throw pizza in one another's face or slip on a banana peel, you're on the way to a healthier and longer life" (Caylor 1978).

Equally peculiar, a Chicago man used television to escape an assault charge. Claiming that watching "Roots" had led him to believe that there was a race war that compelled him to kill people, he won acquittal of a knife attack on a store manager and employee by reason of insanity (United Press International 1979).

Whether helping us live longer, keeping us out of jail, or providing a conspicuous location for the display of our bowling trophies, tele-

Routine Problem Solving

In everyday life we routinely solve problems, for every situation that we enter poses different problems for us. We can never completely frame situations, however, before entering them; we cannot fully anticipate how we will feel, what will be our capacities to act, or how others will act. Unexpected, seemingly random elements may further hamper our framing capabilities. Yet most of us can routinely work through and negotiate these situations as though no problem existed.

We can do this because we have developed problem-solving skills that enable us to adjust to most situations. More often than not, we make these adjustments so effortlessly and adroitly that we may never experience the problems that we are solving or become consciously aware of the solutions that we are applying. The term *routine problem solving* refers to this everyday adjustment to situations.

What do we do when we solve everyday problems? Usually we use one or more of the four framing styles discussed in the last chapter. They allow us to create a personal identity for ourselves, to personify other people, and to assess the seriousness of situations. To accomplish these tasks, we must often negotiate with other people. Sometimes these negotiations go badly. Sometimes the cues provided by others are ambiguous. A situation that we at first see as nonserious may suddenly start to look serious. How can we induce others to personify us as we want to be personified? How can we develop a clear picture of who another person is trying to be? How can we resolve an ambiguous situation and determine how serious our actions should be? These are questions that our skills in everyday problem solving enable us to answer.

vision and all of the mass media help us solve problems that confront us every day. Sometimes the problem solving is simple and obvious: To decide what to wear for the day, we might listen to the weather on the radio or read the day's forecast in the newspaper. Sometimes the problem solving is more subtle and complex: To deal with a problem situation—a first date or job interview, for example—we may consciously or routinely call into play solutions that we have acquired from the mass media.

In most instances, our problem-solving skills are so well developed that we can identify a problem and impose a solution without any conscious awareness that the problem existed. Everyday problem-solving skills enable us to take much of our daily activity for granted. But how are these skills developed and used?

One way is by use of mass media representations and the experiences made possible by that content. But these representations, guided by the LCD principle of programming, permit only a limited range of skills and solutions. Consequently, we move through our everyday lives imposing oversimplified solutions on problems that we do not realize we have. We buy the soap for people who like people, or we put our money where our mouths are. Only when these solutions fail in some dramatic way do we become aware of the problems. It may be difficult by then, however, to find more useful solutions. Mass media provide superficial problem-solving skills and pseudo-solutions. The solutions offered tend to work only for short periods of time. They often get us through the situations in which problems first arise, but when we continue to apply them without much thought or planning, we inevitably make serious mistakes. Simple solutions to everyday problems consist of routinely performed actions structured by some type of keying.

7.2 Dangers of Simple Solutions to Everyday Problems

Simple problem solving has two important characteristics: First, there is little conscious awareness that a problem exists; and second, there is little awareness that a solution is being applied. An everyday situation suddenly becomes a problem when the frame that we try to impose is inadequate.

How are the unclear actions of others to be explained and coped with? A child who has learned to use violence as a routine means of resolving problems, for example, will become aggressive when faced with ambiguous situations. Others will see this aggression as inappropriate and may try to stop it. Adults may assert authority and force the child to act differently. But coercion may only confirm the child's framing of the situation as hostile and needing to be physically challenged. A breakdown in negotiation of social action occurs because no compatible frames can be agreed upon. The simple solution of using violent actions routinely to cope with everyday problems is clearly inadequate for dealing with most of the problems that children face. It results in much unnecessary violence and produces confrontations with adults who are responsible for controlling certain situations.

How many of the everyday solutions that we use to cope with problem situations are like the child's simple solution of violence? How often do we routinely impose solutions that interfere with the negotiation of everyday situations? How often do our solutions lead us to act in ways that others will regard as inappropriate or even irrational?

The development of public communication has permitted the creation of many ambiguous public situations that need to be collectively framed. In simpler societies, simple solutions tend to be traditional and taught by social authorities. But that is not the case in our society. Public situations require participants to negotiate in order to resolve framing difficulties. When we apply the simple solutions learned from

---

Simple Solutions to Everyday Problems

A simple solution to an everyday problem consists of routinely performed action structured by a keying. It lets an individual continue framing a situation using that keying despite the continuing presence of ambiguous cues and events, even when other people become upset or when actions fail to accomplish what they were intended to achieve. Simple solutions permit us to avoid becoming consciously aware of everyday problems and thus enable us to avoid taking constructive action about them. They enable us to continue doing things as we have routinely done them in the past, and we avoid the necessity of questioning routinely experienced self-identities, personifications of others, or the seriousness of situations. Simple solutions persist because they are not contradicted by experience in everyday situations.

The routinely performed action that is part of a simple solution can sometimes be interpersonal or intrapersonal communication. The child who has learned to use violence to cope with ambiguous situations will act interpersonally with aggression when confronted with ambiguity. Adults are more likely to impose simple solutions that involve intrapersonal communication. When a woman experiencing job discrimination tells herself that it is her own fault, for example, these thoughts about herself have become routinized and are applied to deal with ambiguity.

But simple solutions tend to aggravate rather than resolve the problems that create ambiguity. Possibilities for collectively negotiating frames are avoided or inhibited. Widespread use of simple solutions restricts the development and use of various forms of public communication; public communication that could encourage and develop skills for reflecting on frames is avoided.

The advantages of simple solutions are many. We would be ineffective social actors if we constantly questioned the utility of the frames we use to structure experience and action. Much of the ambiguity that we encounter in everyday life is not worth taking account of. All of us know people who are oversensitive observers of everyday life, who constantly agonize over what they are doing and how others are viewing them. They may interpret another's fatigue as personal rejection or another's self-anger at some clumsiness as animosity toward them. We say that they are always jumping to conclusions, conclusions that are rarely useful because they are based on misinterpretations of unimportant cues.

Simple solutions give us a means of protecting ourselves from extraneous cues. They direct our attention away from ambiguity and can make our daily lives more stable. They allow us to continue acting as we have acted in the past, preventing rapid and radical changes in our actions.

Figure IV   Model of Simple Solutions Learning From Mass Media

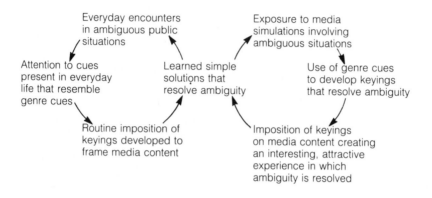

mass media to these situations, we escape the necessity of negotiating; but we then risk acting in ways that do not complement the actions of others. We risk alienating others who expect that negotiation will take place.

The most important forms of public action require negotiation in public places to frame situations collectively. Various forms of public communication have been developed to facilitate this negotiation. But when we routinely impose simple solutions learned from mass media, we avoid public communication. Figure IV represents the way in which simple solutions (various keyings) learned from media content can intrude on everyday life.

The solutions that we learn for resolving troublesome situations may be a product of the cues presented in media content. When we frame an everyday situation using the keyings learned in media content, we risk acting inappropriately; we risk imposing inadequate solutions.

7.3   Aggression: A Simple Solution to Everyday Problems

One simple solution to everyday problems that has been extensively discussed and researched is aggression. Many people feel that this possibly media-learned solution may be replacing public communication for problem solving in important, often unpleasant ways. Television, in particular, has been singled out for criticism.

The best answer yet developed to the television violence question is that some types of programming affect some people in some ways some of the time. While this scientifically and logically irrefutable statement on the effects of television violence has been accepted as truth, it tells us little about how some people indeed learn to behave aggressively in certain situations.

For centuries it was thought that people were innately aggressive. If so, television violence would seem to have little impact on subsequent viewer aggression because "that's the way people are." Media programming is rendered effectless and therefore blameless. This simple *drive theory* (i.e., that people exhibit aggression because they are innately aggressive) still has some important contemporary proponents; but most theorists now believe that "complex behavior (such as aggression) does not emerge as a unitary pattern but is formed through integration of many component activities of differing origins" (Bandura 1978).

A second popular explanation of why people choose to solve some problems through aggression is an extension of drive theory called the *frustration theory,* articulated by Dollard et al. (1939), among others. In essence, when frustration results as a function of some occurrence in the environment (a problem), an aggressive drive is produced that in turn motivates and is satisfied by aggression. You are reading in your room or apartment, for example, and the people next door are playing their stereo at maximum volume. You have asked them to turn the sound down a bit, but they have ignored you and you find it impossible to read. This frustrating occurrence in the environment creates an aggressive drive. The anger wells up inside you, and that feeling motivates you to pound on their door and scream at them. This aggressive act makes you feel better—the drive has been sated.

Again, media portrayals are rendered effectless according to this theory because aggression is seen as the natural response to a problem that creates frustration, not as a media-learned simple solution. Moreover, because this drive must be satisfied, some media researchers have argued that media violence actually serves to reduce viewer aggression because the individual can vicariously get rid of that aggressive drive (see Feshbach 1956). This *cathartic* view of media representations of violence enjoyed a good deal of attention and credibility in the 1950s and 1960s. The 1972 *Surgeon General's Report on Television and Social Behavior* (Comstock and Rubinstein 1972), however, effectively countered the arguments of the catharsis proponents, as has a good deal of other work (see Goranson 1970). This latter research has demonstrated that what was accepted as catharsis in previous work was in fact the learning of nonaggressive behaviors or the functioning of factors that inhibited aggressive acts—not a media-induced reduction of the aggressive drive.

Even if we accept the notion that an aggressive drive exists that is the product of some frustration, however, it is obvious that not all people reduce that drive with aggressive behavior. Some people count to ten, some take long walks, some play the saxophone, some do crossword puzzles.

Social Learning Theory of Aggression

This theory not only helps explain why different people react differently to various problems but helps us see the limiting nature of media representations in providing information for problem solving. Social learning theory argues that aversive or problem situations produce an emotional arousal that calls for action. The behaviors elicited to solve that problem or deal with that aversive situation are a function of the solutions that the individual has come to *learn* for dealing with those situations.

Albert Bandura, a prominent social learning researcher (1971a, 1978), argued that there are many ways to deal with aversive experiences (i.e., ambiguous, threatening situations): dependency (asking for help), achievement ("I will overcome"), withdrawal and resignation, aggression, psychosomaticization ("What problem?"), self-anesthetization (taking of drugs and alcohol), and constructive problem solving. He argued that our selection of a given solution depends on what we have learned and how effective we regard that solution in the given situation.

Inasmuch as the resolution of ambiguous situations is the essence of most drama, the mass media could be an excellent source of useful keyings. Instead the media offer us a very limited array of simple solutions from which to choose: People in commercials deal with headaches through the use of drugs, businesspeople need "a double shot," and action-adventure heroes outshoot, outfight, and generally outaggress the villains.

Social Learning from Symbolic Representations

The first serious look at learning through observation was offered by psychologists Miller and Dollard (1941). They argued that imitative learning occurred when observers were motivated to learn, when the cues or elements of the behaviors to be learned were present, when observers performed the given behaviors, and when observers were positively reinforced for imitating those behaviors. In other words, people could imitate behaviors that they saw; those behaviors would be reinforced and therefore learned.

However, instead of presenting a means of understanding how people learn from models (including media models), Miller and Dollard simply described an efficient form of traditional stimulus-response learning. They assumed that individuals behaved in certain ways and then shaped their behavior according to the reinforcement they received. They saw imitation as replacing random trial-and-error behaviors. Imitation simply made it easier for an individual to choose a behavior in order to be reinforced for making it. It was that reinforcement, however, that ensured learning. But this insistence on the operation of reinforcement limited their theory's application for understanding how people learn from the mass media. Its inability to account for people's apparent skill at learning new responses through observation in the absence of reinforcement limited its applicability to media impact.

The efforts of Miller and Dollard, however, were not in vain. Two decades later, their ideas on social learning and imitation were sufficiently developed to become valuable tools in understanding media effects. Where Miller and Dollard saw social learning as an efficient form of stimulus-response learning (with the model providing information that helped the observer make the correct response in order to be reinforced), contemporary social learning theory argues that observers can acquire symbolic representations of the behavior, and these "pictures" provide them with information on which to base subsequent behavior (Bandura 1971b). In terms of the mass media, media characters (models) can influence behavior simply by being. The audience member need not be reinforced or rewarded for exhibiting the modeled behavior; observation of the behavior representation is sufficient for learning if there is successful functioning of these four processes:

1. *Attentional processes.* Observers must be able to attend to, recognize, and differentiate the distinctive elements of the modeled behavior. They must see and understand what is on the screen.

2. *Retention processes.* Because observers must store the representations or pictures of the modeled behavior, they must be able to recall them in order to exhibit that behavior at a later time. They must remember what is on the screen.

3. *Motoric reproduction processes.* Even if observers attend to and retain the information offered by the media model, that information cannot manifest itself as behavior change if the observer is physically unable to perform the modeled behavior. They must be able to perform, to some degree, what is on the screen.

4. *Reinforcement and motivational processes.* The likelihood that observers will actually demonstrate the modeled behavior (even if they have learned it) depends on the motivation and reinforcement value they learn to associate with that behavior. They must want to do what is on the screen.

Media viewers, then, can have their behavior changed by a given message if they attend to the message, retain it, can perform to some extent the behavior offered in that message, and are significantly motivated to do so.

Social Learning from Media Content

One useful way to understand how social learning theory manifests itself in terms of the mass media is to view its operation as a function of our substitution of media representations for everyday communication.

Traditional or operant learning theory holds that people learn new behaviors when they are presented with stimuli (something in their environment), make a response to those stimuli, and have those responses reinforced either positively (rewarded) or negatively (punished). In this way, new behaviors are learned, or added to people's *behavioral repertoire*—the sum total of an individual's available behaviors.

Two things are clear, however. First, this is an inefficient form of learning. All of us know, for example, how to deal with fire. If each of us had to learn our fire-related behavior individually, we would have crowded hospitals and super-rich bandage manufacturers. Each of us, when presented with that stimulus (fire), would render a chance response (put our hand in it) and be negatively reinforced (burned). We would then add avoidance of fire to our behavioral repertoire. This is very inefficient. Instead we *observe*, in a variety of settings (mass mediated and otherwise), the operation of that stimulus, response, and reinforcement chain; and we, in turn, add avoidance to the store of behaviors that we can call into play when confronted in everyday life by that stimulus. In essence, then, we have substituted a representation of an experience for an actual (and, in this case, painful) experience.

A second obvious point is that we do not learn in only this manner. We have all experienced learning through simple observation even when there has been no reinforcement, either to us or to the person in the representation. Observation of a behavior is sufficient for people to learn that behavior (provided that there is successful functioning of the four processes of attention, retention, motoric reproduction, and reinforcement and motivational processes).

Using media representations of everyday encounters as a substitute for everyday communication, then, is an efficient way to learn a wide range of behaviors and solutions to problems that we would otherwise learn slowly, not at all, or pay too high a price to learn in the actual environment.

This social learning through the use of media representations operates in one or all of three ways (see Bandura 1971b for an excellent extended discussion):

1. *Observational Learning.* Consumers of representations can acquire new patterns of behavior by simply watching those representations. All of us know how to shoot a gun, although many of us have never performed or been reinforced for that act. Many of us probably even think that we can hijack a plane. We have seen it done.

2. *Inhibitory Effects.* Seeing a model in a representation punished for exhibiting a certain behavior decreases the likelihood that the observers will make that response. It is as if the viewers themselves are actually negatively reinforced. We see the man in the black hat punished for his evil deeds; we see J. R. Ewing hated by the people of "Dallas" because of his meanness and greed. Our likelihood of responding to various real-world stimuli in similar ways is reduced. In fact, experimental studies using representations of people being punished for various behaviors have shown that these representations can inhibit, in observers, such things as aggression, exploratory behavior, and antisocial interaction with peers.

3. *Disinhibitory Effects.* A media representation that depicts reward for a threatening or prohibited behavior is often sufficient to increase likelihood that the consumer of the representation will make that response. We see Kane successfully defend his Oriental heritage through the use of kung fu; we see Fonzie surrounded by beautiful girls because of his adroit utilization of antisocial or eccentric behavior. Again, experimental studies using film and television representations of various threatening and prohibited encounters have successfully reduced fear of dentists, dogs, and snakes; and increased aggression by reducing viewers' inhibitions toward those actions.

Vicarious reinforcement is central to this notion of social learning through the mass media. It is true that observational learning can occur in the absence of any reinforcement, vicarious or real. In one laboratory experiment, children were shown a film of a young boy pummeling a large plastic punching doll in various unique and novel ways while shouting "lickitstickit" and "wetosmacko," all in the absence of any reinforcement, either in the film or everyday life (Bandura, Ross, and Ross 1963). Observational learning seemed to occur. When put in a playroom, many of the children performed those same pummeling behaviors and shouted those same strange words.

Some, however, did not. All of the children probably learned this way of interpreting action, those behaviors and words; but only some chose to act out or exhibit those behaviors. This is where the concept of *vicarious reinforcement* becomes important to our understanding of how learning from media representations affects our behavior. Vicarious reinforcement is the operation of reinforcement, although the observer is not actually reinforced. Observation of a model's or character's behavior-reinforcement combination often serves as an actual reinforcement for the observing individual. Observation may be sufficient for learning from the media, but the reinforcement contingencies we see associated with the represented behaviors may dictate whether we actually use these behaviors in our everyday life. For example, when we see a television character rewarded or punished for some action, it is as if we ourselves have been actually reinforced, either positively or negatively. This vicarious reinforcement tells us where to place the observationally learned behavior in our behavioral hierarchy—the likelihood that we will choose a given behavior. When presented with certain stimuli in our environment, we will be likely to choose a highly placed behavior for demonstration. One that promises punishment will be given a lower place in that hierarchy. We do not actually have to experience those rewards and sanctions; we have done it vicariously through the use of media representations.

Clearly there may be times when we ignore the negative vicarious reinforcement and perform a behavior that we have seen represented as associated with punishment, such as running into a burning house. In these cases, sufficient incentive is presented in the everyday encounter (saving a child from the flames, for example) to move that behavior higher in our behavioral hierarchy to a point where we can choose it from among a number of alternatives.

A Synthesis of Frame Analysis and Social Learning Theory

Social learning theory is quite compatible with frame analysis theory. Social learning is one of the four possible styles for framing situations. It provides a simple, often effective means of adjusting to situations. It is especially useful to children who have not learned to frame situations from the viewpoint of others. Lacking insight into how others view the social world, they tend to rely on the most prominent, often-repeated cues in situations. Parents often encourage social learning from media content by approving or simply tolerating framed actions that use keyings provided by media.

Children who learn a keying from media content will probably use it to frame everyday actions because they cannot differentiate between everyday and media representations. When these keyings are used in everyday life, they may provide a useful means of structuring actions. Parents may be amused by a child who imitates Superman by imposing a keying learned from the movie. But they will be upset when they find that the keying results in the child's attempts to fly from the tops of chairs, tables, or roofs. Parents know that such flying is unreal—an action possible only in fantasy. But children often demonstrate a remarkable ability to ignore the dangerous consequences of actions structured by keyings.

One of the weakest elements in social learning theory is the concept of reinforcement contingencies. It is difficult to explain why some reinforcements are effective for some children under some circumstances, while the same reinforcements seem to be ignored by other children. Reinforcement contingencies are reinforcement values that people come to associate with certain behaviors.

Reinforcement contingencies are best regarded as cues or sets of cues. These cues have no inherent significance, no universal meaning. To interpret a particular cue, one must frame it. A set of cues implies the frame to be used for interpretation, but ambiguous media content contains conflicting sets of cues. This ambiguity is often not apparent to adults who have learned to pay attention to a limited set of cues that permit a simple frame to be imposed. They find children's programs boring because the cues are too obvious and the experiences created by framing them too predictable.

Great potential exists for a child to learn many keyings, however, because mass media action is presented so dramatically and is accompanied by a seemingly infinite variety of sounds and visual images. To adults, these sounds and images are all variations on a well-known theme, as familiar as a television jingle played with a new melody.

Perhaps the most common error committed by early social learning researchers, then, was to assume that certain elements in media content have a specific meaning that can be interpreted by using adult keyings. When adults view a superhero program, for example, they can see actions presented either positively, negatively, or both—if they know how to impose the most commonly used keyings. But it is misleading to assume that children will frame these actions in the same way. They do not know adult keyings.

We should not be surprised, for example, to find children identifying with crooks in television programs. Social learning theory, as traditionally applied, would imply that children will be reinforced by criminal actions only when those actions are presented with positive consequences. Since this rarely happens, crime drama should have no effect. But what consequences does a particular child perceive when viewing these actions? Will punishment always be associated with crime just because it is presented? Will the routinely imposed, moralistic adult keyings always be used by children? We often wonder why children get so excited about seemingly trivial media representations. But is this excitement so strange? Children viewing television representations are attempting to make sense of ambiguous content. They are coping with problematic situations, learning an elaborated code consisting of sounds and visual images. They are learning to use this code to construct keyings that create experiences for themselves. Is it surprising that they frequently make mistakes? We do not expect four-year-olds to read, but somehow we are ready to assume that they will appropriately frame television programs. We know how to use the elaborated codes of television with some sophistication, but they do not.

What consequences do children's mistakes in interpreting media content have for their adult action? One fear of some media critics is that children may learn violence from watching television, then continue to be aggressive as adults. Is this fear justified? Thus far, social learning research has produced contradictory answers to this question. Experimental research can demonstrate short-term learning of violent action but cannot prove that these actions will continue as children mature (Bandura, Ross, and Ross 1963, for example). A handful of studies of growing children have found some correlation between viewing of violent television programs and adolescent aggression (see Comstock and Rubinstein 1972). But the link has not been made directly, and these findings have been systematically attacked by industry researchers.

One thing is clear, however: Some children will use keyings that frame television violence for routinely framing ambiguous everyday situations. Two consequences are likely. Some children will passively anticipate being the victims of violence in ambiguous everyday situations, while others will see these situations as places for their own aggressive action. Either keying is a simple solution that routinely deals with ambiguity, but neither produces the kind of society one would like to live in; and neither produces a universally useful course of action for the individuals involved. The fearful child will remain passive and less likely to learn how to cope with ambiguity, while the aggressive child will tend to find that adults are as hostile as expected. Aggression will be met with aggression.

These keyings will be employed whenever the social learning style is used to structure action. When a child learns to use reference others, generalized others, or personal values to frame actions, such keyings will become less important and less frequently used. They are unlikely, however, to be totally forgotten; when the other three styles of framing fail to provide useful frames for problematic situations, these keyings may be routinely used. Since much media programming is best enjoyed using a social learning style, frequent use of violent content will probably permit these keyings to be imposed over and over, even when they are not being used in daily life. The media present us with highly ambiguous situations that the other three styles of framing cannot easily cope with. We are encouraged to use the social learning style and the keyings that we have developed using this style. Simple solutions may retain their relevance for us long after we cease to routinely apply them in everyday life. In a crisis, we may turn to these solutions for a means of structuring our actions.

7.4 Three Types of Simple Solutions

Most of the simple solutions that we usually apply to everyday problems are more subtle than overt aggression. Three can be differentiated and related to our use of the mass media: stereotypes, motive talk, and communication talk. All involve routinized intrapersonal and interpersonal communication. They differ primarily in the purposes that they serve for us.

Stereotypes are simple definitions consistent with the routine frames that we use to categorize other people and objects. When we enter stores, we routinely expect to interact with people whom we define as sales clerks, not friends. We want to make our purchases efficiently without engaging in an elaborated social conversation in which personal identities are established and recognized. We may be upset with chatty clerks who insist on asking unnecessary questions about our experiences.

Motive talk serves to make sense of our own or others' actions so that we can continue framing situations in certain ways, even when much ambiguity is present. We are constantly being asked by others to explain why we are doing certain things. Whenever our actions fail to achieve some short-term objective, we ourselves tend to question what we are doing. In both of these cases, we will tend to answer these questions with routine descriptions of our motives. We defend our actions with motive talk—routine explanations of what we are doing. We and others will normally accept these descriptions and explanations. Most of us have learned many commonsense descriptions and explanations of motives so that we have no difficulty accounting for actions of our own and others that may seem inappropriate in a given situation.

Finally, we use our routinized knowledge of communication to make sense of troublesome communication. Much everyday *communication talk* consists of simple solutions, descriptions of communication that provide little insight into the communication taking place but which serve to justify the continuous framing of situations in certain ways. It is talking about communication.

Stereotypes

Stereotypes permit us to regard discrepant elements of situations as unimportant and nonserious. We can develop stereotypes of people and objects. When we stereotype people, we are quickly labeling them as unworthy of the additional attention that would be necessary for us to develop an understanding of them as unique or complex individuals. We do this all the time. We stereotype most of the people we meet in low-context public places, and we meet too many of them to be able to define and recognize each one as a unique individual.

Stereotypes provide us with a means of easily and quickly explaining to ourselves people whose presence implicitly demands our attention and evaluation. When we impose a stereotype on them, we reduce them to simple social objects that can be easily taken for granted no matter what they later do or say. Any actions they make that are inconsistent with our stereotype will be ignored as unimportant. The truth of our simple solution is taken for granted and is not easily contradicted by our experience in situations. We easily stereotype our professors, for example, as serious, scholarly, smart, boring people. It makes our interaction easier with a wide variety of different professors; we know what they are like. When we see them in stereotype-breaking situations—sitting in a student bar and drinking, for example—we find it difficult to frame the situation. Should we ignore them? Should we extend a courteous but distant welcome? Should we approach them as we would other drinkers in the bar? That same stereotype that made dealing with them in class so easy is now challenged. We will probably ignore them. Even though drinking at a student bar, they are probably serious, scholarly, smart, and boring.

We stereotype objects as well as people. Stereotyping of objects has received much less attention from researchers than stereotyping of people, but it may be important. We live in an environment cluttered with objects. Many of us create living spaces filled with trinkets, souvenirs, appliances, toys, sporting equipment, books, television sets, radios, furniture, and so on. Most of these things are meaningful to us because objects can acquire meaning as we use them in situations. But an object can have a meaning for us that transcends its use in any specific situation. The object has been stereotyped. We begin to take its meaning for granted.

We can learn stereotypes for objects without ever personally using them if we see them used by others. This can happen when we see objects used in mass media representations. We constantly see products being used and demonstrated in commercials, but we also see products being used in dramatic or even in news content. Car manufacturers are aware of the importance of this phenomenon. They are willing to negotiate with television producers to assure that their cars will be used by the heroes of programs while a competitor's cars will be used by villains. We come to understand things by seeing them used, just as we come to understand types of people by seeing them displayed as social objects in situations. Once an understanding has developed, it will persist unless contradicted by later events. But these later events must overcome the stereotype already developed. Maybe our stereotype of professors would change if only we would sit and have a drink with them.

Much of the research on media-created stereotypes has been concerned with how minority groups and women are portrayed. It is argued that the demeaning portrayals of these people reduce them to social objects that can be treated in routine, often inhumane ways. Blacks find their own portrayal in media content demeaning and have expressed much frustration about it (see Efron 1972). Characters such as Rochester, Stepin Fetchit, and Amos 'n' Andy were a source of amusement to blacks and whites alike for decades. But the sets of cues that whites associated with these characters served as a basis for developing or maintaining powerful stereotypes that blacks have found difficult to contradict in everyday situations. These stereotypes are especially useful to whites when they want to ignore the actions of a black person and continue imposing a frame that they find useful. Thus, nonserious representations of characters may have serious long-term consequences when used as a basis for developing stereotypes.

Women have fared just as badly. In prime-time television, women occupy less than 30 percent of the speaking roles. One recent study indicated that 30 percent of the children's television shows then available contained no female characters. And about 70 percent of all male television characters are depicted as employed, while only 40 percent of the female characters hold jobs (see Miller and Reeves 1976 for a review of this literature). What stereotypes of women are men and children likely to develop from these representations? Even more important, what stereotypes are women likely to develop of themselves and other women?

Stereotypes may be an important source of social stability, maintaining the power of certain types of people in a social order. Thus far we have considered stereotypes suggesting that certain types of people are nonserious and should be ignored. But there is another set of stereotypes: We do not stereotype only powerless people—we also stereotype those to whom we attribute power. What do these stereotypes allow us to do? Whenever we encounter someone possessing the attributes (cues) we associate with social power, we can routinely look to that person to indicate how to frame the situation. We can cease any conscious effort we might otherwise have made to define a situation and passively accept the powerful person's definition.

There is a fairy tale about the emperor who wore no clothing. In our terms, he was so well-stereotyped by his citizens that almost all of them saw him dressed in the finest of robes even though he was nude. Only a little boy, who clearly did not know the stereotype, was willing to question what he saw. The stereotypes we have developed of people who hold power may have a similar blinding effect upon us. They enable us to avoid looking closely at people in authority, and they prevent us from seeing them as human beings like ourselves. People who have power can rely on these stereotypes to help them maintain power. It is unlikely that others will raise questions or contradict the powerful. Those with power find it easy to enter new situations and have others take their power for granted. When the chairperson of the board walks in, it is ordinarily unnecessary to establish his or her authority. The framing demands of that person are readily accepted by others.

Stereotypes, like all everyday solutions, function to preserve an existing social order. They enable us to categorize both serious and nonserious people quickly and act accordingly. We are able to ignore nonserious people and impose the frames we want, and we at once respect the serious people above us in the social order and permit them to impose whatever frames they choose. When we seek to contradict these stereotypes, we are likely to encounter great difficulty.

Motive Talk

Motive talk is another simple solution that we apply to everyday problem solving that may be influenced by media representations. Stereotypes provide us with explanations for certain types of people, especially strangers. But when we know the other person well, for example, we may be reluctant to impose stereotypes on him or her. Hewitt and Hall (1973) stated that in these situations, we begin to speculate to ourselves about our friend's motives for acting in a given manner. If an individual's behavior threatens a frame we want to impose and it cannot be protected through use of an applicable stereotype, attributing motives to that behavior may be a useful means of preserving our frame.

Suppose you are seated on the subway and the person seated next to you starts pestering you with silly questions, telling you stories about her or his life that do not interest you at all. If he or she is over sixty-five, you might quickly stereotype the annoying person as a "senile old fool." But if the person happens to be a friend, simple stereotyping will not work. Instead you will ascribe motives to the friend. You might say, "He's just letting off steam," or "She's putting me on." These motives explain the disturbing action in a way that denies its seriousness and allows you to ignore it as unimportant.

Similarly we often find ourselves in situations where we have to interpret our own motives. We may find ourselves behaving in a manner that is inconsistent with our own routine behavior. We may pester someone on a bus. It may be necessary, for the sake of preserving our frame of the situation, to attribute a motive to our own action that excuses us from full responsibility. Or, in some cases, we may be asked by other people to explain our behavior, because as we threaten our own frame, we may be threatening theirs as well.

Although the research evidence concerning motive talk is less abundant than evidence concerning stereotypes, media representations may be a valuable source of talk about motives that can later be applied to simple problem-solving. While persuasive arguments might be made for the presence of a wide variety of media representations of motive talk ("To get that girl, get this car," "To get that guy, use this toothpaste"), most of the available empirical evidence centers in the areas of aggression and altruism.

Media representations of violence, regardless of the medium, are virtually always presented in context; that is, within the story or presentation we will be offered motive, act, and subsequent ramification. We are shown the social relationships surrounding actions. Even when apparently senseless violence occurs, it is depicted as being motivated by lunacy or whatever. Such are the demands of good drama. In fact, the National Association of Broadcasters' *Television Code* (1979) requires its subscribing stations to present some reasonable motive for all depicted violence: "Violence . . . may only be projected in reasonably handled contexts, not used exploitatively. Programs involving violence for its own sake . . . are not permissible" (p. 4).

Just as media representations may provide us with stereotypes for explaining unexpected actions of individuals, these depicted motives for aggression may offer us routine labels for other forms of unusual behavior. Much research evidence indicates that the motives associated with mediated violence play an important role in influencing subsequent behavior. Berkowitz (1962) argued and effectively supported his hypothesis that the viewing of justifiably or appropriately motivated media violence led to reduced inhibitions toward aggressive responses in the viewer's own environment. Providing a socially acceptable label for an unusual action may serve to justify that action and encourage us to accept it as appropriate. The label quickly resolves ambiguity. Equally important, Berkowitz discovered that the viewing of unwarranted or unjustified media violence led to greater inhibitions of those aggressive responses. Berkowitz used fictional film violence in his work (a boxing scene from the movie *The Champion*). The same relationship was found between portrayed motives and subsequent aggressive behavior in college students (Meyer 1972) and in young children (Meyer 1973) using real film violence (i.e., a 3 November 1979 CBS newsfilm report of the execution by knife of a North Vietnamese prisoner by a South Vietnamese soldier). In this latter work, the findings led Meyer to note that the portrayed motive "plays an important role in the formation of children's judgments of the acceptability of violence" (p. 331). In other words, justified portrayals of violent action may encourage the integration of aggression into everyday frames. Motive talk provides a frame-protecting judgment of potentially threatening actions; it helps us see where they fit. This also serves to make these discrepant actions part of the frame by establishing their relationship to other, previously framed situations.

Talking to ourselves about motives, then, gives us valuable *frame-preserving* and *frame-elaborating* solutions to problems. Why would a normally sane driver tailgate a speeding car with high-beam headlights aglare? Recklessness threatens the frame we may have developed for driving. If we are careful and courteous, we will be safe. But we see something that threatens to destroy this reassuring frame. If we see a careless driver cut another car off on the highway and the second driver is behaving recklessly, we attribute a motive: "That other driver cut them off." This potentially frame-threatening response (reckless driving) is easily explained by attaching a label to it—nothing really unusual is going on.

In a disturbing extension of this logic, Sanford and Fetter (1979) have argued in their book, *In Defense of Ourselves*, that media portrayals of rape inadvertently reinforce that age-old motive for attack on women: They secretly want to be raped. "There is little doubt in the viewer's mind," wrote the authors, "that the woman deserves it. We must remember that rapists see these movies too. The scenario that women secretly want to be raped and end up loving it is played out for them as well." What better way for a rapist to preserve and elaborate his frame of a quite ambiguous situation than to believe he understands the secret motive of his victim?

The utilization of motive talk presented by media for labeling good behaviors is equally well documented. The viewing of representations of well-motivated (acceptably labeled) altruism and badly motivated (negatively labeled) selfishness was found to increase the altruism or giving behavior of young children in a number of research studies.

Bryan and Walbek (1970) presented third- and fourth-grade children with either a lecture on the value of sharing or television representations of well-motivated sharing actions. Those children who viewed the sharing with its appropriate motives donated more one-cent gift certificates to poor children than those children who heard the talk about the value of giving. The language of television was more powerful than the discourse on values. A situation in which they are asked to give up their hard-earned money (in the Bryan and Walbek study, the certificates were won at a bowling game) can certainly be viewed as a problem for children. But the problematic behavior of giving away what is theirs to a stranger can be understood as a routine action because it is motivated by a greater good called sharing. Giving up personal possessions may not be a routine action for most children in public situations, but they can resolve that ambiguity by assigning motives that label that action as appropriate for those situations.

Communication Talk

Motive talk involves labeling actions so that they can be routinely defined in terms of their significance for the situation frame we are using. Most motive talk serves to explain away deviant actions so that we can go on imposing a routine frame. There is an especially important type of motive talk that deserves special consideration. We often talk about how we are communicating. This *communication talk* serves the same purposes as motive talk. It enables us to explain our communication to ourselves. But communication talk differs from motive talk in one important respect. Communication talk involves talk about talk. It is *metacommunication*. In our society, communication is often a problem. Ambiguous conversations that occur in low-context, public situations often need to be explained. We want to know "Why is he saying that?" or "What is she implying by that remark?" Is he trying to use his talk to impress us? Is she trying to say that we are doing something wrong? Communication talk enables us to impose routine labels on these conversations—it provides answers to questions about talk.

The most common outcome of everyday communication talk is that any apparent ambiguity in messages will be explained, and the routinely imposed situation frame will continue to be imposed. Participants in a situation may agree that their communication has been faulty. They may say when questioned that they "didn't really mean that" or that they really intended to voice agreement, not disagreement. Ironically, communication talk often serves to prevent useful analysis of situation frames and inhibits changes that could improve communication. But it can also serve to prevent unnecessary dis-agreements over mistakes in communication.

A second outcome is also possible. When a situation becomes ambiguous, an authority who can serve as a useful source of com-munication talk may be sought. The authority can provide us with labels that help us interpret what we assume is problematic commu-nication. Research evidence exists that television is respected by many people as a source of information about communication. Walters and Stone (1971), for example, discovered that many married couples use conversations they see on television as a basis for their own everyday conversation. Clearly we need to know much more about how the mass media may influence the way we communicate about communi-cation.

7.5 Alternatives to Simple Solutions

Conscious problem-solving provides an alternative to the simple solu-tions of everyday life. Conscious problem-solving refers to any sys-tematic, formalized procedure for reflecting on frames. If more of us used mass media content more often to engage in conscious problem-solving, we might realize and overcome problems that we now avoid by using simple solutions—we might overcome racial prejudice, dis-crimination against women, mistaken notions of how to communicate, and inappropriately categorized motives. People who engage in con-scious problem-solving tend to be more objective. Their systematic efforts to engage in reflection based on the best information available from many sources allow them to formulate the best possible solutions to their problems.

But conscious problem-solving in everyday life is hindered by the same limitations that result in inadequate framing of situations. People who depend upon the social learning framing strategy will use situ-ation cues to aid reflection; those using the looking-glass–self strategy might choose topics for reflection that they think reference others would choose; people using the generalized-other strategy will reflect on frames based on their conceptualization of their generalized other; and those who have developed a personal value system will base their reflections on their value system.

In our society, conscious problem-solving procedures are taught in schools, and the assumption is that a particular generalized other should be used as a point of reference. The generalized other for educators is the academic community as a whole and scientists in particular. Students are taught that they should try to apply scientific reasoning on their own, but if they fail they should turn to scientists for expert help. Scientists and other academic professionals are to be relied upon as sources of information to be used in solving problems. Newspapers can be used if the sources of information in news stories are professionals who have adequate academic credentials. Most television content is defined as having little or no usefulness for conscious problem-solving.

American educators have long struggled to reform the mass media industries. Their efforts are based on the assumption that most of the commercial entertainment content supplied by media is unsuited to conscious problem-solving efforts. Industry professionals, however, usually respond to this criticism by arguing that most people do not want to engage in conscious problem-solving using television and that it would be undemocratic to force them to do so. They usually offer the Nielsen ratings for informative programs versus entertainment programs as evidence. The high ratings for purely entertaining shows prove that Americans do not want information, they claim.

Perhaps many of the problems in American education stem in part from a conflict between the explicit elaborated codes taught by traditional academic curricula and the implicit elaborated codes found in media genres. Both types of codes provide frames for everyday experiences. The media genres provide their frames inadvertently and implicitly as a necessary part of creating representations of everyday communication play: social conversation, stories, and drama. Academic codes purport to allow the objective and systematic framing of social situations. Children who learn academic codes—reading and writing, the scientific method, geography, social studies, mathematics, and the other traditional areas of academic curricula—should be prepared to enter everyday life and act effectively so that they can serve society as well as themselves.

But these codes have little relevance without the generalized other that provides a point of reference. They are little more than formulas for consciously analyzing fragments of everyday life—why should students respect these frames more than the stories they see in the mass media? The media representations are compelling, dramatic simulations of everyday life, while the abstract representations of life produced by academic codes are much harder to relate to and understand.

We face a curious paradox. The genres used by the mass media produce representations of everyday life that are clearly inadequate and often very fallacious. They lead to the development of many simple solutions that undermine the quality of everyday life and inhibit useful social change. The academic codes produce frames for bits and pieces of everyday life that are adequate by academic community standards but are found to be irrelevant by most people who lack an academic generalized other.

We seem to have trapped ourselves in a very dangerous dilemma for a democratic society. On the one hand, we admit that a particular way of understanding everyday life—formal education—produces the most useful and adequate (serious) representations of that life, but these representations can only be understood by a few dedicated, quite serious people. On the other hand, most of us—the public—prefer representations that are merely entertaining (nonserious) because we tend to be nonserious. The logical solution to this dilemma is one that is difficult for people in a democracy to accept: Since most of us are nonserious, we cannot be depended upon to control our own lives or the lives of others; we should surrender control to the experts who can use the abstract, powerful representations that we cannot understand to control our lives for us. Must we, however, accept this logical conclusion?

There is an alternative. Public communication is closely related to the development and use of the reflective-self style of framing. Public communication alone, however, will not facilitate the use of this style. People must seriously intend to use it in certain ways. Publics can create and collectively reframe public situations if public communication is seriously used. The reflective-self style of framing can permit individuals to integrate and reflect on frames implicit in public situations. Through this integration and reflection, individuals can develop and apply unique, personally meaningful systems of values.

The widespread utilization of the reflective-self style of framing, however, is made difficult by the predominance of media-created cues that facilitate unreflective framing. And if we cannot take our mass media creations seriously—if these products cannot offer useful insight into social situations—then we will find it difficult to take ourselves seriously. Human beings always find themselves in communication play with others—in the conversations, stories, and drama of everyday life or in the mass media creations that simulate this informal communication play. We fashion our knowledge and presentation of ourselves, our knowledge of others, and our understanding of the situations we enter. When we do this, we imitate the creations of others. This personal art inevitably reflects the artistic representations that we have chosen to take seriously.

We need to develop our ability to reflect critically upon artistic representations. We cannot rely upon the cues supplied by media professionals to provide us with a reference point. Media professionals have become very skilled at selling us a product, their art—so skilled, in fact, that we often do not bother to be concerned about it. We take it for granted as a routine part of everyday life. We consume it, just as we consume quarter-pounders and buffered aspirin, with little concern for long-term consequences. Novelist John Gardner (1978, p. 100) wrote:

We need to stop excusing mediocre and downright pernicious art, stop "taking it for what it's worth" as we take our fast foods, our overpriced cars that are no good, the overpriced houses we spend all our lives fixing, our television programs, our schools thrown up like barricades in the way of young minds, our brainless fat religions, our poisonous air, our incredible cult of sports, and our ritual of fornicating with all pretty or even horse-faced strangers. We would not put up with a debauched king, but in a democracy all of us are kings, and we praise debauchery as pluralism.

We need a basis for moral reflection on situation frames. We need a framing strategy from which to communicate and to understand communication. Then we can be serious and productively nonserious about ourselves in ways that are meaningful, that will permit us to take serious actions that have the long-term consequences that we intend. This is the objective of the reflective-self style of framing.

7.6   Conclusion

Our everyday adjustment to and solution of problems is called routine problem-solving. We constantly engage in it; every situation we enter poses different problems for us. Mass media representations and the experiences they make possible help us develop our routine problem-solving skills. These representations, however, permit only a limited range of skills and solutions to be developed.

One simple solution to everyday problems is aggression. Many people feel that the use of this possibly media-learned solution may be replacing public communication for problem solving. The social learning theory of aggression, for example, argues that aversive or problem situations produce an emotional arousal that calls for action. The behaviors elicited to solve those problems are a function of the solutions that the individual has learned for dealing with those situations. Inasmuch as the media offer much problem-solving information that is centered around aggression, they are seen as leading to increased viewer violence.

This social learning is said to occur when four processes operate: The viewer must see and understand what is being shown (attention), must be able to remember what was seen (retention), must be able to perform to some degree what was seen (motoric reproduction), and must want to do it (reinforcement and motivation).

Social learning from mass media can manifest itself in one or all of three ways: (a) Observational learning is the acquisition of new behaviors by simply watching media representations; (b) inhibitory effects occur when we see a media character punished for exhibiting a certain behavior, decreasing the likelihood that we ourselves will exhibit it; and (c) disinhibitory effects occur when we see media models rewarded for prohibited or threatening behaviors, increasing the likelihood that we will exhibit those behaviors.

We obviously do not meet all situations with aggression. We encounter and solve most problems very much out of our conscious awareness. Three simple solutions to these problems are stereotypes, motive talk, and communication talk. Stereotypes enable us to categorize other people and objects by using simple definitions that are consistent with the frames that we routinely impose. Motive talk is routine explanations of what we and others are doing, and we use it to frame situations in certain ways when much ambiguity is present. Finally, our routinized knowledge of communication helps us make sense of troublesome communication in our everyday lives; this is communication talk. A wealth of research evidence suggests that the mass media are powerful agents in the creation and maintenance of some of these simple solutions.

An alternative to the imposition of these simple solutions is conscious problem-solving, a systematic, formalized procedure for engaging in reflection on frames. If more of us used media content more often to engage in conscious problem-solving, we might become aware of and overcome problems that we usually avoid through the use of simple solutions. This is difficult, however, because the genres used in mass media are usually inadequate and fallacious simulations of everyday life and, as such, may offer little in the way of useful cues for framing.

Increased utilization of the reflective-self style of framing will help in the more effective use of media content; and public communication can help us in the reframing and redefining of much problem-solving activity.

References

Bandura, A. 1971a. *Aggression: a social learning analysis.* Englewood Cliffs, N.J.: Prentice Hall.

———. 1971b. *Psychological modeling: conflicting theories.* Chicago: Aldine Atherton.

———. 1978. Social learning theory of aggression. *J. Communication* 28: 12–29.

Bandura, A.; Ross, D.; and Ross, S. A. 1963. Imitation of film-mediated aggressive models. *J. Abnormal Soc. Psychol.* 66: 3–11.

Berkowitz, L. 1962. *Aggression: a social psychological analysis.* New York: Mc-Graw-Hill.

Bryan, J. H., and Walbek, N. H. 1970. Preaching and practicing generosity: children's actions and reactions. *Child Dev.* 41: 329–53.

Caylor, R. 1978. TV's laugh shows can help you live longer. *National Enquirer,* 26 September 1978, p. 24.

Comstock, G. A., and Rubinstein, E. A., eds. 1972. *Television and social behavior (Reports and papers, volume 3: television and adolescent aggressiveness).* Washington, D.C.: U.S. Government Printing Office.

Dollard, J.; Doob, L. W.; Miller, N. E.; Mowrer, O. H.; and Sears, R. R. 1939. *Frustration and aggression.* New Haven: Yale Univ. Press.

Efron, E. 1972. Excluded, distorted, manhandled and exploited. *TV Guide* 20: 44–49.

Feshbach, S. 1956. The catharsis hypothesis and some consequences on interaction with aggressive and neutral play objects. *J. Personality* 24: 449–62.

Gardner, J. C. 1978. *On moral fiction.* New York: Basic Books.

Goranson, R. E. 1970. Media violence and aggressive behavior: a review of experimental research. In *Advances in experimental social psychology, vol. 5,* ed. L. Berkowitz, pp. 1–31. New York: Academic Press.

Hewitt, J. P., and Hall, P. M. 1973. Social problems, problematic situations, and quasi-theories. *Am. Sociol. Rev.* 38: 367–74.

Meyer, T. P. 1972. Effects of viewing justified and unjustified real film violence on aggressive behavior. *J. Pers. Soc. Psychol.* 23: 21–29.

———. 1973. Children's perceptions of justified/unjustified and fictional/real film violence. *J. Broadcasting* 17: 321–32.

Miller, M. M., and Reeves, B. 1976. Dramatic TV content and children's sex-role stereotypes. *J. Broadcasting* 20: 35–50.

Miller, N. E., and Dollard, J. 1941. *Social learning and imitation.* New Haven: Yale Univ. Press.

National Association of Broadcasters. 1979. *Television code, paragraph 4 of the program standards of the 22nd edition.* Washington, D.C.

Sanford, L. T., and Fetter, A. 1979. *In defense of ourselves.* Garden City, N.Y.: Doubleday.

United Press International. Insanity plea accepted in race attacks. *Houston Chronicle,* 10 January 1979.

Walters, J. K., and Stone, V. A. 1971. Television and family communication. *J. Broadcasting* 15: 409–14.

Additional Readings

Problem Solving

Bandura, A., and Walters, R. H. 1963. *Social learning and personality development.* New York: Holt, Rinehart & Winston.

Baran, S. J. 1974. Television as teacher of prosocial behavior: what the research says. *Pub. Telecomm. Rev.* 2: 46–51.

Hewitt, J. P. 1976. *Self and society.* Boston: Allyn & Bacon.

Johnson, N. 1972. *Test pattern for living.* New York: Bantam Books.

Kidd, V. 1975. Happily ever after and other relationship styles: advice on interpersonal relations in popular magazines, 1951–1973. *Q. J. Speech* 61: 31–39.

White, R. W. 1972. *The enterprise of living.* New York: Holt, Rinehart & Winston.

Social Learning

Bandura, A. 1965. Vicarious processes: a case of no-trial learning. In *Advances in experimental social psychology, vol. 2,* ed. L. Berkowitz, pp. 3–55. New York: Academic Press.

Baran, S. J., and Meyer, T. P. 1974. Imitation and identification: two compatible approaches to social learning from the electronic media. *AV Comm. Rev.* 2: 167–79.

Cowan, P. A.; Langer, J.; Heavenrich, J.; and Nathanson, M. 1969. Social learning and Piaget's cognitive theory of moral development. *J. Pers. Soc. Psychol.* 11: 261–74.

Flanders, J. P. 1968. A review of research on imitative behavior. *Psychol. Bull.* 69: 316–37.

Aggression

Baker, R. K., and Ball, S. J. 1969. *Mass media and violence: a staff report to the National Commission on the Causes and Prevention of Violence.* Washington, D.C.: U.S. Government Printing Office.

Bandura, A., and Walters, R. H. 1959. *Adolescent aggression.* New York: Ronald.

Berkowitz, L. 1965a. Some aspects of observed aggression. *J. Pers. Soc. Psychol.* 2: 359–69.

———. 1965b. The concept of aggressive drive: some additional considerations. In *Advances in experimental social psychology, vol. 2,* ed. L. Berkowitz, pp. 301–29. New York: Academic Press.

Chapter 8

Media Fantasies and Moral Planning

CBS has dropped its plans to produce a dramatized miniseries on the Symbionese Liberation Army, the terrorist group that abducted heiress Patty Hearst in 1974. The network had spent an estimated $50,000 on the project, called *The Voices of Guns*. William Self, vice president of TV-movies and miniseries, says that the scripts were good, but they presented too many legal and factual problems.

CBS executives made their decision after receiving 75 pages of factual questions on the scripts from a special group established eight months ago to scrutinize the accuracy of docu-dramas. In addition, CBS was concerned that the telecast might prejudice the upcoming trial of SLA members Bill and Emily Harris.

8.1 Introduction

Americans talk a lot about planning. We plan vacations, weekend trips, trips to store or supermarket. We even plan our use of mass media. We buy *TV Guide* or read the television logs in the newspapers. We plan to listen to radio when we drive to work or when we return from classes. We count on reading the newspaper over breakfast, or we plan to read a book in bed to help put us to sleep. Students reserve time during the week when they take their textbooks seriously and study.

The purpose of planning is to allow us to do what we intend to do—to make certain that good intentions are carried out. And all of us are aware that some of us plan more effectively than others.

How has mass communication altered our ability to plan our lives? Has it increased our ability to reflect usefully on our actions and thus allowed us to assume more control over them? Are media simulations of everyday action useful in planning our own actions? Newspapers, for example, claim to tell us about the most important events going on in the world so that we can use their stories in planning our decisions. But how useful, actually, is this information?

Commercial mass entertainment and news are usually inadequate forms of communication on which to base planning. Some of these inadequacies are obvious. Anyone who plans to live like a television or movie character is asking for trouble, and few of the thousands of discrete news events reported to us have any relevance for our own lives. But the influence of mass communication on our planning may be more subtle and pervasive than we realize. Most of us, for example, do not rush out and buy the items we see advertised on television, but when we pass them on a supermarket shelf we tend to reach for them. It is usually hard for us to explain why this happens. We have feelings about these products that motivate our purchases. We trust them more than those that are not widely advertised.

How does buying attractive, heavily advertised products relate to planning our futures? We may be willing to admit that a skillfully done ad campaign that uses several mass media is able to influence some of our short-term planning. We may rearrange our priorities and buy some things rather than others. We may occasionally buy a few things on impulse as we pass them in a store. We still have control, however, over our long-term actions even if we allow these short-term goals to be manipulated. Moreover, this is a pleasant form of media influence; we occasionally enjoy indulging our whims. It is true—we do "deserve a break today." Life is too short to be lived too seriously. Make yourself happy today, some advertisements whisper, and our country's founders guaranteed us the right to pursue happiness. The pursuit of short-term pleasant experiences, however, does not usually lead us to the achievement of significant long-term objectives.

8.2 Planning and Pseudoplanning

An effective mode of planning can be defined and differentiated from commonsense styles of planning that often involve the imposition of simple solutions. Effective *planning* involves the use of a complex framing process to anticipate and develop conscious expectations of future situations and to consider the possible consequences of personal actions. The role of conscious awareness in this framing process is likely to be limited but important. Simple plans involve anticipating a few situations that are likely to be entered soon and that will not affect our action in later situations. We can use simple plans to prepare for an evening out with friends, and we can use complex plans to prepare for a lifelong relationship with another person or a particular career.

Even simple plans, however, can involve somewhat complex framing problems. We must become aware of the situations that we are likely to enter and frame them so that we can form expectations about how we will identify ourselves, personify others, and assess the seriousness of the situations. We can greatly simplify the framing process if we impose many simple solutions and rely on stereotypes, motive talk, and communication talk to provide us with easy answers about what is likely to happen. Such planning that relies on simple solutions is *pseudoplanning* because it does not involve adequate reflection on the frames being used. Simple solutions are routinely imposed as though the answers they provide are the only possible answers. But these solutions often provide arbitrary, useless, or misleading answers to our questions about future situations. We often make serious mistakes when we fail to question those solutions.

Reflection and Planning

Effective planning requires at least minimal reflection on the frames being used, ordinarily possible by considering alternate keyings for future situations. We can envision these situations developing in different ways involving different self-identifications, personifications of others, and degrees of seriousness. We can playfully ask ourselves: "I wonder what would happen if I act this way tonight?"—"How would others act toward me?"—"How appropriate will these actions be?" Most important, we can consider the consequences likely to result from our behavior. "Can these actions help me reach meaningful or important objectives?"—"If not, are there other actions that might be more useful?"

This reflection will only be as useful as the keyings that we have developed for the specific situations. If our knowledge of the keyings is limited, if we know only a few primary frames or a handful of simple solutions, we will not be able to plan effectively.

Planning is a complex art form that permits framing of the future. It is an art that demands skill. We must be able to impose keyings creatively on situations that have not yet occurred and that may never occur. This skill can be developed through communication play in which many different types of keyings are learned and playfully imposed. It is easily short-circuited if we rely on simple solutions or a small number of primary frames. When we do, planning becomes routine, a means of easily imposing typical, commonsense keyings on the future. It may appear to be effective as long as the routinely imposed keyings result in socially acceptable actions that have expected, short-term consequences. But when we plan in this way, we cannot assume personal responsibility for our actions. We allow ourselves to be controlled by simple solutions offered by others and by the mass media.

8.3 Personal Responsibility in a Mass Society

We live in a society that makes it easy for individuals to evade personal responsibility for action and to avoid planning. There are many reasons why this situation exists. Media representations, for example, provide us with simple solutions, stereotypes, motive talk, and communication talk, all of which permit us to construct routine explanations for the future and allow us to easily label other people and their actions. These simple solutions usually divert our attention from the problems and ambiguity that develop in our lives and blind us to information that we should take into account when anticipating the future.

Our stressful time makes many demands on us. But we have developed solutions for most stress that help us cope. One common solution for many of us is use of the mass media. When we find it difficult to create meaningful experiences for ourselves in everyday situations—when these situations cannot be made routine by imposing simple solutions—we can always retreat to our television sets or pick up a newspaper and enter a world of prepackaged communication that routinely allows us to create satisfying experiences. When we create these experiences, we routinely learn more simple solutions, making pseudoplanning even easier and more likely.

In spite of the stress we sometimes encounter, we can see our society as a very positive one. We have an abundance of material wealth. Most of us live everyday lives in which there is little physical danger and where our basic physical needs are easily provided for.

We turn on our water faucets and make regular trips to the market to meet needs that, for thousands of years, required long hours of work.

We are no longer bound by rigid traditions that dictate how we act in certain situations. Our children can aspire to social roles that are different and sometimes more important than those of their parents. The power of social authorities over our lives is limited by explicit elaborated codes that define which situations they can and cannot directly control. We have a rich heritage of public communication, including a history of social revolution that legitimized it and limited the power of social authorities to control it. We have at our disposal the most effective, efficient technologies for the transmission of information.

In spite of this material wealth and great discretion in the control of our personal lives, however, many of us find planning to be difficult and frustrating. Why? In part, because we seem to have so little control over major social events that inevitably disrupt even our best formulated plans. Couples who have saved for years for a down payment on a house may find their planning wasted if interest rates soar and the requirements for making a down payment increase. Students planning certain careers can suddenly discover that their chosen field has been closed to new entrants because of oversaturation.

How do we cope? Most of us adjust by imposing simple solutions provided by the media. Only rarely do we feel compelled to engage in public communication. News stories help us anticipate the impact of elite actions on our everyday lives and help us cope with these changes. If unemployment soars, we can count on television news to show us people standing in unemployment lines to get assistance checks or apply for new jobs. If gasoline is short, we can be amused by the problems of others forced to wait in long gas lines and prepare ourselves to accept the shortage as routine. The news stories assure us that something is being done about the problem. The president and Congress are taking action, a government commission or two is investigating, a federal agency is hard at work. We can do our part by simply coping as best we can until the bureaucrats and professionals manage to work the problem out. Our responsibility is to stay cool (impose simple solutions) and wait for the return of normalcy.

There are, however, some critical questions about the absence of personal responsibility for action and the way in which social orders inhibit its development. Why is the range of personal action that is available to us often so limited? Why are most of us unable or unwilling (except occasionally) to engage in public communication in times of ambiguity? Why is it possible and perhaps necessary for our leaders to deal with us as masses of individuals having many routine

Media Fantasies

A *media fantasy* consists of a set of interrelated simple solutions to routinely experienced and anticipated everyday problems. Individuals learn them as they use media content that features various combinations of simple solutions. *Fantasy theme* refers to a specific combination of solutions that is related to other combinations. It is possible, for example, to define several broad and pervasive media fantasies in American society that link the consumption of goods and services with personal happiness. Within these overall fantasies, we can differentiate many different themes dealing with various types of consumption. There is the Playboy, the Sports Fan, the Thrifty But Conscientious Housewife, the Luxury Car Driver, the Counterculture Freak, and even the Animal Lover.

Each of these fantasy themes consists of many stereotypes, forms of motive talk, and types of communication talk. They take on personal meaning when we use them to anticipate how we will frame our personal lives and plan the structure of our daily experiences.

These fantasy themes also structure much of the content in mass media. A continuing problem that faces content producers is to discover and create fantasy themes that will attract and interest large audiences. The more that individuals use them to structure their everyday lives, the more attractive these themes become, and more audiences will seek out content that offers them.

An important relationship develops between the producers of media fantasies and the mass audiences that consume their art. Each is quite dependent on the other. Producers of content are dominant to the extent that they alone have the skill to encode fantastic messages using implicit but elaborated codes. Audience demand for their product enables them to sell it for high prices. But there is always the possibility that audiences will lose interest in particular fantasy themes; and there is the long-term danger that an entire fantasy may lose its attractiveness (a fate that has befallen the white-hatted good guy in television and movie westerns and the conscientious liberal social-service worker in movie disaster films).

---

needs and desires rather than as members of publics holding consciously framed objectives?

One answer may be that the simple solutions offered by mass media constitute *media fantasies* that lead us to develop many routine expectations of the future that can best be satisfied by mass production and distribution of material goods and services. We can use these fantasies to guide both short- and long-term planning. As long as our societal production and distribution system does its job, our planning succeeds. As long as we can ignore the social and personal problems inherent in this system, we can use fantasies to plan effectively.

These plans, however, depend on the mass production and distribution system that, in turn, makes us dependent on the bureaucratic and professional elites who administer it. They have the responsibility of attempting to coordinate many types of social action throughout the social order. They inevitably seek out efficient strategies for coordinating action of large numbers of people. The creation and transmission of media fantasies provide an efficient means of structuring mass action. A new fantasy theme can be used to discourage certain forms of social action and encourage other forms. Advertisers and public relations people have often successfully used media fantasies to control social action—the buying of products, improving corporate images, voting for certain candidates. Other elites (many religious organizations, for example) are also finding that media fantasies are more effective in coordinating social action than are various forms of public communication.

8.4 The Consumption Fantasy: An Example of a Theme

A classic example of a fantasy theme is provided by the Playboy. He is very popular with women, knows to order Chateau-neuf du Pape with his goose, drives a Porsche, hunts with a double-barreled shotgun that he crafted himself, and will never order Johnny Walker Red when Black is available.

This fantasy theme illustrates the typical structure of most such themes and the use that we tend to make of them. Few of us have actually been Playboys (or Playgirls, for that matter). Some may find that this fantasy simply structures an occasional pleasant experience as they read *Playboy* magazine. But we all tend to use some consumption fantasy themes if only to make our routine purchases more meaningful and their planning more enjoyable.

How does someone utilize the Playboy theme? The successful Playboy is an expert in impression management. He strives to create and control certain situations by pseudoplanning using simple solutions. The apartment, the car, and the singles' bar are the spaces that he seeks to control by carefully arranging objects. The most critical of these objects is himself. He must present himself with care so that others will appropriately personify him. Fortunately he has many readily available simple solutions learned in mass media use to aid his efforts. Advertising, especially for hard liquor, clothing, and cigarettes, features the stereotypes, motive talk, and communication talk that aid him in routinely solving impression management problems. The would-be Playboy has only to develop his skills in applying these solutions and he will be stereotyped as he wants, and his motives and communication will be properly categorized. The essence of Playboy planning is self-control so that certain, specific consumption experiences can be achieved. The Playboy succeeds when he is able to consume goods and services with style.

Media Fantasies and Everyday Life

This discussion of the Playboy theme highlights two of its essential characteristics. First, such a media fantasy provides arbitrary but routine representations of social relationships that are neither inherently true nor false. Second, it represents social relationships in ways different from the codes of everyday life. This is what makes them fantasies. They simplify the meaning of everyday action; they imply that certain stereotypes, motive talk, and communication talk have specific meanings and uses. A powerful new media fantasy theme can organize and make sense of other simple solutions already present in previously learned media content. Sometimes the same simple solutions can be integrated into different fantasy themes or the same media content can be used to develop several different themes.

We may come to use a media fantasy as a basis for exercising control over ourselves and our everyday lives. Media fantasies become formulas for routine personal planning. They enable us to simplify our understanding of ourselves and our lives so that we can control our experiences and achieve specific objectives. Some fantasies are simple and involve only a few simple solutions, while others are very complex.

Seriousness and Fantasies

In general, the fantasies offered by the media are useful in anticipating and framing the more or less nonserious situations in our lives. This is another reason for use of the term "fantasy" rather than another, more serious word like "ideology" or "information." In some respects, though, a fantasy is similar to what some social theorists have defined as ideology, and fantasies in news stories (such as portrayals of a hard-nosed police captain or repeated showings of certain minorities as criminals) do convey information. A media fantasy provides an individual with a biased and arbitrary world view. But this view is created for different purposes than either ideology or information. Fantasies are often not intended by their creators to be used to frame serious everyday situations. An ideology, on the other hand, is a set of ideas created by a public and intended to be used to frame serious situations with the purpose of producing specific consequences. Ideologies are produced by publics striving to achieve certain objectives through the use of public communication; fantasies are created by media professionals striving to attract the largest possible audiences through the use of various genres that convey popular simple solutions.

Once we have learned a media fantasy, we are free to apply it to whatever planning for which it may prove useful. We can use it to anticipate our purchases before shopping. We can use it before driving to work to make the drive more meaningful. We can use it prior to dates or before "hanging out" with friends.

But we have gradually learned to respect and even fear the power of ideology to control social action. Publics created by ideologies can easily gain control over ambiguous public situations and structure the actions of both members and nonmembers. Once embraced by a public, an ideology can be used to anticipate and explain a wide variety of social action and impose social control on members and nonmembers alike. By contrast, media fantasies seem to be innocuous and trivial. But like ideologies, they serve as a basis for social control.

Control is not exercised by an elite public in the same way as when ideologies are used. It is exercised by professionals using elaborated codes to create fantasy themes, which, in turn, structure the actions of mass audiences. The age of ideology may have ended, but we have entered an era of media fantasy.

The power of professionals using media fantasies to structure social action has greatly increased. The rise of complex industries to conduct advertising and public relations provides evidence of this transition in power. Even our highest elected officials surround themselves with advertising and public relations people to manage their campaign and image fantasies.

The Confusion of Media Fantasy and Ideologies

How has the power of publics been eroded by the rise of media fantasy? The answer may lie in the widespread confusion of ideologies and media fantasies.

One of the most vexing, pervasive problems of modern publics in our country arises because their ideologies are often transformed into media fantasies and repackaged for mass audience consumption. The women's liberation movement offers one example. It appears to have been disrupted by media fantasies that have capitalized on its ideology and transformed it. There is, for example, the Superwoman theme that suggests it is not only possible but necessary for a woman to be both successful mother (keeps her family well fed and happy, the house is clean, no ring around hubby's collar) and successful career woman (respected by co-workers, has serious responsibilities, has "come a long way"). The fantasy of the Superwoman is a complex combination of simple solutions. A brief look at *Ms.* magazine (especially the advertising) shows what many of these are. Superwomen dress in certain ways (for power), they utilize certain stereotypes of themselves (I am strong), they attribute certain motives to themselves (I work because it is self-fulfilling), they use certain communication talk (avoid being one-upped); and consequently they structure their consumption in certain routine ways (smoke certain cigarettes, use certain brands of liquor). In this way, an ideology is transformed into yet another theme consistent with the consumption fantasy.

The Superwoman theme has many appealing features for women. It says that it is possible for them to do what they now do but do it better, as well as do something else that is even more important. The Happy Homemaker theme is now rejected by many women. Nobody likes to wash clothes like the women in old-fashioned commercials. Nobody likes to clean kitchen floors or wash windows. Even the promise of magical assistance from Mr. Clean and the White Tornado is not enough to perpetuate the Happy Homemaker theme. Modern women want more from life, and the Superwoman fantasy provides them with the assurance that what they want can be achieved.

The social movement that gave rise to the Superwoman theme, the women's liberation movement, began as a middle-class, urban public engaged in public communication. Like most movements, it started with a relatively small public in which most members knew each other and had some direct or indirect contact with one another. Thus it began as a public capable of generating a context for its own communication. That context included much everyday coding, as well as the more elaborated coding provided by the public's explicitly formulated ideology. The everyday coding provided the context that made interpretation of the ideology in specific ways possible. In our society, however, ideologies are soon separated from their contexts. Women's liberation ideology was featured by the mass media in news stories and entertainment programs as a set of radical new ideas that threatened old ways of thinking about women. As this out-of-context ideology was gradually absorbed by the mass audience, it was transformed into fantasy.

Today's Superwoman is not necessarily a part of any social movement. She accepts most of the traditional values associated with being a wife and mother, but she accepts the new feminist values as well. She does not need the guidance and public communication provided by other women who share feminist goals. These are taken for granted as worthwhile. Why meet with a group to discuss motherhood or sisterhood? Whatever information might be necessary to help her become a Superwoman can be found in media content.

Ideology and Fantasy Equal News and Entertainment

Fantasy and ideology are often mixed and confused in mass communication. Publics are often tempted to rely on existing fantasies as a means of arousing interest in their communication. The Superwoman fantasy attracted many women to the women's liberation movement. News stories stimulated audience interest in feminists in action. But the fantasy created widespread misconceptions about the movement. The media fantasy proved beyond the control of the movement leaders.

Ideologies created by publics are vulnerable to removal from their contexts and transformation into media fantasies. They provide artistic material for media professionals intent on creating provocative news stories or entertainment programs that fit certain genre formulas and involve certain fantasy themes. Inclusion of innovative ideas from ideologies and unusual characters drawn from social movements is a means of increasing the attractiveness of media fantasies. Paddy Chayefsky (who wrote the Howard Beale speech that opened this book) satirized this tendency in his movie *Network,* depicting the creation of a television program in which a radical leftist group stages weekly violent revolutionary actions for the television cameras. The satire was a bit extreme, but not too far wrong. Soon after, CBS began planning a docu-drama centered around just such a group, the Symbionese Liberation Army (SLA). A few years later, a group of Iranian terrorists took a page from Chayefsky's script and overtook the American embassy in Iran, staging daily "demonstrations" for cameras of the networks' nightly news programs.

How did most of us come to know and understand that first group, the SLA? It is a safe guess that nobody outside the SLA truly understood its ideology. But most of us were exposed to media content—news as well as entertainment—that transformed this group and its ideology into media fantasy. If Hollywood scriptwriters had tried to write a better tale than the one created by news reporters on the SLA trail, they most certainly would have failed. Remember the SLA—the Patty Hearst kidnapping, the leader Cinque? This group of black and white revolutionaries robbed California banks in 1974 in order to fund their revolution. They were ultimately traced to a Los Angeles bungalow, where a handful of their members engaged police in a lengthy gun battle in which all of the group were killed.

Why was the news about the SLA so fantastic? In part, it was because the members were trying to make news and had a good working knowledge of the genres used by reporters to create stories. The SLA wanted news coverage and got it, but SLA members even-

195

tually became victims of the stereotypes of themselves that they helped the news media create.

Was it necessary for the Los Angeles Police Department to surround the SLA's small house with an army of men and to use tear gas and machine guns to liquidate this small group of people? Perhaps the SLA fantasy created by news stories influenced police officials to act the way they did; the fantasy may have left them no choice.

The coverage of the SLA is one example (although extreme) of what often happens when news professionals cover events that are artfully created by people to secure attention from the news media. These occurrences are called *pseudoevents,* and they are increasing in number—plane hijackings, the taking of hostages, high-profile kidnappings and assassinations, census-form burnings, and so on. Reporters cover events where publics engage in communication; then editors edit carefully selected segments of this communication into news programs. Public communication becomes part of a presentation controlled by television producers who are ultimately concerned with attracting large audiences. They select those bits of communication that can serve as cues to audiences looking for the fantasies implicit in the day's events. Public communication is transformed into skillfully edited reports that leave viewers with the impression that they have been informed in an interesting, useful way about important events. Publics know this, and they structure their own communication accordingly.

When publics stage events for cameras, they do so with the knowledge that television producers like certain cues and not others. If they want their event covered, they must recognize the constraints imposed by the appropriate media genres. In the late 1960s, draft-card burning in opposition to the Vietnam War had become a staple of television news coverage of the antiwar movement. As such, some women in the feminist movement were tempted to reduce their meaningful women's liberation ideology to a foolish fantasy consistent with this genre definition of news—they burned their bras for the cameras.

Media fantasies disrupt the work of publics in several important ways. They provide the context used by audiences to understand publics. This makes it difficult to recruit people who have not already developed possibly misleading and inaccurate impressions of what they are trying to do. The ideology of a public is boring when compared to media content, so publics sometimes make their communication more interesting by using media fantasies to illustrate their ideologies, and this leads to further confusion. The feminists' bra burnings, for example, probably did more to hurt the women's movement than to help it. It was seen as a silly act, and it provided the basis for much sexist humor and derision.

Publics are tempted to gain quick recognition and rapid growth for their movements by creating pseudoevents that bring widespread exposure. But this usually results in their being contextualized (put into a certain context) by media professionals using fantasies. In time, the public must devote ever-increasing effort to overcoming the misconceptions that these media fantasies may create.

Finally, the danger exists that when audiences lose interest in a particular fantasy theme, a given public will be of no further interest to news media and will disappear from mass communication. For many publics, dependence on media exposure is high. Movement leaders depend on news stories to confirm the movement's importance and success. Members judge the worth of their group, its seriousness, and its likelihood of achieving serious objectives by looking at media coverage of it. When coverage stops, it is as though the power plug has been pulled and the fantasy-dependent movement ceases to be. What media professionals give, they also have the power to take away. Social movements based on media fantasies survive only as long as the fantasies survive. As long as the fantasies are popular, movements grow; when the fantasies become routine, movements fade. Leaders can aid reporters by creating pseudoevents that link them to fantasies and achieve national prominence, but that notoriety can easily disappear when reporters ignore them or use negative fantasies to contextualize them.

8.5 Planning and Morality: An Alternate Perspective on Communication

Planning makes it possible for people to assume responsibility for the consequences of their actions. We can be only as responsible as the skills that we have developed for planning permit us to be. In choosing actions and in anticipating their consequences, for example, we can choose those that we know will have negative consequences for others even though they may result in personally desired ends. Or we can choose actions that will be harmful to us but might benefit others. Our planning must be judged against some standard. We can be responsible only if we act with the knowledge that certain chosen consequences are worthwhile and others are to be avoided.

These judgments must be made in terms of a *value system,* a set of interrelated priorities for action. We must consciously determine that some consequences are more desirable than others and that our plans should enable us to achieve these outcomes. The development of such a value system can be difficult. It is easy to assume that the simple solutions that we routinely impose provide us with an acceptable value system. They justify a wide variety of routine action. In our society, for example, much of our consumption of products is routinely defined as good and worthwhile by the simple solutions that we learn from mass media content. But these solutions do not permit an individual to assume personal responsibility for action any more than the traditions of a folk community enabled its tribespeople to be personally responsible for their actions.

For planning to be moral, it must be accomplished by a value system to judge the consequences of anticipated actions. For an individual to assume personal responsibility for planned actions, the value system must be more than a set of simple solutions; it must consist of values that the individual has consciously chosen and used as a means of reflecting on and evaluating plans of action. This value system can also be used to evaluate the actual consequences of actions.

Is moral planning by use of value systems possible? It is a very difficult task, and our social order does little to encourage it. Although we have forms of public communication that may encourage moral planning, we have developed sophisticated forms of mass communication that inhibit it. Few social groups or bureaucratic organizations encourage moral planning because they usually rely on ideologies, professional codes, or media fantasies to structure action in the situations they control.

Every social order that now exists has underlying values. They are implicit in the simple solutions offered to members, and they are widely shared in the social order. We can anticipate what will happen in most everyday situations because we know and routinely accept the values implicit in them. People who engage in moral planning, however, may decide to use different values. Their actions may be difficult to anticipate. How will they fit into an existing social order? If many people begin to plan in this way, will the existing social order break down? These are questions that we cannot answer. For now, moral planning is an ideal that is worth striving toward.

Moral planning as the basis for determining how societal communication should be structured is not a totally innovative idea. It has guided thinking about communication in the past. The best and most relevant example is libertarian theory. Chapter 2 discussed libertarianism and its influence on the development of modern mass communication.

Libertarians sought to resolve the conflict they perceived between what is best for individuals and what is best for society. They recognized that if individuals are freely allowed to communicate in certain ways, an existing social order might be endangered. They argued, however, that it is sometimes necessary to endanger a social order when circumstances warrant.

Borrowing from libertarian logic, moral planning may be an ideal that is more important than the preservation of a specific, arbitrary social order. It is an ideal that may create communication that, in turn, may structure action inconsistent with the social order. It is therefore an ideal that must be given serious consideration and evaluation. Moral planning may be a beginning point for seeking alternatives to existing forms of communication that seem to be inadequate, but it cannot be accepted without question. One failing of most communication theories has been their inability to articulate an alternative to existing forms of communication. Viewing communication in terms of moral planning and public communication, however, may generate new thoughts and subsequent articulations of valuable alternatives.

Toward Moral Planning Through Criticism of Communication

The development of the reflective-self style of framing is essential if we are to live surrounded by sophisticated mass communication messages. Personal responsibility for action will be possible only if reflective framing skills are developed. In the absence of these skills, even the most reasonable individual may be easily led to accept the routine answers to everyday problems that are offered by media content.

The framing style that we use will determine how seriously we take media fantasies and the role we allow them to play in our lives. If we adopt the social learning style, for example, we will rely on cues provided by media professionals to assess the usefulness of a media fantasy. We will probably learn the simple solutions associated with the fantasies. News stories and entertainment programs will contain cues suggesting that their fantasies are useful in framing our everyday lives. Similar problems might develop with the use of the looking-glass–self and generalized-other styles.

Much of the confusion of modern life arises because we are surrounded by artistic representations that simulate everyday communication. The intrusion of so much mass communication into life and the transformation of so many aspects of life into mass communication make it easier than ever to reflect on the codes that we use to organize our everyday experience. But we have developed simple solutions that permit us to ignore these intrusions, and we therefore define them as nonserious.

The first step toward developing reflective insight is to take these intrusions seriously. This is the overall theme of this book. We need to increase our sensitivity to the intrusion of mass communication into our lives. As we reflect on these intrusions, we can develop our awareness of how we allow communication to shape our experience. We can start to formulate an answer to the question of the consequences resulting from our use of mass communication. Does it create a basis for long-term action plans that permit the realization of important moral values? Or does it create pleasant experiences that are amoral but distract us from long-term planning?

The best and most useful media representations have the potential to intrude on our lives in very important ways. They intrude by providing us with reflective insight into social relationships, with visions of new solutions to problems that we were unaware of. They can be viewed as moral visions made possible by specific codes, media technologies, and content genres. To understand and use the media's art, we must develop our knowledge of genres and technology. We need to understand how we can use communication to achieve long-term objectives that are moral.

Communication has the power to transform our experience. We need to develop skills that can bring this power under control and direct it toward humane objectives. Mass communication offers representations of experience that enable us to reflect on that experience. We need to use this reflection with care and nurture the skills that make it possible.

8.6   Conclusion

The purpose of planning is to allow us to do what we intend to do—to make certain that good intentions are carried out. What influence, then, have the mass media had on our ability to plan?

Commercial mass entertainment and news are usually inadequate forms of communication on which to base planning. They help us plan for pleasant short-term experiences, but they usually do not lead to the achievement of significant long-term objectives.

Effective planning is possible when we use a complex framing process to anticipate and develop expectations of future situations. In that way, we can consider the possible consequences of our actions. Pseudoplanning, on the other hand, results when we rely on stereotypes, motive talk, and communication talk to provide us with easy answers about what is likely to happen. These simple solutions to planning problems are often learned from mass media. Effective planning is a complex art form that permits the framing of the future; simple solutions that allow us to frame the future arbitrarily in routine or nonreflective ways limit our ability to plan well.

When we allow our planning to be controlled by the simple solutions offered by others and the mass media, we lose personal responsibility for our behavior. These simple solutions divert our attention away from problems and ambiguity in our environment. When they are repeatedly presented in the media and when they lead us to develop many routine expectations of the future—in our society, these expectations are best met by the consumption of goods and services—they become media fantasies.

Media fantasies enable us to simplify our understanding of ourselves and our lives so that we can control our experiences and achieve specific objectives. We use them to guide our short- and long-term planning. Thus much of our reflection on the future is dependent on frames provided by media professionals.

Serious problems sometimes result when we confuse media fantasies with purposeful ideologies communicated by publics. Publics are often tempted to rely on existing fantasies as a means of arousing interest in their communication, and media producers are always anxious for new ideologies, communications, and publics to transform into content. Publics, however, run the risk of having their ideology obscured by the fantasy that comes to represent their true communication. Ideologies are vulnerable to decontextualization and transformation in the hands of media professionals.

Media fantasies and the simple solutions on which they are based often make it difficult for us to develop a value system that can be used for planning. It is easy to assume that the simple solutions that we routinely impose provide us with an acceptable value system. They justify a wide variety of actions. But for an individual to assume responsibility for planned actions, the value system must be more than a set of simple solutions. It must consist of values that we consciously choose and use as a means of reflecting and evaluating plans of action. Mass communication offers representations of experience that can be used for reflection and evaluation. We need to use it wisely.

Additional Readings on Planning and Fantasies

Barthes, R. 1973. *Mythologies.* London: Granada Publishing.

Douglas, M. 1975. The meaning of myth. In *Implicit meanings,* ed. M. Douglas, pp. 153–72. Boston: Routledge & Kegan Paul.

Duncan, H. D. 1968. *Symbols and society.* New York: Oxford Univ. Press.

Gardner, J. 1978. *On moral fiction.* New York: Basic Books.

Jewett, R., and Lawrence, J. S. 1977. *The American monomyth.* Garden City, N.Y.: Anchor Press.

Mankiewicz, F., and Swerdlow, J. 1978. *Remote control.* New York: Ballantine.

Real, M. R. 1977. *Mass-mediated culture.* Englewood Cliffs, N.J.: Prentice-Hall.

Chapter 9

Mass Communication Policy and Research

I believe television is going to be the
test of the modern world, and that in
this new opportunity to see beyond
the range of our vision we shall
discover either a new and unbearable
disturbance of the general peace or a
saving radiance in the sky.

> E.B. White writing in 1938, quoted in
> *Look,* 7 September 1971

Don't bother to finish telling me the
story. If it's got people dressed up as
dogs, it can't miss.

> NBC president Fred Silverman's
> reaction to the script for a 1979
> television pilot offered to his network,
> quoted in Ben Stein's "The Unmaking
> of a Sitcom," *Penthouse,* November
> 1979

9.1 Introduction

We may see as much change in mass communication technology in
the next two decades as we have seen in the past century. By the year
2000 we may develop a completely new system of mass communication. We may see, as some observers have predicted (Grunwald 1979),
the rapid decline of broadcast television as we know it. Cable companies could grow, linking most cities with television services far more
varied and specialized than even the most sophisticated systems offer
today. Among these services might be news programming that would

make newspapers obsolete. In addition to audiovisual versions of news stories, cable could offer us printed copy as well. The rise of these new media services could produce a dramatic transformation in the audiences for media content. Existing audiences could fragment again and again into small, specialized segments served by very specialized content.

The technology that could bring about most of these transformations either already exists or is the simple extension of existing technology. Three important new technologies whose potential is unlimited are being linked into communication systems: cable television, communication satellites, and computer technology. When these are joined, it will be possible to create national banks of media content stored by computers and made accessible to media users via satellite through cable-equipped television receivers. These services are already being used by large companies to make information available to their employees. Prototype services supplying information to home consumers in Great Britain are already being tested.

The problem that faces the media industries in our country, however, is not how to invent new technologies that can serve existing needs more effectively. There is no mass discontent with current service that might force change. Instead, these industries are in the difficult situation of already possessing new technologies while making enormous profits from existing ones. The presence of these new technologies has become a threat to a very satisfactory status quo, and critics have already begun to accuse the industries of slowing down technological change to protect their investment in existing equipment. Industry spokespeople, on the other hand, argue that they are proceeding cautiously because they do not know how willing the public will be to accept and pay for the new services they can offer. They profess a willingness to exploit the profit potential of new technology only if this potential can be conclusively demonstrated.

The greatest barrier to technological change, therefore, is not the invention of technology but the absence of the specialized communication needs or purposes that could be served by it. Our capacity to be technologically creative has exceeded our creative ability in developing new purposes for communication. As a nation, we appear to be satisfied with mass news and entertainment content. Ever-growing audiences for existing content and industry surveys of audience preferences provide strong evidence that these forms of content have not yet lost their attraction. Consequently when new technologies are developed, they tend to offer us even easier access to a greater variety of mass news, entertainment, and advertising. All-news radio stations are created, for example, and cable television offers us first-run movies and Las Vegas entertainers. We get what we have already been getting to a greater degree.

Thus mass communication policy makers, both inside and outside the industry, are right in asking, "Why introduce change if the public does not demand it? Why introduce change if it may lead to declines in profits and possibly disrupt advertising?"

We can be excited by the potential for innovative use that new technology offers, but we must also be aware that this potential is likely to be lost. Contemporary procedures for setting national mass communication policies are unlikely to lead to productive change. Audiences for media content are unlikely to rise up and demand new forms of content; the media industries are unlikely to invent them and then educate people to use them. Libertarian theorists envisioned a self-righting media system that would evolve gradually according to natural laws, but they did not reckon with the technological change that we are experiencing.

The marketplace-of-ideas concept was based on limited printing technology. The libertarians believed that publics would form around the most truthful ideas and would advocate and transmit them in print. Widespread public involvement in societal communication would ensure that this communication served to advance true ideas and inhibit falsehood. But mass communication seems to have created passive mass audiences that enjoy prefabricated experiences. They are unconcerned about the truth or falsehood of the content they consume. Even if they were concerned, they would quickly discover that media content is fundamentally amoral and cannot be judged by moral standards.

One basic problem of mass communication today is how to bring about productive change in the way media technology serves us. To do this, we do not need more inventions; we need to reassess our purposes as individuals and as a society in communicating. If we are satisfied with what we are now doing, however, we can proceed on our present path and create a wired nation with coast-to-coast access to ever more attractive media fantasies.

Developing new purposes for mass communication will be difficult because our past usage of mass communication may not provide useful direction. Our present media system is built around the simulation of simple forms of communication play. It has been tremendously successful in linking them to a particular form of economic development. As noted in Chapter 1, this success has been due in part to the development of administrative communication research that increased the effectiveness of advertising and public relations. If we begin to dismantle this media system and replace it with a new one, what might the consequences be for future economic development? What role can communication research play in the development of this system?

9.2   Policy Making on Mass Communication

In the history of media policy formation, the public has had little input into the decisions that led to policy. That process was dominated by, and largely restricted to, three major participants: the Congress, federal regulatory agencies (such as the Federal Communication Commission and the Federal Trade Commission), and the media industries themselves. These were the focal points of a closely knit triangle of pressure, cooperation, and shifting alliances. This balance of forces, however, has recently been altered by the "increased involvement of three more participants in . . . regulatory policy making: the public, in the form of citizens' groups; the White House, by means of special advisory bodies and governmental bureaus; and the courts, in the form of judicial opinions" (Krasnow and Longley 1973, p. 36).

With attainable and significant changes in the structure, function, and subsequent impact of the mass media now technologically possible, several heterogeneous entities are now engaged in clarifying goals for mass communication: public interest groups, Congress, federal regulatory agencies, other governmental bodies, the media industries, and the courts. Each has and will continue to have various amounts of influence. But to what extent is the public represented in the process? Is it true that elite public interest groups are now being accorded more influence in policy decision making than ever before? How these elite publics frame their media interaction and how they come to understand media theory and effects may help them clarify and articulate goals that will produce public-serving, as opposed to industry-serving, policy. But will these groups pursue policies of interest to nonmembers? Can they be expected to articulate public purposes for mass communication that will serve people outside their own groups?

Recent Policy Making: A Case Study

The development of cable television policy offers a good case study in the problems of creating policy for mass communication. In 1959 the Federal Communications Commission was faced with the task of developing policies to regulate cable television. By that year, there were over 600 different CATV systems operating in this country, and broadcasters complained to the commission, claiming that new policy was necessary to protect their interests. The FCC undertook an examination of this new technology and decided that it had no jurisdiction over cable. The Communication Act of 1934 gave it no such power; cable systems were neither common carriers nor broadcasting and thus were outside commission control. The commission refused to create rules and regulations for an independent industry simply because it had some negative effect on broadcasters. The commission wrote, "In essence, the broadcasters' position shakes down to the fundamental proposition that they wish us to regulate in a manner favorable toward them . . . any nonbroadcast competitive enterprise" (26 FCC 403 1959).

The commission did feel, however, that the development of sound policy could ensure that CATV would develop to its fullest potential for social good. They reasoned, though, that this policy should come from congressional legislation and not from commission mandate.

The FCC said that the goal of CATV policy should be the development of the new medium in the public interest. Broadcasters, however, foresaw a different goal—their own protection. Cable was allowed to grow unfettered by restrictive regulation for several years, but in 1966 the FCC, accepting the arguments advanced by broadcasters, granted itself the power to create cable policy, which naturally reflected the goals of the broadcasters. In its *Second Report and Order on CATV* (2 FCC 2d 725 1966), the FCC asserted its right to regulate "to the extent necessary to prevent cable television from frustrating the Commission's policies and regulations relating to broadcasting."

In that same document, the FCC initiated an inquiry into possible rule making for the direction of CATV development. This inquiry led to a 1971 meeting under the auspices of the Office of Telecommunications Policy in which the commission, representatives of the cable and broadcast industries, and copyright owners attempted to clarify the direction of subsequent cable policy. No representatives of interested publics were present.

The policies that resulted reflected the goals not of the cablecasters or the public, but of the broadcasters. The number and type of distant television station signals that could be brought into an area by a CATV system were limited and times of importation were restricted. CATV systems were required to open their facilities to any person or group that asked for access, and they had no right to deny it to anyone. This origination of public-access programming, while attractive on the surface, was a financial blow to young cable systems because it required large investments in new and different equipment and personnel.

In effect, the goals of several entities conflicted. The most powerful agent, the broadcasters, had the strength to impose its own wants and self-serving policy on an industry that once promised the benefits of an information-rich wired nation. Through all this, the FCC maintained that it was operating in the public interest, that it was requiring significant new services that would ultimately benefit the public.

We may, however, have an opportunity to express new goals for cable policy. A 1978 U.S. Circuit Court of Appeals decision, popularly known as Midwest II, ruled most of the FCC's restrictive CATV policies to be unconstitutional. The 1980s, then, could be significant years in the development of new, constructive CATV policy. Problems of clarifying and articulating goals will no doubt remain, but involved publics may be able to play a more effective role in that process. Prospects for this, however, are not good. Public apathy about policy making in general has long been characteristic of our society.

Creating Public Communication About Policy

The promise of cable, pay-television, home video recorders and discs, satellite retransmission, home computer information systems, the re-writing of the Communication Act of 1934, and increased judicial involvement in media issues present the opportunity for new policy formation. They offer the chance for Americans to practice politics, to engage in public communication about policy. That communication should address itself to several important questions. What will we gain from more tightly regulated mass media—more socially responsive industries, or industries denied useful freedom of speech and press? Would a less strictly regulated system of mass media have beneficial consequences? We have developed a commercial system of broadcasting that sometimes serves us well. Should new policies be designed to protect the commercial and financial structures that allow it to serve us in these ways? Or is it that same commercial and financial structure that keeps its content mired in banality?

Selecting a course of action to develop and implement worthwhile media policies by weighing probable consequences of the various alternatives will be difficult. Our ability to weigh those consequences is hindered by the absence of a wide variety of competent, recognized, clout-carrying publics who represent a broad spectrum of the population interested in long-term, useful media policy. Action for Children's Television and Ralph Nader's National Citizens' Council for Broadcasting are the only two that have received any significant attention; as good as they are, they represent relatively narrow, middle-class interests. Might social science, then, be useful in creating and encouraging public communication on mass media policy?

9.3 The Role of Communication Research in Policy Making

For several reasons we are likely to be dependent on social science for the formulation of policies that will guide and govern the mass media in the 1980s. Social science has given us our past understanding of the mass media, and it has helped formulate current policy. Sadly, broad-based public communication on policy is unlikely to develop on its own; in its absence, social science may be able to articulate important public purposes for mass communication, help design policies to achieve them, and thus create and support public communication.

What should be the role of the social sciences in policy making? If the politics of policy making involves continuing moral compromise (as suggested by Bauer 1968, for example), what is the role of a social science that bases itself on fundamental moral values (that is, a humanistic social science)? To what extent is policy making presently controlled by a relatively small number of elite groups that use it as a means of pursuing self-serving goals? Does the pursuit of self-interest undermine the policy-making process so that broader human purposes cannot be served, or is the pursuit of elite self-interest consistent with the public good?

These concerns are central to understanding mass communication policy because the pursuit of private self-interest is very apparent in mass communication policy making. The FCC has historically defended the interests of broadcasters at the risk of compromising those of the public at large. It frequently assumed that what was in the interest of the industry was in the interest of the public.

Consequently, public policy in mass communication was more often made in corporate boardrooms than in the FCC, Congress, or the White House. Reasonably high levels of public satisfaction with broadcasting (as shown in the industry's administrative research) were used to defend the status quo, and the commission tended to accept industry research without question.

There is need, however, for a new policy-making basis concerning mass communication. Narrow self-interest–based policy making will tend to perpetuate the existing media system, which may be incapable of providing more useful forms of communication. But what alternatives to this type of policy making do we have? The traditional role of social science in policy making does not provide a useful alternative. Ideally, social scientists would provide objective, broad-based factual evidence on which public policies could be founded. This, however, did not happen. Many social scientists simply served interests of the groups (usually businesses) that paid for their research.

This administrative research has now developed a relatively well-accepted track record in the eyes of various governmental policy makers. Like the FCC, they have relied on it to justify their decision making for several decades. Their main problem has been to make sense of the sometimes conflicting facts provided by industry sources.

Critical Research for Policy Making

It is important, then, to begin developing an alternative basis for the creation and evaluation of public policy on mass communication. Decisions made in this decade could be very crucial. The application of administrative research is likely to perpetuate the status quo, the dominance of existing corporate interests over media technology and programming. Critical research based on a reconceptualization of the role of human values in decision making can offer an alternative. A critical research alternative would seek theoretical frameworks that can explain (not just predict and control) complex communication processes (not simple linear processes) as part of an ongoing, evolving critical effort to evaluate, communicate, and implement broadly important human moral purposes. This explanation of communication processes would be from the perspective of many different types of individuals and social groups committed to implementing moral values in their lives. This critical research would favor the creation and verification of theories that are useful to individuals and social groups in planning and realizing long-term moral objectives.

Instead of looking at the ways in which contemporary media systems do and do not serve us, we need to examine who and what we are as people and as a society. Once we better understand ourselves in terms of the communication environment in which we live, we can conduct the additional critical research necessary to improve that environment and make it more responsive and useful.

What are the drawbacks of this alternative? Why might it fail to be implemented? One answer lies in its fundamental opposition to the usual notions of policy making. Traditional policy planners argue that politics is the art of compromise and that all human values are only relatively important. They are realists, not moralizers or activists. They portray people who, in terms of morally based policy, are suffering from the "complacency of easy virtue and the illusion of omnipotence." Policy making, they feel, must be the product of the "intellectual and moral discipline of policy making" (Bauer 1968). But what is this "moral discipline of policy making"? It seems to be the discipline required to deny the usefulness of morals in formulating policy and to seek instead the most practical solution. Traditional policy making is cost-effective and action-efficient. It seeks more bang for the buck—better television technology for the consumer's dollar—more public interest programming in exchange for more commercially lucrative programming.

Are these compromises necessary? What is being compromised? In whose interest are they being made? A critical research approach assumes that fundamental human purposes can be articulated and pursued by using new forms of communication. And though these purposes change, the values that underlie them do not—we are all uniquely human, and we are each defined in terms of our culture and our communication within it. Traditional policy making involves sorting out the differences between competing purposes, all of which mean to achieve the same basic ends; the emphasis, however, should be with finding the most useful ends and then seeking ways to implement them.

A humanistic social science of communication based on critical research, then, would view media technology as a means of educating individuals to participate in the creation of new forms of communication, and it would seek ways of making their participation easier and more attractive. In the space of thirty years, administrative mass communication research greatly facilitated the production and distribution of manipulative media fantasies. Is it too much to expect that humanistic mass communication research might serve as an important means of reversing this use of the mass media and help replace it with creative public communication about human values?

9.4 Barriers to the Development of a Humanistic Science of Communication

Many barriers must be overcome if communication science is to achieve these goals. One of the most obvious barriers is opposition from competing participants in the policy formation process. But the greatest barrier is not external resistance but the historic, continuing fragmentation of scholarship on communication. Communication research is currently conducted by scholars from every existing social science discipline, as well as by researchers in the humanities. The only well-organized and predominant tradition of scholarship in the United States is that of administrative research. Scholars using this tradition are at least united in their acceptance of research methodologies even when deeply fragmented by their choice of discrete theories to guide their work.

Other scholarship has often been forced to define itself in terms of the administrative research tradition and, when judged by this standard, has been labeled tangential at best, merely speculative at worst. Consequently much existing work is pursued in relative isolation, and there is surprisingly little communication between scholars. Many excuses have been offered for this situation. Perhaps the most common is that communication research is still an infant discipline. But as the infant ages, this argument becomes less persuasive.

Sources of Fragmentation

Fragmentation of communication research was encouraged by a variety of ideological disputes in American society and interdisciplinary disputes within the scientific community. As noted in Chapter 2, deep divisions developed between social scientists and humanistic scholars. Social scientists were anxious to separate themselves from colleagues who insisted on advocating subjective values. While social scientists did not openly reject humanistic values, they did suggest that such values were too abstract and biased to guide research. Scholars in traditional humanistic disciplines resented the intrusion of the social sciences into academic life and were suspicious of the education they provided. The growth of college and university social science departments often came at the expense of other disciplines. In some cases, long-established areas of scholarship were threatened or eliminated.

Methodological disputes broke out that further increased fragmentation. Social scientists were divided in their loyalty to either experimental or survey research methodology. They were further divided by their preference for certain mathematical or statistical models. In extreme cases, certain methods of data collection and analysis were linked to specific theories so that the only way these theories could be evaluated was through the use of specific methodologies. These were considered so complicated and their careful application so important that, researchers argued, only people with years of training and apprenticeship could be relied upon to apply them. Nonspecialists were forced to accept the usefulness of this research without question.

Critical scholars, too, were divided in their use of research methods. Marxists advocated the use of dialectic analysis as a means of analyzing societal conflict. Structural functionalists constructed grand theories. Pragmatists preferred to generate complex explanations for various forms of human action that assumed people could become rational. Scholars in differing schools rarely used the same concepts; and when they did, they disagreed on how these concepts should be defined. Humanists tended to specialize in their study of various communication genres or other art forms. Some specialized in certain forms of literature, others in film, others in poetry or drama. Different concepts were created to analyze different forms of communication content and the genres used to generate it. Disputes arose concerning the propriety of applying a theory created to analyze fiction or drama to the analysis of film. Differing interpretations of various humanistic values also created conflict.

Prospects for Integrated Research on Communication

Two recent trends in communication research, however, offer some future hope of increasingly integrated research on communication. First, the confidence of empirical communication researchers in the usefulness of their approach for theory construction is declining. After more than two decades of hope that broad theory would emerge to unite discrete middle-range theories, some researchers have begun to argue that alternatives should be considered (see Budd and Rubin 1979). Discontent with the administrative approach has led to a growing openness toward some alternative modes of theory construction that can be found in humanistic research.

The second reason for optimism, then, lies in this increased acceptance of alternative approaches by American researchers. This happened, in part, because British researchers have already begun to demonstrate the utility of combining American research methods with European approaches to theory construction. Foreign scholarship may now be influencing American research despite more than two decades of relative isolation from such influence.

The most innovative and challenging humanistic and foreign research has a common theme that may help integrate future scholarship. It involves the investigation of communication's role in changing social structures and the way in which different forms of communication facilitate the perpetuation of particular social structures.

This theme has emerged with the gradual reacceptance by many communication scholars of longstanding humanistic conviction that human beings can create themselves by creating culture (the artifacts of their society)—that cultural changes can lead to the creation or change of social structures. This view of a powerful culture suggests that it can transform social and psychological structures.

If culture is indeed powerful, it must be taken seriously, and the links between it and social structures must be studied with care. A culture that merely reflects but cannot change social and psychological structures can be ignored. But a powerful culture that can influence those structures is worthy of the kind of scrutiny and criticism that might help it develop in useful ways.

9.5 Conclusion

This chapter has detailed the reasons for believing that the emergence of a humanistic science of communication would prove useful. It can play an important, innovative role in the formation of policy on mass communication, a matter of ever-increasing importance as decisions are made concerning the implementation of new technologies. But this role in policy formation would be only part of a larger effort to educate the public about the necessity for new forms of public communication. These new forms of public communication are essential to the development of a morally responsible society in which media technology assists rather than impedes moral development and dialogue. The creation of a humanistic science is a very real possibility if present trends continue, but efforts at its creation face many barriers.

The goal of developing a nation of reflective and active citizens capable of articulating moral purposes and engaging in communication on them so that a useful consensus can emerge as a basis for planning action presently appears somewhat optimistic. But it is no more idealistic than the dream of the early propagandists to use mass media to expand the influence of minor ideologies. It is no more idealistic than the 1930s and 1940s dream of creating a mass economy based on advertising and public relations techniques.

We can be pessimistic about the potential of new technologies to consolidate the power of existing social structures over human action. Or we can be optimistic about the creation of innovative and liberating forms of culture that will transform those social structures. We can be paralyzed by fear or encouraged by hope. It is time to begin taking our culture seriously and using our science in the service of our most valued objectives. We can each contribute to this effort in our own way. We can become more critical of our personal communication and more consciously aware of the coding schemes that we use to organize our experiences. We can use simple solutions less routinely. We can initiate dialogue with people whose values are different and be more respectful of the role that those values play in their lives. We can take ourselves more seriously and begin to plan our own futures more effectively. In all of these ways, we can make communication personally serve us better and can encourage the development of forms of mass communication that will better serve our society.

References

Bauer, R. A. 1968. The study of policy formation: an introduction. In *The study of policy formation*, ed. R. A. Bauer and K. J. Gergen, pp. 1–26. New York: Free Press.

Budd, R. W., and Rubin, B. D. 1979. *Beyond media; new approaches to mass communication*. Rochelle Park, N.J.: Hayden.

Federal Communications Commission. 1959. *Inquiry into the impact of community antenna systems*. 26 FCC 403. Washington, D.C.

————. 1966. *Second report and order on CATV.* 2 FCC 2d 725. Washington, D.C.

Grunwald, D. 1979. Breaking the television monopoly. *Penthouse,* August 1979, p. 53.

Krasnow, E. G., and Longley, L. D. 1973. *The politics of broadcast regulation.* New York: St. Martins.

Additional Readings

Policy Formation and Social Science

Lerner, D., and Lasswell, H. D. 1951. *The policy sciences: recent developments in scope and method.* Stanford, Calif.: Stanford Univ. Press.

Lippman, W. 1951. *The phantom public.* New York: Macmillan.

Macrae, D. 1976. *The social function of social science.* New Haven: Yale Univ. Press.

National Science Foundation. 1969. *Knowledge into action: improving the nation's use of the social sciences.* Washington: U.S. Government Printing Office.

Robinson, G. O. 1978. *Communications for tomorrow: policy perspectives for the 1980's.* New York: Praeger.

Schorr, A. L. 1971. Public policy and private interest. In *The use and abuse of social science,* ed. I. L. Horowitz, pp. 155–69. New Brunswick, N.J.: Transaction Books.

Williams, R. 1974. *Television: technology and cultural form.* London: Fontana.

Humanistic Communication Science

Bernstein, R. J. 1976. *The restructuring of social and political theory.* Oxford: Basil Blackwell.

Carey, J. W. 1978. Social theory and communication theory. *Comm. Res.* 5: 357–68.

Carey, J. W., and Kreiling, A. L. 1974. Popular culture and uses and gratifications: notes toward an accommodation. In *The uses of mass communication,* ed. J. Blumler and E. Katz, pp. 225–48. Beverly Hills, Calif.: Sage.

Gouldner, A. W. 1976. *The dialectic of ideology and technology: the origins, grammar, and future of ideology.* New York: Seabury.

Hirsch, P. 1978. The relevance of humanistic models to communication research. *Comm. Res.* 5: 235–39.

Sackman, H. 1971. *Mass information utilities and social excellence.* New York: Auerbach.

Worth, S., and Gross, L. 1974. Symbolic strategies. *J. Comm.* 24: 27–29.

Index